More
or Less

More
or Less

Stephen W. Redding

Illustrated by

Meurcie Katherine Redding

&

Valerie Landon Ryan

iUniverse, Inc.

New York Bloomington

More or Less

iUniverse books may be ordered through booksellers or by contacting:

iUniverse
1663 Liberty Drive
Bloomington, IN 47403
www.iuniverse.com
1-800-Authors (1-800-288-4677)

ISBN: 978-1-4401-6121-6 (pbk)
ISBN: 978-1-4401-6120-9 (ebk)
ISBN: 978-1-4401-6117-9 (cloth)

Printed in the United States of America

iUniverse rev. date: 8/14/2009

Dedication

To all of us,
those who were there in the beginning
and remain even today.

Contents

Acknowledgement

A staying love for this world, guided by the multiple edge experiences of my life, along with the support of special people, family, and friends has at long last found in me the courage to extend these words, thoughts, and experiences in the hope that the journey of life might continue.

Where to look and how to see
the wondrous More of which
our lives and our world
are deserving to be.

Foreword

The first time I met Stephen Redding, he was the guest speaker at our nondenominational Sunday Celebration. His presence exuded peace, and his words expressed deep wisdom. Descriptions of his multi-world experiences took us beyond the realm of the known, allowing us to peek into other existences. While listening with fascination to his accounts of surviving numerous brushes with death, and coming back from the edge, I was stunned into deep silence. From within this silence, I knew his soul had experienced the Beyond, the Space Between, the Something More. It was obvious that Stephen's journeys into the depth of the More left him with an extraordinary understanding of what is really important in life.

Since then, I had the privilege of getting to know Stephen as an amazingly gentle, thoughtful, and wise man. This arborist by trade is a sage who honors life within every being, whether it is called a tree, flower, animal, amphibian, insect, or human. He lives what he writes about so eloquently.

More or Less encompasses many dimensions: the seen and the unseen. Stephen's message "life does not stop at the end of our personal bodies" is beautifully and skillfully conveyed in this, his second book. Life continues. The essence of who we are remains intact even after apparent earthly death. We continue to exist in a wonderfully fluid state, in that Something More space, which connects us with all dimensions.

For me, this book contains a timely message. Seek life and light while being mindful of preserving your energy. It seems that when we allow our life to be filled with doing, running, and accomplishing, we lose focus of what is truly important. Where is our center of attention? Do these activities allow us to perceive the whispers from another realm? Have we made time for reflection? When our minds are filled with chatter and to-do lists, how can the still small voice of transcendent nature be perceived?

Stephen's words have reminded me to honor Space. I have learned to appreciate that this is the essential element to expanding my life-perception beyond the obvious. It allows me to notice incredible beauty, and most importantly, who we really are. We are more than meets the eye. We are so much more!

Allow *More or Less* to enhance your life as it has mine by integrating the message into your heart.

Thank you, Stephen, for sharing your wisdom!

Rev. Hannelore Goodwin, Founder

Circle Of Miracles Ministries

Introduction

The previous book, *Something More*, articulated a longer and broader view of life. It spoke to the incredible journey of creation and how we are connected to it. Drawing from extreme and unusual personal experiences, a vision of multiple worlds to which we belong was extended. The implication is that there is more, much more, to the experience of life than we might expect. Not only is there more available to us, we can begin to know it personally. As we come to experience and understand the More of our lives, deeper meaning and personal value will be added to our every day.

This work, *More or Less*, attempts to identify what we can do to allow this More into our lives. If we begin to reach and prepare for the More of life, we will be imbued with a sense that we are more important, more lasting, and more precious than we ever could have known.

This work also touches on the fragility of life in these times and how we must begin to understand what can be done to protect it. Doing nothing, which could leave us with less than what might have been, is no longer an option.

The river of life seems to be at a dangerously low level, and the life that we highly value may be in a time of subtraction. The process of loss and decline of life is proceeding more quickly than is the force that infuses more into the expressions of living.

It is such a time
to once again believe
in things as yet unseen.
Something More is available to us,
which will warm us against the cold of night.

The More side of the title reminds us that we are the eyes and the hope of all of those that came before us. There are other rooms in our house of life, and our contemporary experience is just one of those rooms.

The Less, as presented in this book, suggests that some of us are living in ways that increase our distance from what truly matters. We may have stuff (and lots of it) on the outside, but are we really empty on the inside?

The following manuscript urges us to reflect upon the implications of Less, which has introduced so much night like darkness into our world. As a result our way has been obscured, which is withholding us from so much More. It calls on us to remember that, although we may have lost sight of our onward journey as we undervalued ourselves, we are not undeserving.

As before, personal experiences that provided me with a longer view of life are utilized to help foster understanding of some of life's mysteries, such as what we are doing here now and what is next for us.

The thoughts and perceptions herein will allude to the possibility that we are in the final days of this dispensation, the age of time and material, and they will help us to prepare for the dawn of a day with a beginning but not an end. Let's do what needs to be done together. It is our birthright. There is much more available to us, and the thoughts and possibilities proposed in *More or Less* may guide us in our quest to find it.

Perspective

Readers should begin this book with the perspective of nothing less than opening themselves to a new world view. If they successfully navigate to the far side of this discourse they will readily agree that there is much more beyond our contemporary sciences, philosophies, and theologies.

In proceeding through this work, old thoughts may need to be subdued while experiential courage is advanced. It's all right if what is true and obvious for the author is speculative for others. If the way these concepts and visions are presented seem offensive to some basic beliefs and ideas, this clearly is not the intention. Instead, the objective is to affirm meaning and value. Its purpose is not to take away from, but rather to add to the wonder of life and our place in it.

How will this work be received? Will its truthfulness be questioned? For this author, the testimony of truth is evidenced by the way a human life was crushed, frozen, and stung to death and was miraculously protected and returned to life, leaving open the opportunity, if not the obligation, to lend the experiences and perceptions herein to this world.

Will the relevance of this work be questioned? Can we benefit from the message without bearing the drama and trauma of these edge experiences? The answer is yes because that which is revealed herein belongs to all of us. No one needs to give it to us, for we in our inception have all belonged to the creative intelligence that has made our life in existence possible. We are all worthy enough. The challenge is to reconnect with the ancient wisdom, which has been lost, obscured, or forgotten so that we might efficiently separate the More from the Less of these times.

The hope is that this book will be viewed from a subjective place. Does it awaken something that feels right? Are there times when it causes the hair on arms and necks to stand up and a shimmer to slide over the skin? Does it cause eyes to moisten with warm tears of hope and gladness that there is More, much More? When the book is closed upon our laps, are we left with a sense of wonder? If so, then this sense of wonder will be forever inseparable from us and will become a most blessed and giving quality of our living experience. If we are set to wonder, then horizons will be extended for us as we wonder even more. If in this our hope is enlivened and our hearts are gladdened then this work must be judged worthy of your time and mine.

In the Beginning

Where we began upon our journey in an age now gone by, there was the essence of life, the mustardo that supported it, and the promise of more life. Enthusiastically and joyfully, we voyaged far and wide, looking to bring warmth and illumination to another realm. We discovered that the darkness, which we wished to illuminate and understand, unexpectedly permeated our beings. Life changed as we knew it, and much was lost in the forgetting. Now an opportunity to remember and retrieve that which was lost or forgotten is before us.

To understand
life's many faces
brings us within
her embrace.

1

Touching Base With Creation

These Times

These times in which we presently live cry out for our understanding and ask that we reconsider our relationship with our living world. Along with the longer and broader view of life as given to me by so many edge experiences, has been a deep, deep regard for our world and the experience of living upon her. In fact it is right here, right now where we are so critically needed to renew our relationship and loving regard for our earthly world of existence. Not as a place to get past, or ascend above, but as a highly valued part of creation.

As we begin opening windows and doors to the More of our lives, life's wonder will be revealed. Compelling experiences and perceptions of where we are now, as well as other spaces and places, will affirm for us the length and splendor of our lives. As this experience and discovery unfolds we will be reminded of who and what we are. Along with these revelations and discoveries we will appreciate the need to care for this world to which we now belong. When we can trust what is before us while embracing where we are, we will indeed be touching base with creation.

And if, in fact, we will not give the necessary standing to our world of earth, then we will lose the very vessel critical to our passage toward a wondrous and beckoning horizon.

There is a sense among many
that something valid is missing from us.

We may open our discovery of More by taking a candid look at our present day world. Less seems to be begetting Less with consequences that are subtracting from the health and vigor of life. Many of these consequences involve taking from the More side of life. This then becomes the less side of things, as we are withholding so much of value from ourselves.

These consequences are not unavoidable. In fact, they have causes that we can do something about. We will attempt to identify and illuminate some of the causes that seem so predominant in the threat to the More of life. With the more side of this work given to a much longer and broader view of life, it is hoped that we may begin to see our place in all of this very differently. Passions may be awakened within us, with life-caring consequences leading to life-giving motives. Passions stoked by emotions of joy can have enormously giving consequences. With this awakened value in ourselves we will be able to supplant so much of what we think we need with the much that we already are. When life is given a longer view, taking away can be replaced by getting along as it pertains to one another and our world.

As a boy I noticed that feeding the beef cattle back on the farm had very different consequences from season to season. In inclement weather hay was delivered to them in the barnyard. Their rations were always the same, but they were much more aggressive toward one another in the winter. They were more inclined to fight with one another over their food when their range of vision was winter white or brown. Springtime brought green meadows into view and their demeanor showed great improvement. In either season they were confined to the barnyard, but what they could see beyond it made all the difference. How much more impulsive and contrary they would be when there was nothing more beyond their fenced in barnyard. For many of us the winter has been difficult and long, but the greening sprigs of spring are now asking us to enter the More before us.

Might the winter season turn quickly into spring for us? If we are allowed to glimpse the additional meadows of this creation, can personal choices with rational thought and behavior lead to consequences of More while holding back this time of subtraction?

When we refer to the time of subtraction, we are implying a precipitously low flow in life's river. The decline side of things overwhelms the up side of life as it pertains to a sustaining and living world. To better understand the tenuous relationship between growth and decline one might benefit by seeing these processes from a structure and function perspective. We may need to consider how both structure and function are vigorous and strong in the living or reclamation of life but express weakness in the decline of life. The history of existence upon our world has always involved a basic design of form and animation, often noted as structure and function. Form is the specific outline of individualized life such as people, trees, horses, and bees, which provides the structure where living is experienced. The animation of forms or structures is essentially equivalent to function, the other basic component of the existence experience.

For me, the tree is a good model from which to view the balance or imbalance between structure and function. It reflects so much about the success or failure of beings living in this existence. Looking from the long-lived and well-managed perspective of the tree, we may gain in understanding the entrapping webs of less, which are withholding so much from us. Before we start with the tree as a model, some may protest that trees do not have minds, are not inter-relational, dynamic, or cognitive, and therefore cannot be intelligent. Instead, they may argue, they are only reactive, static, and predictable.

While trees are not the same as humans, I feel very connected to them and have lived much of my life attempting to understand them. I do believe we can gain a great deal of insight into our relationship to one another and to our world from them.

If intelligence means expressing complex ideas and accumulating factual information, then perhaps the tree may not measure up as a comparable entity in some people's thinking. However, if being possessed of intelligence implies having an effective and staying integration into their environment, then trees are very wise indeed. In this case, intelligence is viewed from a holistic perspective emphasizing its life-giving and sustaining attributes.

The things that trees achieve and demonstrate speak to an intelligence that is fully integrated throughout their small beginnings as a sprouted seeds as well as their larger, mature manifestations. The way they manage their lives is key. They remain continuously alive for countless years while being functional parts of their environment. All the while they sustain and are sustained by millions of smaller life forms such as soil organisms. For me, trees must be considered one of life's ultimate and finest examples of the universal intelligence which underlies the existence experience.

The secret to the intelligent way in which they live and manage their lives comes back to their rooted connection to the world. Their many incredible functions of exchanging carbon dioxide for oxygen, fruit production, providing habitat, cloaking the earth, and providing us with fuel, medicines, and building supplies benefit us without diminishing or taking from our world. (see 'Wonder of a Tree,' *Something More*)

In trees structure supports function while function builds more structure. It is the very balance of this relationship that effectively allows the trees to manage their long lives. In these times, however, the human condition evidences that our function of living our lives has often proceeded without true appreciation for the structure of our world, which makes our life functions possible. Without giving standing to other living life forms, our function may be greatly diminished.

It is said that we can't live our lives backwards, but looking back may help us find our way forward. We may need to relook at ways of thinking that may have been involved in life's subtraction. The ways we have thought about our world have led to ways of seeing our world, which have often led to the manipulation and consequent loss of so many of our living earth systems. Regardless of how much we factually know and can predict about our interactive behavior, it does us no good if we don't continuously factor in a healthy and sustaining relationship with our earth.

Continuing to borrow from this analogy of our arboreal friends, in trees new and living tissue is built upon old wood. A tree's internal scaffolding of old wood provides the structure that allows support for the dynamic expression of living tissue, which delivers life-giving and life-sustaining functions. In a sense, a tree is forever only one year old, regardless of however many hundreds of years it may have existed in a continuous way upon the earth.

The eyes which lift these words from this paper are in many ways ancient eyes. As a tree's new life is built over old wood, you also are built upon many generations of human expression which has preceded you. In the human condition the 'old wood' is not so stiff or hard as that of a tree but instead resides in phantom-like ways. (There will be more on this as the wonder of life unfolds in these coming pages.)

Its new wood of growth is built over its old wood. From a functional standpoint the tree is always new. From a structural standpoint it may be very old indeed. If the structural health of the tree is compromised at any time in its history by lightning, storm damage, human calamity, insect infestation, or invasion of decline organisms; decay will set in, function will be compromised, and the tree may fail before its time.

Among humans, the earth is the structure upon which life is lived and new lives are born. Human function heretofore relied on the existing structures of the natural world such as rivers, wildlife, minerals, forests, and seas to be that primary locus of function. Almost every act of living implied participation in the natural arena, including gathering of materials and food, acts of celebration, and expressions of worship. Stars, moon, and sky were invoked while feathers, scales, and precious minerals adorned their bodies. Not unlike the results of injury to the structure of a tree, the unwelcome consequences for our world have resulted from invasive wounding, excessive taking, and polluting of these earthy structures. The function of our lives cannot be satisfying and will ultimately be lost entirely if our host is continually beaten low. If the functioning of our collective lives continues to injure our world, the resulting decay may soon culminate in the loss of both our vessel and us. The implied wisdom of a tree in distinction to the said intelligence of human behavior is displayed in the way that the functioning aspects of a tree seldom cause deterioration to its structure. The function of our lives must be held equally to this standard of non-degradation of the natural world's structure, upon which our lives depend.

How and why have we introduced so much decay to our world? The way we have managed, or mismanaged, our lives has often been very damaging to the surrounding world. We have caused wounds that have led to systemic decay, which is becoming very obvious in this time of subtraction. Most of the ultimate wounding has been caused by loss or threats to this world's living life forms. Its effect has been to drain off the necessary vigor that underlies the entirety of the existence experience.

In place of seeing the damage and understanding its danger, humans have tended to look for alternative resources to satisfy our needs. Rather than extending ourselves to heal or make things right, we have forged ahead in an urgent attempt to take precious life-sustaining energy from somewhere else.

Over time, expressions of our intelligence such as cognition, ideas, and beliefs became like proxy structures that we lived around and valued, and little by little we lost our sense of responsibility and connection to the animate and living planet. As this has occurred a psychic sense of alienation and loneliness has encouraged us to go-it-alone, to care for ourselves by ourselves. Although this is now what we accept as right and normal, it was not always this way. The greater part of human history evidences a close kinship with our world and the many life forms upon her. A deep respect along with social taboos encouraged a close, if cautious, relationship to our natural world. Indigenous and native peoples expressed a day-to-day reverence toward the world they took from and lived upon. Their gods were often here in this world with them. Their great spirit was in the very air they breathed. The Sun God looked down upon them with light and warmth, and the Goddess of Fertility gladdened them with her children. In this way they were never alone, and at the same time they were always being watched and monitored by their deities. In almost every native community waste was taboo. They worked to achieve what they needed but nothing more. Time was set aside for celebration and ritual with expression of thanks and gratitude for the giving earth, sky, and sea as its first purpose. Celebrations and taboos constantly reminded these cultures to value and thus protect the very structures of the land that the wellness of their lives depended upon. They were connected. Psychically and emotionally they felt secure and satisfied in their oneness with their world and the circle of life. The earth was well, her life forms secure, and our vessel was allowed to make her way upon the etheric sea.

> The natural world would
> never leave empty
> a life which has
> loved her.

To this some might say, "We are so much better off now. Life means more to us." But does it really? And if so, why are we squandering the world to which we belong? Is there any evidence that prehistoric man fought any less strenuously than we would today to preserve his life? Instead, it is my belief that life always matters and then, as now, every effort was and is made to preserve it.

What happened? We must reflect upon this question. There are some things we can draw forth if we are willing to look behind us a little. Must we sometimes go backwards a bit to find our way forward? Did humankind take a wrong fork in the road?

Did we become impatient with the pain of illness and the uncertainty of dying? Did we fail to remember that the nature of our journey implied these hardships, which could not, at this time, be avoided? The journey of life was not asked to circumvent the darkness. Instead, it was directed to pass through it, and as a result a great deal of confusion entered in. So much of the More of our lives was forgotten, but hopefully it was not lost.

If there is any clarity to be gained from the story of Eden, we must remember that the torturous first act was to eat of the fruit from the tree of knowledge. By implication, this justified our mind's ascendance, leaving the integrated whole and creating mental structures that were thought to have more value and a better future than the real, if unpredictable and sometimes hostile, world. With this mindset, in place of celebrating the natural world we celebrated our ever-increasing hold over it. Unfortunately leaving the garden by losing our intimate connection to the natural world guaranteed that our hardships would only worsen. It extended the duration of our voyage through darkness and even brought question to our destination. And so it is when we dare to look back. Our minds may have gained a hurtful ascendance, often operating in a proxy world of thoughts and ideas that has little regard for the sanctity of the living world. Our cognition broke out of its integrated place in our presence and often suggests that it is equal or greater than its source. Along with the rise of language and mathematics, which we hold up as our greatness, so much goodness has been lost.

As our intellect gained its predominance over our once indigenous and connected presence, our language, mathematics, and ideas created beliefs, which soon acted as structures upon and around which our function was expressed. These new structures of thought often closed out the natural world altogether, except when we wanted and took resources from it.

In this mental world of thoughts, ideas, truths, and discoveries we say that we have learned very much. But is there any real truth in any of this if we are forfeiting our kinship with our world and destroying bits and pieces of our living vessel? Regardless of how intelligent we say we are, we know very little if our thinking behaviors look past caring for what we already have and can't do without. In the matters of life, truth is not so much static facts as it is values that guide our behavior. Thoughts, ideas, and formulations, regardless of how cognitively true, can be means of wrongful manipulation if they foster unnecessary taking from our natural world.

How do trees respond to injury, which always leads to decay? Unlike in human and animal beings, which attempt to repair or replace wounded tissue, trees rush to wall injury off. Immediately upon being wounded, bio-chemical barriers are set up in the tree surrounding the site of the damage. The purpose of these barriers is to prevent decay from spreading to other parts of its structure. Decay fungi are always present in the world of trees, just as infectious bacteria are always present when wounding occurs in the animal-human world. Trees never attempt to replace a wound site with new tissue but instead encircle the area of decay with a strong fiber known as wound wood.

How can we humans wall-off the huge wounds to our animate world inflicted by our excessive appetites that are supported by our belief that it is ours for the taking? A salient belief in the journey of life, which values the creation as necessary to our safe and sustaining passage, may be the prescription for what ails us.

As the story of *More or Less* unfolds before you the value of touching base with creation should excite and gladden. The following truths and queries, some of which may have been lost or forgotten, provide us with options with vastly different consequences for our consideration:

~ We have been present in one way or another for the entirety of this long andextended journey of life.

~ At our seeming death, dying here may also be living on.

~ Our present world of existence is connected to other worlds and realities that we may have an opportunity to glimpse, even in our time upon the earth.

~ How are the darkness and unknowing so obvious in our world today different from us?

~ How we live and value our lives will make all the difference regarding whether we continue to slip into the ghostly spaces of Less or choose to have more of life and life always.

Seeing more, understanding the longer view of our lives, and knowing the many ways that we do matter will go a long way toward diffusing our feelings of being unfulfilled and separate. These two subjective emotions have a huge impact on the way we live our lives and thus the consequences that are leading to Less in these times of subtraction.

If there is to be any ultimate truth or value in our extensive use of cognition then it must be immediately turned toward appreciating and supporting our living world.

If our home and future
is spent
then where will our thoughts and ideas
be lent?

When we calculate and form ideas and thoughts about our world, we are always only regarding pieces of it. Many so called facts and truths may be amassed that are predictable and even dependable. But

13

when we are discovering predictable facts and relationships we are only looking at a part of a much larger whole. Regardless of how we break out the parts, one essential quality always remains that can never be separated or divided: life. Without this essential quality nothing else matters.

Other ways in which our loss of connectedness to our world might be glimpsed when looking back involve beliefs that may be distorting our vision of what matters. In this case, what we need to value and protect may be overlooked.

If the Great Spirit was thought to live in the atmosphere in which we were immersed, as opposed to existing in some distant heaven, our behavior toward this world might be very different. Removing our God from this world and putting him/her/it in a distant heaven has allowed so much disregard and misuse of our vessel. These beliefs have allowed manipulative thinking to transform our critical earth to a temporary stop on our way to heaven. We may have implied that the earth really doesn't matter much, because it is just a lowly place we need to endure until we are called above to the astral habitat of rarified air. Let's hang out with the angels and rest eternally in a selected place where some, but not all, are welcome.

Dominion and manifest destiny are two other beliefs that were born from disconnected people with overly active minds. These beliefs stood in for what the early peoples knew to be tried and true structures. Instead of promoting integrated function in and upon the earth, these self-serving human ideas have allowed so much wounding behavior to be tolerated. From these beliefs dangerous behaviors have been justified and condoned:

~ We are God's children and we above all else matter.

~ Man has dominion over all the earth and the creatures thereof.

~ At almost any cost we can manifest our own destiny.

Taken together these cancerous beliefs have allowed us to justify our deeds while ignoring the much of life we have taken away. In this way manipulation of and taking from our animate world gained acceptance and momentum as 'God's children' held on here until they were elevated and received through the pearly gates of heaven.

As time has passed, this out-of-balance intellect envisioned and justified this world of ideas. Instead of valuing our world, celebrating our existence, and using our minds to skillfully integrate within the intricate patterns of life's many expressions we choose instead to own and control. To this end we have often misused the tools and technologies born of our inventive and capable intellect to accelerate our taking of that which would function to assure our high place.

From a breathing-earth perspective, these fabricated structures of ideas and beliefs have been supported with ever more sophisticated functions, effectively and dangerously serving these alienating beliefs. The consequence has been to quicken the onset of loss and injury to our very necessary vessel, introducing the days of reckoning to our front door.

Disentangling the webs of wrong thought and behavior are a must if we are to enjoy the wide and giving horizons before us. Without looking back, we may not be able to return to where we once belonged: completely connected and integrated into life's fabric of warmth and protection. Clearly that which will allow us to get unstuck and leave this valley of not enough is awaiting our willingness to relook and assess what we truly value. Knowing and remembering the grandeur of life's promises should go a long way toward affording a renewed reverence for our world and our place in it.

There is a sense among many that something valid is missing from us. This leaves us yearning to know of it. Instead of filling these empty spaces within our psyche with the stuff of this world, we should be responding to this thirst through discovery of more. We have long looked out and beyond ourselves for something more, and the time may be at hand to give meaningful effort to this deep longing.

If we can agree to return to a caring connection to our living world, we will benefit greatly. The collective wisdom and ancient intelligence of creation's grand design will lift us up, heal our wounds, and secure our many fears and losses. The warming connection to our world will not easily remain obstructed by our willingness to stay cold in our endless dialogue with human thought and ideas. We will again, as we once did, begin to feel a gravitational pull upon our minds, psyches, and souls of a greater harmony within us. This will lend us a sense of wonder that excludes none of life and finds us no longer alone or disparate, nor on the outside of anything. Inseparable from our vessel, grounded in our destiny, and comforted within the embrace of the circle of life, we will have come back to where we once belonged. Thank goodness life is calling and we are on our way again!

In Life's Fabric

Do not sit by the window
nor fear to open the door,
for
the mysteries of life
will be found and discovered

as we live in her fullness
and play in her gardens.

Numerous worlds set out together
upon this incredible journey.
To each a unique design
and multiple realities.

2

The Story

Regardless of the level of acceptance of the concepts in this story, please note that nothing is being demanded of anyone. No one is being asked to believe anything out of hand, nor to buy into a particular belief system, or even to express a faith in things not seen.

The first book, *Something More*, closed with a reference to 'The Beginning.' This manuscript, *More or Less*, intends to further value our life and to help us learn how we might make more of it by understanding how it was, what it is, who we are in all of this, and where we might go from here.

More or Less suggests differing implications based on humankind's willingness to respond in these days while there is still time. Nothing is completely new here, but there is much that needs to be remembered. The emphasis of these words and expressions will reaffirm that the quality of our lives is the only thing that matters. Life, and more of it, will be the only thing that will make the struggle worthwhile and may ultimately allow life's eternal embrace to encircle us.

The way to remembering and awakening will ask that we make some difficult, but not impossible, choices and attunements in our personal lives. As we begin these considerations, so much more of the possible will be open to us. Jettisoning our excessive material fortunes and lessening our dependence on mental-only ways of seeing, while reappraising our bottom-line orientations, may be some of our most difficult adjustments. If in lieu of these we are allowed to feel, believe, and share more of life, we will want to have more of it as we live it completely.

In the ending parable in *Something More*, mankind was struggling against a great storm upon the open sea. As the winds abated, a single light shone and the sailors called out for help. A voice responded to them, "Care for your vessel, and remember that you were given all that would be needed to cross the great sea." Clearly their vessel, earth, was imperiled, and their course had lost its bearing during the long night in which a mighty storm blew. Yes, the storm continues, and this text is put forth with hopeful anticipation of fostering understandings that might assist us in righting our vessel and best setting our directions. Thus we might free ourselves from the troubled waters, reclaiming a basic trust and an inner faith strong enough that the promises of our parting, offered to us so many ages ago, may soon be realized by all of us. So, let us begin to marvel.

Life matters.
Be good to it.
Support it.
Don't take from it.

If this simple thought is already a part of our everyday lives then there is a grand promise that goes with it. The promise is that there is much, much more life available to us. If we do not find it in this world, we will surely meet it at the door to the next. Belief in the extraordinary will make this promise more fun and meaningful, but we really don't need to believe in anything, as believing alone will not get it done. Rather, it is how we live our lives that will place our signatures on 'yea' or 'nay' to the More or Less before us. Along the continuum of belief to disbelief, certain attitudes toward our lives and our places in this world will be significant.

Those who will find the following experiences and visions most comfortable are those who view themselves as belonging to the circle of life. All life matters to them, and caring for those whose lives are diminished by basic needs is a priority. The expression of life in the natural world is equally important to them. If there is a special role for human beings in all of this it is to steward the circle of life. Life and its expression is the 'pearl of great price.'

Progressing along the continuum of belief will be those who agree that life matters, but for whom human life matters more than the other life forms. These people will express a love for the world but will place themselves in the center of and just above life's circle. For them a humanistic notion of God and creation will belie a preconscious (if not conscious) worldview that, "God gave us dominion, didn't he? We must use this special status as we see fit!"

In a spot further along the scale toward disbelief will appear a superior and sometimes detached attitude toward the surrounding world. The living world takes on the form of a pyramid, with humankind elevated high above the 'lowly' life forms at the bottom. This perspective allows that, not only has the Almighty granted us dominion, but also we must conquer and subdue a dangerous and sometimes heathen world.

At the far end of the continuum, where we encounter those with even less belief, there will be little if any value or comfort found in the following notions. Here reside those who feel nothing special for this world. They see it as a place we need to be saved from, a place where we need to shed some karmic debt, be forgiven, and move away from the fallen around us until we die and go to heaven … or, God forbid, end up in hell. Manipulating, taking, and using the world around them is how they get ahead. Voracious consumption is not only okay, it's necessary. These people can be cold and callous toward life in general for it is only theirs that matter. Specific belief systems with very clear prerequisites entitle them and only them to the stairway to heaven. Their way is the only way to their God and eternal salvation.

Alongside these, but with a different worldview, will be those embodying an equal lack of belief in the More of life. They will suggest we have evolved strictly by accident or chance. From their view, since everything resulted from coincidence and now follows mere physical laws, nothing follows this existence. Faith or belief for these beyond this here and now is a distraction.

For those among us who sense that there is More, we must not allow this time to pass us by. Other worlds and meaningful realities are within our reach. Ripples from these are reaching out to us and initiating this awakening in us. As we sense this connection, curtains will be lifted which will allow a thirst quenching seeing and knowing of how it is that we do belong. Instead of accepting the little of the much that we are, the longer view of life and our place in it will gladden our hearts.

Time

From the very beginning of life's journey, time was a critical component. Time was always important, and now it is even more so because it is limited. Let us suggest that we may be in the final days of this dispensation. The age of time, place, and separateness may soon be redefined.

Time as a measure between the two most important events of our journey, our inception and our destination, will begin to dissolve, even though we may not be where we expected to be. This is an important focus of this work. Boundaries, which have separated worlds and realities from one another, begin to break down. The curtain is being lifted. As such, these times are pregnant with the unusual. Understanding how we are connected to the More of life is becoming comprehendible to us. In particular, those who came before us are now being represented by our eyes and hopes and are knocking at the door.

Let me in, let me in.

Do not question.

Do not fear.

We are together again!

Among others, these could include past family members or friends. We know they died, but here they are again! They may briefly appear as we walk, or whisper our name from an adjacent room. They may manifest themselves in our dreams too often to be ignored. The fact that they have passed on may not mean that they are absolutely dead. In influential and perceptible ways they may still percolate into our lives. Their presence may startle us, but it should also gladden us. We may even know some of them by name, provided we are ready to receive them. They may come to us as playful phantoms by night or helpful

Benginers by day. As we allow them in, more color and motion will be stirred into our lives.

The following text will explore this phenomenon. Depending on our openness and basic trust, the unusual may be received in different ways. In this present year of 2008, under an early afternoon sun and a cool breeze of late October, four regal wild turkeys presented themselves.

Wild turkeys tend to be very secretive and frighty, but this foursome walked confidently up to three fellow workers and me. A great deal of human chatter was forthcoming from the firewood crew as different degrees of doubt and even fear were expressed. Although it took some time for the workers to become comfortable with the turkeys, it was immediately obvious that the turkeys were comfortable with us. While the crew's many questions and comments went unanswered, I had no questions as I have been blessed with this type of visitation before.

Soon the four turkeys encircled me with heads held high, looking proud as each in turn spoke to me in an interworldly gobble-type language. I could not decipher what they were saying; but I smiled, said hellos, and reached out and stroked their backs. It was a breathtaking experience. Who they were, what they were doing there, and where these turkeys came from remains a mystery.

We were being visited in the here and now by the presence of four beings who gathered up these turkeys, calmed them, and utilized their chestnut brown plumage to greet us. At one point I sat down and all four came up and placed their heads in my lap while I quietly stroked their necks. I asked them who they were, but they didn't tell me.

A little more firewood was needed to complete filling the truck, and as I climbed up on a pile of logs to cut the wood, they climbed up with me. They stood three feet away, watching and murmuring. The noise and danger of the chainsaw failed to deter them. After visiting for approximately four hours, these magnificent beings departed as quickly as they had arrived. Exactly what presence was reaching out from this feathered four I may never know. The men who witnessed this remarkable display are still wondering what, how, and why. I felt blessed to receive this gifted life that had come from afar into this reality dressed in the splendid feathers of a wild turkey.

A second visit by these mysterious turkeys occurred during a cold afternoon in early January of 2009. Once again they seemed happy and satisfied to present themselves among us. On this occasion they were seen running in earnest toward the approximate space of their first visit. We were pouring concrete for the base of a horse barn when they strutted through the wet pour to greet us. In all the splendid regality and color of a native wild turkey we were touched and received. Coming within inches of our eyes with their eyes, we looked deeply and intimately within one another. Celebration and wonder was again in the air. How unusual it was to receive distant guests in the same way through an earthly form wrapped in the plumage of a wild turkey. Ah!

My impression, and the collective view of many others derived from the persistent signs offered by the phenomenological just beyond our windows, suggests that these are our final days. Before us there remains only a small fraction of the great amount of time that has passed and is now behind us. As these last days play out and the boundaries between worlds become more porous, we need to be available. If we are reluctant to believe and resistant to see we may miss much of the joy of discovery. Again, a great part of the impetus of this work will be to prepare us for the joy of these opportunities so that we are not shrouded in fear. "Why would I want this?" you might ask. "Why want more?" Because we are more. The opportunity to connect with and belong again to the larger whole is before us. Our elliptical voyage of separateness is coming close to a rendezvous of interconnection. The psychic antennae of many are being aroused by these possibilities. There has long been a yearning to resolve life's mysteries that live in many of us. This is an opportunity, not a time to be feared. We must allow this wonder to play out openly before us. It is what we have longed for, what we have lived for and died for. So much more is becoming available; we must not withhold it from ourselves. If we behave in the manner of a doubting Thomas and are reluctant to see and trust, these opportunities may still avail themselves to us, though perhaps only in very subtle places until we are ready to receive them. We may need to give up old habits of thinking and taking that have gotten in the way of opening windows so that we may see beyond, and the beyond may look back at us.

The End of Darkness

The stars will again truly shine,
instead of being out of reach in the distant sky.
They will guide and warm us on the ground.
Darkness will no longer all surround.
A heartfelt cry of happiness,
we will know
we are being recovered,
being found.
This is the common refrain,
"Awake-awake!
It is late - it is late!"
This is our chance to do it here,

to do it now.

There is much of life in our grasp,

and it may never come this way again.

"Get up - get up!

Don't get stuck – don't get stuck!"

The light that greets us
along our way
Is where life is or was,
not what's lost or taken away

Why do so many undervalue their lives and this world to which we belong? It is my belief that many are disillusioned with what this world does with their existence. It grants them life by birth then seemingly takes it away with death. Neither are particularly enjoyable experiences, even if we have faith that there is more. For myself, even as a young farm boy, I could not accept that things that were alive should have to die. My mother reminded me of how, at two and a half years of age, she found me sitting on a dead cow. By its mouth I had laid a pile of fresh corn. Sitting upon its bloated stomach I was begging for it to get up. On another occasion I had dug up a barn cat that she had buried the previous day. Being undeterred by the smell of death, I was carrying its dead body around with me. It was the following summer when the farm tractor seemingly crushed the life out of me. I had been unsuccessful in coaxing life back from death, so my new strategy was to attempt to protect it. In this case I was running ahead of the farm implements to preserve the lives of rabbits and pheasants. My zeal for protecting the most innocent of creatures had put me in harm's way. And so it was on this summer day in 1951 that my life would be given some protection. From this miracle in the hayfield to others, a new worldview would be shared with me, which I now humbly share with you.

Why I was chosen to be this conduit I really can't say. Could we say that the farm boy went to the edge and brought back some understanding? Clearly the knowing that I was given was enriched considerably by my numerous edge experiences. It is also possible that another world would utilize that farm boy to look back into this world to assist us as it could.

Most of the longer and broader views of life as shared in this work were given to me during my eighth year experience of being frozen in a blizzard and during two edge experiences later in my life. These would be the fifty days long fast seeking the preservation of trees (lightly touched upon in *Something More*) and the attack of yellow jackets ('The Sting' in *Something More*). In these incidents, I experienced subjective awareness of being in this world while I was simultaneously elsewhere. I seemed able to slip in and out of earth's reality while being protected and guided in parallel worlds.

From each such experience something was added, making the design more complete. Today I am comfortable with the mosaic. Here is a part of what life would want this world to know.

The Beginning

During these different edge experiences I've been given the same point of view or perspective of what I've come to understand and believe is the elongated view of life's journey. It is a difficult perception to put into words, but I will attempt to convey this powerful vision with worldwide implications in the pages of this work.

Judging by the number of times this scene was repeated during my edge experiences and in my most revealing dreams, I am left with this impression: life is a voyage and much of the pain, unknowing, repetitive dying, and other hardships are a result of our struggle upon this voyage. The purpose of this voyage is to bring the way of life into a sea of great darkness in order to illuminate it and come to know it.

With this basic belief comes much hope and value for our lives. We have been here from the beginning. Yes our faces have changed along the way, but there always was and still is a purpose to what we do. There is a lasting, possibly eternal, value in doing this life well!

~ ~ ~ ~ ~

We stood there at the edge of today looking back into yesterday. I say we because, although I could not see another, I clearly felt that I was in the company of others. While the illumination at the edge of today was opaque, even dark; a brilliant, blindingly bright light shone from the portal where yesterday began. I sensed that the very beginning of time was declared from whence this incredible light shone. Being unable to look directly into this light, I focused on an area some distance away from it and observed numerous heavenly bodies suspended in an amoeba-like space. There were numerous spheres with a bubble-like presentation and they moved toward us. Each of the bodies in the cluster appeared to have density and was surrounded by a clear space. As they moved along, the spherical bubbles began to shrink and lightly wobble, taking on a form not unlike popcorn. Off to the right a dark cloud appeared. It loomed so large that I could not see beyond it, nor could I see very deeply within it. A gray area surrounded it, but beyond the gray this large cloud became darker than coal. The popcorn-like masses, looking more and more like vessels, continued to move toward the darkness. Oh how beautiful these numerous bodies were! Most of them were colored, with red-blue-green light coming from them. A few were perfectly clear. One in particular, a smoky blue-green, touched me as though it was my home, the vessel of earth perhaps. These planetary bodies moved ever more closely toward the deep darkness. I was troubled by the enormity of this blackened space, so completely different from the brilliant light from which they came. As these different planetary bodies, moving like vessels, entered the gray zone bordering this very dark space, a whitish fluid settled upon them like a skin. This white, skin-like substance seemed drawn from the spaces that separated one world, or vessel, from the other. Time would allow me to understand more about this sticky fluid. I came to understand it to be mustardo, the very essence of life itself.

Mustardo

It is that
which keeps and supports life itself.
The vigor and the spirit
the hope and the prayer.
As we would come to thirst
it would be the quenching something.
It would be both
the water and the well.

Slowly these vessels seemed to set their own course as they entered the blackness into which I could not see. Crashing sounds with loud cries of concern could be heard coming from the inky sphere. Loud echoes spoke of multiple collisions and reverberated within and around the darkness. The fire and force of great impact burst forth with overwhelming shock from this dark, inky realm. It was not just a dark and empty space. Something was there that would have to be considered. Something was getting between the vessels and threatening the voyage. But what it was, and what it wasn't, could not now be completely known.

~ ~ ~ ~ ~

For me if there was a point in time when the big bang of the astrological sciences could be identified, then this would surely have been it.

A certain amount of insight into this darkness may be gained by sharing an account coming from the realm of Benginers. These truncated versions were shared over a period of time from the delightfully alive phantoms who reside in the fluid space adjacent to the physical confines of our planet. They always seem to be so concerned with us, and I am beginning to understand why.

These are people-like phantoms who can claim a continuous existence from the beginning. I am introducing them briefly because of their accounting of life's voyage, its hopes and promises, and its losses and vulnerabilities. Unlike us, they seem to have a clear understanding of the length of time they have been in existence. A large part of the longer view of how it was and how it is was communicated to me while in their company. They are willing and capable of sharing the bigger picture as they step into and exit from our world of existence. Their present place of residence is a fluid realm very close to our present reality of earth. More so than any others, these phantom people were and are human-like. They are such close cousins to us, and we to them. My experience with them has revealed that they are kind and helpful when present. They constantly express their allegiance to life, and they long to be recovered, to reclaim their place in existence. Subsequent passages will reflect more upon the Benginers, who they are, what they see, and how we are connected.

In their words, "We were once upon life's deck, guided by the light of day, as you are now. Beware of the encroaching sleep, which surrounds and even now occupies your vessel. Don't allow your lives to be taken away! We also," with a sweeping expression of inclusion meant to imply the entirety of their milky-fluid realm, "came this way as you have come. We preceded you in our time but have lost our world. Many who came with us are lost as well and have lost communication with us." In hushed voices, as though fearful of being overheard, they continued to communicate their travails, pointing into the deep and distant darkness far beyond us. "That was and is our vessel. A protective and molten fire protects our one-time world from the troubling sleep that entered our vessel near the end of our time. Now those of us who are left behind could not endure the scorching fire that blazed from our world. If that very hot flame can burn through the overwhelming darkness from which the sleep came, then we still have hope as you have hope of the open and lasting sea beyond this deep night. Your vessel of earth is still at the edge of the vast darkness. Continue to navigate in your circuitous route. Do not allow yourself to sink more deeply into this blackened space or your fate may not fare any better than ours!" Wow!

Barely able to hear more but wanting to continue this opportunity to know how it was and how it is, I fumbled with my questioning thoughts. "So it's ... not just a star?" I queried, pointing toward that which they identified as having been their world.

What has fired those
distant stars?
Have they been where
life once was?
If they have been
taken from,
is that what's left
of what was begun?

"Yes, it is a star, but it was and is also our home. As we were being squeezed mightily by the night in our last days, our vessel erupted into a scorching fire so that it might escape the night. Now we can only trust that it will." And the fuel that feeds this fire? My suspicion was confirmed. It was indeed their world's mustardo, liquefied and ablaze; temporarily, at least, taken from all the life that once resided on that vessel.

Any promise of one time life was now suspended deep within the hold of their fleeing star. Those that were left in the milky, shadowy realm in the space between our world and the great sphere of darkness were left with very little mustardo. It would only be enough to sustain them in a static condition until life might come their way again. I wanted so much to reach out and hug them, but there was nothing solid there and my arms moved through them like a warm knife through butter. Still, I wondered, wouldn't it be nice if our world could somehow allow the marooned sailors a place in or around our vessel? Perhaps we could utilize their experience and understanding of this foreboding darkness to help free us of the night!

The Benginers began moving away from my range of perception while I felt myself returning to the terra firma of my world. Here again came what would become a familiar refrain from their phantom realm:

> "Get up! Get up!
> There is yet time.
> Get up! Get up!"

As one hand touched again my home on earth, another reached out and touched their murky realm, leaving my heart to resonate with this deep appreciation.

Always Day_

We must again place our hand completely in life's way.
Living apart from life threatens to take our face away.
As we have lived in both the night and the day
we have known both the beauty and frailty of it.
But clearly, life is worthy enough,
and the call has gone out.
Embrace what is ours and leave all the rest.
Now we will have life eternal or eternally a nighttime guest.

Some have asked, "Did you meet God personally during your adventures to the edge of life's fantastic voyage?" No, I can't say that I did. I have never thought to personally seek God out. God has always seemed present in goodness and life wherever I met it. But should God have a place of residence, I suspect it might be at the source of the blinding light noted above. Another question often asked is, "Is there a particular belief system that seems to be 'more right' than another when regarding life and its expression?" I don't feel confident enough to attempt an answer to this question. I will add with assuredness that the quality of faith seems central to all true belief systems. Faith and its extension of basic trust are critical to becoming open and receiving the More of life. It is cause for concern that among the numbers who profess to believe, so many are often absent from the places where we might be expected to practice our faith. Houses of worship, meditation, prayer, and reflection allow us to be receptive to feeling and sensing what may be asked of us. These places and preparations provide us with an opportunity to quiet our busy minds and utilize other faculties so important in direction and discovery. It is impossible to overstate the value that faith and trust will play at times of uncertainty during our recovery from the clutches of the bottom-line way of living. We are at a time when a certain amount of belief will be necessary to successfully clarify what we are and what we aren't, as well as who we were, who we are, and who we will choose to be.

What specific things do I remember about those different worlds when I entered the specific realities that belonged to them? Very little. Most of these interworldly travels took me to places where my mind could not follow. I am left to assume that our cognition belongs to this world and the adjacent realities connected to it. It would follow that inter-worldly travel may seem to wash our minds clean. Who I was, what I was, and where I was while being there was gone from me. Leaving here and going there was often accompanied by a breathtaking view of our world just before my mind was disconnected. The same was also true of the return, leaving there and coming here. There were a few exceptions, however, when my subjective sense was that I occupied two worlds simultaneously. Or maybe it was two realities of the same world defined by different frequencies.

Did I have any guides? Not that I could see and specifically identify. I did not feel alone, however, and may have indeed been assisted.

Are there any particular obligations and opportunities necessary to receive the grand promise noted above? The only obligation is to support the pulse of life. Should you disbelieve or doubt the message within *More or Less*, that may be okay. Your purpose may nonetheless be full and complete if you are living a caring life. The opportunities are many, none more so than to fulfill a function as a Sailor of Fortune. As such, you will feel great value in facilitating others in awakening from the layers of darkness that may surround them. Your task is to carry a light so they, too, may see the many beautiful possibilities before them. If this vision from outside and beyond the sphere of contemporary knowing becomes you, then a seeable, believable overview of who we are, where we are, and where we are going from here will be most comforting.

Made by the Maker

Life, the essence from which we are, never knew a time when it wasn't. Yes, the existence experience of what we are now a part abides by the parameters of time. There was a beginning in time for this existence experience as we journeyed upon the earth. Hopefully we will satisfy the promise of our parting and manifest beyond time. There was purpose and value in its inception, and there is much hope (both within existence upon this world and others, as well as the realm from which we were sent before time) that the intention of our beginning will be confirmed.

How things might have been in our very beginning, the inception, is open to conjecture. The collective visions and perceptions of our journey garnered from the edge experiences of my life have not given me a complete view of this beginning. The only intention is to suggest how it could have been, to put a few words to this unknown.

> The creative moment was said to be God
> The shaker – baker – more of life maker!
> From the all of life our way has been given.

As creation's grand chef, God has stirred the ingredients of life into a great batter with intention and purpose. A fuel was added to our promise, mustardo. Mustardo is the underlying dynamic qualities of life; vigor, power, and passion that powers life itself. With this fuel we were sent out toward the edge of night. Upon the vessel of earth and over time the mineral, plant, and animal kingdoms established relationships and expressed themselves in many life forms. The intention was that this batter would manifest into a viable and staying life expression. The hope was that it would also seed itself into the great night and bring life, light, and warmth into the distant darkness. Life would be lent upon this voyage and emerge upon different levels and realities. These different realities would be of varying design and substance. Some would be firm existence experiences, while others would be fluid and reside in the space between where the magic and mystery live. While each reality would be of its own singular design, all would share the percolation of the spirit, or mustardo, of life's breath in different ways with a unique design for each reality or world. These multiple realities represent the differing ingredients in our beginning and are part of the single voyage with the wondrous promise of our creation. It also must be noted that threat or failure in any of these realities or layers imperils the entire voyage.

In some ways our voyage is more fluid than form. Our purpose is the complete expression of life here and now while we carry the qualities of this life into the dark and unknowing space that surrounds our voyage. The darkness that now challenges us is the same night-like sphere to which our bearings were set in our beginning. The voyage to which we belong is referred to as the existence experience and is a multilayered creation with different realities of form and space. This includes us, our earth, and the here and now.

Among these multiple realms, our existence experience and its expression of life and well-being are now in question. That this unique expression of life is being measured and revalued upon the planet of earth is our comfort and also our great concern.

So much is at stake here in these times. While the existence experience moves onward, its well-being seems threatened. So much of life, which fuels this reality, seems to be lost, subdued, and taken away. While the other layers or realities of this creative voyage are not so immediately threatened, they are connected like bark is to a tree and are not easily separated from us. The health of any one of the realities of this voyage of life affects the well-being and promise of all the rest.

Where are we now? Our existence experience is identified as being two thirds from the center of a disc-like galaxy of approximately two billion stars. Incredibly, it is said that our galaxy, the Milky Way, is one of countless billions in the yet to be quantified universe.

Fortunately for us, it is not these vast physical distances and intergalactic spaces that we need to traverse or even completely understand. Our concern is for the place of earth and the realities or worlds interconnected with her, along with the space that supports them.

We have not journeyed here before.

We are now

where our life has never been.

If we are lost,

we may need a door.

For life has

never

gone

here

before.

The current expression of our life within this existence experience is essentially the expression of being-ness within time and place. It is our greater hope that this being-ness will successfully complete its voyage, arrive in protected harbors, and be granted the eternal nature of itself.

Take from this what you may. It really is life and more of it that we will regard. This habit of dying, and all the unknowns that go with it, has gotten old. Enjoy the unfurling of this most amazing story.

Our common prayer is that the storm will desist as we lift the night from our vessel and ourselves. Navigation and protection will return to us in the light of day, allowing us to awaken to who we are and, simultaneously, to be separated from whom we are not. It is to this end that the thoughts, feelings, expressions, and experiences of this writing are lent.

Our Common Prayer

That we may together receive
just one glimpse of the morning light
that would be enough to carry us
through the remainder of this night.
And we shall then surely know that a beginning with an end
life would never willingly send.

In this way we will become acquainted again with our larger selves; to that which we may have forgotten but to which we do belong. For we do belong to so much more. It is the hope of so very many that this story, which has now begun, will continue forever to unfold.

Life has not an edge
and knows never of an end.

Perhaps the much that we are will best be revealed as we come to see and awaken to the wonder of life's sweetness.

Stephen W. Redding

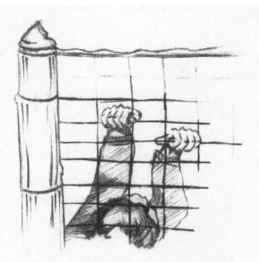

The blizzard blew in on an early March day.
A young boy's body was frozen to a fence
and covered in snow.
Without help from just one reality away,
It would have been said
that he died that day.

3

We Are Not Alone

(Their Eyes Are Now Our Eyes)

While awakening to the discovery of Something More in our lives it must be remembered that it is life, and more of it, that will equal the More. For the purposes of getting to the More it will be helpful to accept (or at least tentatively believe) that life and the experience thereof is a many-layered thing. As a living being, there are many layers of life to which we belong. We are multifaceted with multiple faces in different places and spaces. We will never really know the all of who we are until we allow ourselves to look into other worlds and are simultaneously open to other realities, which may be connected to ours. This implies a willingness to come to the windows and eventually open the doors that separate one world or reality from another.

For the purpose of our discovery, we can distinguish our present state of being from the many others. The present day earth is a world of time and place. As noted it will be referred to as the existence experience. It is a world of great expression and relatedness. The dynamics of this existence involve a fairly slow vibration but with almost endless beauty and expression. Time has always been a defining quality of this existence experience, during which the different forms and functions of life-expressing beings extend their many faces and textures into the space of this world.

Another important part of this existence experience is the connectedness we as individual beings have with the entire history of this world's journey. Many things of value and many beings have preceded us, and they still belong in one way or another to our common journey. In a mysterious sort of repository way these beings are still with us. We are now their eyes into the world. Our hopes are also their hopes. As we experience joy they also celebrate, and when we suffer they also have pain. We are not alone, and our presence here affects many others who have come before us.

Some of the beings that once lived upon the earth as we do now occupy a space that is very close to ours and possess the ability to become available to us. These beings, referred to as Benginers, are beings that have been here from the beginning. In one way or another, they have been connected to the entire history of life's existence. They were there in the beginning, and they are still here today.

These beings that previously worked and played upon the deck of planet earth are now adhered to other layers or realities of this experience of life. If they were to actually greet us or reveal themselves to us, they would most likely manifest as phantoms or even ghosts (friendly ones, of course).

This leads us to the assumption that no one who stands upon the deck of life should allow themselves to think that they are a being of happenstance or that they are a spirit just arrived. Instead, we must consider the long journey we have been on. The vigor and inertia that represents our lives is, in part, also the momentum of the onward journey built up by all those who have come before us. So even while we are relatively new faces turned toward the sun, much of the wind that fills our sails is also ancient wind.

At this point, the opportunity to care as life cares and the obligation to stand in for all those who came before us merge into us and are nurtured collectively with our hopes and visions. The joyful obligation is that we are now the willing eyes and voices of all that have preceded us throughout this existence experience. Many now see as we see.

They Are as We Are

From behind our eyes
they too look into the world,
seeing as we see
feeling as we feel
hoping as we hope.

The opportunity here is that we might infuse their resting essence with a loving confidence that the journey continues still. In hope and expectancy, we represent life's longing to become free of the night while giving value and continued meaning to their times.

Once Upon the Earth

Occasionally we will be greeted by a personal-type likeness of one or some of those whose highway is now our highway. Dreams, clouds vaporizing, and molten embers of a fire are some of the fluid mediums that may allow the unseen to look briefly through a window into our day. I shall never forget a recurring face and nighttime voice I would hear as a farm boy of eight to ten years old. The strong and wise countenance was written upon a lady's face and often came in my dreams. A soft yet compelling voice would sometimes accompany that face while I rested with my head on my dog Judy's belly in the hayloft. I would hear a familiar voice, "Get up! Stay up! Look up!" The message was short and cryptic, and up was always a part of it. After a period of time I grew weary of this recurring face and was frustrated that I could not do anything with it. At that time it had no relevant meaning for me. One day that changed while visiting my maternal grandmother, Mona, in the house of my mother's birth. Mona asked me to walk the wooden staircase with her so she could introduce me to the pictures of some of her family and thus my ancestors and kin.

I was most uncomfortable with this stairway because every picture, and there were many, was a likeness of someone who was already dead. I hated to deal with dead things! I was still recovering from Grandpop's funeral, which had occurred a few weeks earlier. I loved and now missed his stories, the music from his harp, and the smell of his corncob pipe. The word of his passing was difficult enough, but the situation was made even more difficult when we went to a house with too many flowers where everyone cried as they stared at him in a box. The box was soon taken away to a pre-dug hole. They covered his box with dirt while people cried some more. I was hoping I might hear one final sound: a word, a snort, a cough, anything that might be a parting signal, but there was no sound except the thudding of dirt thrown upon the box. Well, this dying and getting buried was something I never wanted to be a part of again!

But on this occasion, with Mona pulling me by the arm, we started the slow assent up the stairway. We stopped on each step while Mona explained about who was looking out at us from behind the glass protected and framed pictures. I had never known so many important people had come before us, and she seemed to know a great deal about all of them. And then, there she was, the face from my dreams. She looked almost regal, but locked in time as she gazed straight at me. I sat down quickly on the step to keep from falling over and stammered to Mona, "That's her, that's her. There she is." After relating her dream-like visitations to Mona, Mona revealed that the woman had been a schoolteacher in a one-room schoolhouse in Lost River, Virginia, and that she had long ago passed away. Perhaps she was still teaching, with the "Get up! Look up! Stay up!" phantom vocals I heard from afar.

It was all a bit much for me there at Mona's house upon the steps. I left those steps knowing that the next time this lady came to me in my sleep or daydreams, I would be able to address her with, "Hello, Gertrude."

How did it become my conviction that no one and nothing that truly lives completely dies? How we come to be their hope and eyes into the world of earth was revealed to me over the course of my life. Certainly the visitations of Gertrude were part of this knowing. This connectedness to those that came before us was even more strongly illustrated in another of my life-edge experiences.

The Blizzard

I was about nine years old and attending the Eisenhower Elementary School in Gettysburg when an unusually harsh late winter blizzard blew into town. The snow had been building from mid-afternoon and I remember how I couldn't wait to get home and tuck my calves into their special stable with a new bedding of straw. Then when the cattle had been watered and fed, I would slip onto a calf's back and ride into the snow. What a delight this would be with the fluffy white precipitation cushioning my certain falls.

"Attention, attention," Mrs. Eden called, "The buses are here. There will be an early dismissal due to the snow. Everyone to your buses! Hurry up now, and find your bus."

Personally, I hated this new school with its many rules, macadam playground, and all the confusion of so many kids and so many buses. It was my second year at the new school, but I never liked it, and I yearned for the one room, wood heated Boyd School with one teacher and eight different grades. I attended the Boyd School for the first and second years of my education.

Lost in thought I boarded the bus. "Hey, kid, you are on the wrong bus!" True, this was not my usual bus driver, Mr. Jingling.

"OK," I said, "Where is my bus?"

"Hurry, he's at the very front of the line!" came the reply. As I exited this bus and ran for my bus, I saw the door close ahead of me, and it pulled out into the snowstorm. All the buses pulled out in turn, and there I stood in the heavy snow without a bus. I was deeply worried. How would I get home?

"OK," I thought, "I know the way. I will walk home!"

No sooner did I get off the school grounds than a large car pulled up, a door opened, and a fat and friendly man was telling me to get in. "I need to get home," I said. "I missed my bus."

To which he replied, "A snowstorm is no place for a boy." Yeah, I thought, five miles would take me a long time. "I'll take you home," he said. Happily, I jumped into the big car. How lucky I was to have someone get me out of the snow and take me home in such a nice, warm car I thought.

It wasn't long however, until something didn't feel right. "This isn't the way to my house," I said, as the gentleman made his way through the side streets of Gettysburg. Soon we were leaving town and entering the battlefield. This was quite the opposite way to my house, but it was on the way to my uncle's dairy farm. "Oh, so we are going to my uncle Bud's?" I asked. There was no response.

Little by little, I was getting more nervous. The man, who had been so nice earlier, didn't seem so nice anymore. He cursed aloud at the snow. His fancy big car was having difficulty negotiating the turns and hills of the battlefield. As his tires spun and struggled with the snow he cursed steadily. When he gained some traction, a stressed face and cracked grin would look my way to assure me we were okay. Then he turned onto another road that would neither take me home nor to Uncle Bud's dairy farm. At this point, I reminded the driver that I really needed to get home, now! The look he gave me revealed a frightening countenance, as he struggled with the snow again. His tires screamed as the car came close to a complete stop.

"I have to go!" I shouted, as I opened the door and jumped into the snow. He cursed farewell to me.

How would I get home from here? I sensed my bearings and out into the open fields and woods I went. The snow fell so densely that I could not see. Darkness began to set in and I knew I was in trouble. Still, I felt relieved to be out of the stranger's car. Something about that man and his big car had stirred considerable fear within me, but now I was facing nature's elements, all of which were familiar to me: the snow, the woods, the farm fields. I thought I would be okay.

The snow continued to fall and walking became more difficult. I left a large section of woods and entered a meadow of thickets. The snow was now up above my knees and walking was almost impossible. I came to a stream. Snow lay on the ice covered portions of the stream but it dissolved as it hit the running water, which was easy to see. What would I do now? I had to attempt to cross this stream even though I knew that if a stream was not completely frozen over, I was supposed to stay off of it.

I would risk it. I was in a bad situation. There was nothing around me but the lonely and empty terrain of the battlefield. To seek shelter among the large, granite boulders was a thought, but I feared spending the night with the pained ghosts of thousands of lives lost too early in the Civil War who, as myth said, could sometimes be heard crying in the night. I had come some distance and my only hope was that there was something beyond the stream.

Slowly and with a great deal of trepidation, I started across the stream. The sound of cracking ice followed each step I took. It was the ominous sound that thin ice makes in the brief moment when it is tested by a weight and either miraculously holds or catastrophically fails. Halfway across the stream, the ice gave way to the frigid water below. I struggled to climb out the far side in water that was shoulder-deep. My clothes quickly froze, making walking even more difficult. Snow continued to fall, the wind blew, and darkness was all but complete. I sensed that I was dangling at the edge of my life. My bodily sensations seemed to disappear. My legs felt stuck in the snow and I leaned over at the waist wanting to pitch into the snow to rest, maybe even sleep. But, wait. Was that a light up ahead? The icy clothing had formed a cast that restrained me. If I could just free myself from its frigid constraint I would struggle to get closer.

Somehow, I did continue to move. Sometime later, a dairy farmer found me frozen solid to his cattle fence just twenty feet from his dairy barn. "I couldn't believe it," he later recalled for the police. "When I left the barn for the house, something attracted my attention to the fence. I thought it was a calf or my dog stuck in the blizzard. I was sure he was dead, completely frozen. I had to cut part of my fence to free his hands, which were in a frozen grip on the wire." He then recounted carrying my frozen body into the house, laying me in front of his wood stove, and removing my icy clothing. At this point I was able to hear and process what was going on around me, but I had not yet returned sufficiently enough from the beyond to respond to it.

My mother and father were also at the farmhouse. I remember my mother telling the police that where I was now, warming by the stove, was the best place for me. I quietly thanked Mom for resisting the talk of taking me to the hospital, remembering my difficult stay there four or five years earlier.

Once again, I had some protection. Without help from another reality beyond ours, that nine-year-old farm boy would have been overwhelmed and fated to die. During this experience I did not have the sense of being lifted into another world, as was the case with the tractor incident and Javunda. Instead, I was somehow guarded and assisted in some inner sanctum of this world. I was comforted and protected until help arrived. In my suspended state of everyday consciousness

51

I had an awareness of earth-like beings assisting in my protection. A clue was given to me when I recognized the face of Gertrude among the caregivers, as she scolded me for daydreaming and missing my bus. Grandpop was also there, telling me that he had tried to warn me about getting into the stranger's car. He and the others expressed how relieved they were when they were finally able to nudge me out of that car. To this day I am amazed at how easily I passed from the frozen, spent earth awareness into a suspended state of safety in another reality that followed passing out in the blizzard.

During my struggle to lift my weighty, water soaked body from the stream and for the short time after that until I fell completely unconscious, the kindly faces and images of people and voices urged me on. "Get up! Get up!" There was that refrain again and that white light that I saw just before losing consciousness to this world. Was it a light from the farmer's house, or was it the entrance to the warm and protective realm of those beings that now protected me?

At first I felt them to be hallucinations of sorts, but some of the images were very recognizable. Grandpop, Gertrude, and a favorite cousin all seemed to call and push me on. I couldn't understand why they were concerned when I felt fine. When my frozen body passed from earth consciousness, the many images became even clearer. I seemed capable of listening to them and understanding how it was on their plane of existence. As my perceptions adapted to the subdued lighting of this phantom space I was able to look deep into their reality. Faces and impressions of beings went on almost endlessly. A warm and agreeable atmosphere surrounded them. Though I could not easily see all of them, I could clearly sense their presence and understand their concerns. They could, and did, constantly monitor the goings on of this world. They could still assist and guide me from where they were.

How much earth time was involved in this exchange with my 'collected kin' I could not say. During their introductions and teachings, I was very comfortable and not at all aware that my body lay frozen in a farmer's meadow or, as I would be told later, frosted fast to his fence.

Not only did my kin and friends from just beyond the veil comfort and protect me until earth help arrived, but they also taught me. I could sense and see how in times of uncertainty there truly may be direction and suggestion put forth which, if we can learn to receive and believe it, can help us along our way. We are not alone! The joy, celebration, and ease of mixing with those many beings was a pleasurable thing indeed. In one way or another, they all belonged to me as I, in part, belonged to them.

Looking back, I know the composition of these friendly people to have been phantoms as regards standards of being in this world. At the time of my frozen state, I felt safe and comfortable in their realm. In fact, I didn't want to leave their company. But, once again, it was not my time and place to be there. It may never be a space where I reside as they do. But what a special space it was! Even now, as I live and breathe in the sixth decade of my life, the certainty of these spaces of wonder and residence is clearer than ever. It gives me such a sense of exuberance to share these discoveries with the physical beings of this existence experience, the people who share the here and now with me.

Reluctantly, I released my consciousness from the Benginers' realm, that space inhabited by all those who have preceded us on this journey and now wait for the resolution of our voyage. I responded to my mother's touch as she attempted to rub the cold from my frozen feet.

The state police soon began to question me intently about what had happened. "You say a nice, fat man in a big car stopped? What did he look like? What did the car look like? You jumped out? He became nasty?" Without further explanation, one of the policemen suggested to my father that the snowstorm may have saved me. I sat quietly thinking that it may have been the unseen kin and friends who deserved my appreciation in this matter. Mom would later advise me that the deep concern echoed by the police arose from the likelihood that this 'nice, fat' man was probably a child molester who had been dissuaded from following through on his despicable impulses as a result of the blizzard foiling his travel plans.

Soon I found myself slipping back to the nether realm, to again encounter the wonderful entities that had held and helped me remain alive at the very edge of earth existence. During this brief return to the Benginers' space, I could hear the police talking to my mother and father with a sense of urgency regarding the stranger who had taken me from school. They also recounted the miraculous circumstances that had surrounded the tractor incident. I found it really difficult to depart the Benginers' space. They seemed so nice, so warm, and so happy to see and help me. Together they and I had so much to celebrate! I attempted to thank them in earth tones, but noise seemed to upset their comfort zone and they withdrew. So with a wide, appreciative, silent smile I left them.

Is this experience so different from wanting to return to a favorite or telling dream? We resist the alarm until the compelling dream completely fades, but for some time we are capable of snatching a little of it and basking in the feeling and the information it left with us.

The police were concerned that I was not responding to their questions, but Mom assured them that I was just resting from a very difficult ordeal. She confirmed with the farmer and his wife that my resting there was okay, and she asked the police to come to the family farm the following day to continue their investigation, to which they agreed. Thus, I had more time to collect myself and allow my earth consciousness to return to me. It also allowed me an opportunity to peer backward into that space of the Benginers and attempt to understand how they joined with us just beyond the veil in the journey of life upon the vessel of earth.

Once I was introduced to their space, I was sure I had met and been comforted by some of them before. In times of loneliness and pain, they had comforted me. In the night of the boogeyman they silenced and assured me. Even in this immediate experience I was certain they had given me the courage to jump out of the car into the teeth of the blizzard. And I am sure they assisted in my climb out of the stream. Did they not help me move the last couple hundred feet to the farmer's fence so that I might be found? And years later, did they not lift me from the stone road and into the stream to help protect me from the venomous sting of the yellow jackets?

On a lighter note, in the aftermath of this frigid drama, a childhood friend nicknamed me 'Popsicle.' In her childlike simplicity she reminded me that only God could have saved me from such a disaster. I could only respond that God has some wonderful phantoms working for her!

Perhaps from the space where they rest and gather, seeing might be more complete. I distinctly remember one earnest declaration from them that thoughts had entered my mind that did not belong there. They did? Which ones?

A unique quality of this kinship with their reality was that, while I could maintain everyday concerns and thoughts, I could not voice them. There seemed to be a filter between my mind and their world.

There seemed, however, to be no restraints placed on the greetings, directions, and information coming from them to me.

Many hours and days were spent sharing these discoveries with Mom. "Mom, we aren't alone," I said.

"I've never wanted to think we were completely alone either, Stephen, but I am so glad to hear your stories about the Benginers. And to think that Gertrude was one of them is even more incredible. Tell me more. Please remember everything that you saw," she pleaded. "But, Stephen, keep this discovery between us for now. People will think that all of this is a thing of your imagination. They'll say extreme cold can do things to people's minds."

It has long been believed by some that other parallel realities do exist alongside of ours, and that good or disastrous forces may inhabit them. For me, I've seen these parallel worlds as being the place of angels or demons, but I do think that at least one exists that is inhabited by people who have come before us. This is most incredible, and it gives our human world great hope and responsibility as well.

Mom was open to my assumption that these Benginers were able to guide and help me as well. This led me to ask, "Why didn't they carry me over the stream or at least keep the ice from breaking?" Mom told me that certain laws and designs govern different worlds. They could only touch me once I touched them. By losing consciousness and venturing to the edge of death, I approached the veil. From there they could intervene in an almost physical way. She went on to conjecture that fluid exchanges between realities would not clash with earth's worldly designs and thus can be spoken to in our dreams or even communicated telepathically during our everyday lives.

Where life once was it still may be.
As we make our way upon this world
Much which is us now preceded and provided,
Now through our eyes they might see,
And guide us through.

Benginers

They have been here from the beginning.
They can help to stir the wind.
They can cause chimes to ring.
They can help birds to sing.
They can see you in your dreams.
They can comfort you if you cry.
They can steady you when you fear.
They can signal you when danger is near.
From behind your eyes, they can see into the world.
And from this world we can know as they know!

At this juncture it may be useful to further define how these Benginers have appeared to me personally. In so doing we may be able to touch upon generalized characteristics of these helpful-type phantoms as they might appear to others. They can mirror human beings so exactly that interactions may occur with them that we don't even recognize.

I now realize that since the early years of my life I have frequently been assisted and quieted by these phantom-type beings. Their adeptness, silence, and cunning timing are quite remarkable. Benginers can show up in an instant and disappear just as quickly. They often manifest as a reflection of oneself or another human being. They may signal their presence by duplicating one of our own tendencies, by pulling an earlobe, running fingers through hair, motioning thumbs up, or displaying a duplicate limp. Their human-like form makes them indistinguishable from others in the crowd. I have evidenced their help and support in both the realm of existence and the suspended state of the space between. My first certain introduction to them occurred during the blizzard experience, but they may have influenced my life even before. How they managed to move me from the stream to the farmer's fence where I could be found I'll never know, but move me they did. While I remained in their fluid space they also counseled me. Their information and directives have supported and guided me over the fifty-some years since the March blizzard of my elementary school days. The occasions upon which I have been welcomed into their realm have been few in number, but their visits to our world have been numerous.

For me, the greatest value of these Benginers seems to be their long-knowing and timely guidance. They often reveal themselves to comfort, steady, and compose us during difficult situations. I'll never forget the gentlemanly Benginer who steadied me during my sentencing at Bucks County courthouse on the trespassing charge I faced for my actions in defense of some grand trees. The situation and looming prison sentence was almost as unsettling as was the powerful voice that flowed through me, "Technology and the greed which employs it have outdistanced conscience!" And then there he was, a man with a kindly but serious face, tapping the side of his nose. A clue. Almost instantly I regained my composure. A sobbing, snotty cry became a gentle flow of warm tears as the voice continued to flow through me, "It is such a time, if we will not agree to be a voice for our natural world then the vessel of earth will not be well enough to carry us into our tomorrows."

Benginers can also show up to assist in the most mundane of things. Sometimes when I am lost upon a highway a car appears. If a kindly, though seemingly emotionless, person makes a small gesture, I follow his car. As soon as I'm on track again he may pull ahead or lag behind, turn a bend, and disappear. It is important to note that, although they may appear, help, or guide us, others around us may not even notice their presence.

When we are broken
or bent low
Life will know
and not forget
Who we are
and what we're not
For we've declared
in our day
Whether the thorn
or bloom will stay.

In Her Words

The following account, sent to me by a lovely lady named Kim, illustrates the More and the goodness that characterize the experience of so many who have seen beyond as a result of extreme shock or near-death experiences. Note the figure with the rose. Was he a Benginer?

"I do not remember leaving my body as the accident took me. I just found myself in a brilliantly white room filled with beings of light. Andy, my deceased daughter, was there, and what I felt was beyond words to describe: incredible joy, a feeling of being welcomed home, recognition of being in exactly the right place, of being appreciated for exactly who I am, and of love beyond all reckoning. I stayed in this state until it was time for me to go, and when I realized I was to leave, I resisted with every fiber of my being. No! I was not interested in even discussing going back! There was nothing there for me; all that I wanted and cherished was here. Gently, I was literally pulled to the doorway. There was nothing special about the door it was just the framed entrance to the room. However, like a cartoon character, I put my palms and feet on the frame and resisted with all my might. All of my efforts were for naught. With great love and tenderness I was placed outside, which is where I opened my eyes in the hospital.

The miracles had not stopped, however. My glasses had been removed, so everything in my sight was very blurry and also dim due to the low light. The first thing I saw was my hands, folded one on top of the other on my chest. They were literally black and grossly swollen. I thought to myself, 'Obviously, I've been injured.' Carefully I moved my back a little. I've had a lot of back injuries in my life, so I needed to take stock of how bad this one was. To my shock and everlasting gratitude, my back was totally fine.

At this point I looked farther out and saw a man sitting in a chair beside my bed. He was tall, blond, and was holding a single, red rose. As I took him in, he smiled and gently asked me if I knew who I was (I did), where I was (a hospital?), what had happened (an accident?), and who he was (the person who saved me?). At my last answer he smiled, rose, and without saying another word, he placed the rose on my bed and left. I felt distressed. I didn't know who he was, I was all alone in a strange place, and I had more questions! It was several minutes, although it felt longer to me, before a nurse came into the room. I asked her who the man was, and she had no idea who I was talking about, no one did. I was left wondering if he was an angel, and the rose was very real."

I am certain that Benginers represent a contingent of phantoms that have a slippery function of showing up to steady and assist those who are attempting to serve life. Are they part of the wedged, unseen people who have preceded us and for whom we are now the eyes that look out into today's world? Yes! Many of us may be accompanied by these helpful phantoms, which are unique to our personal highway. These phantom-like beings are part of a personal contingent of unseen figures awaiting our willingness to allow their assistance. While we are now their feet on the earth, they may be a source of great assistance in the hope that this journey will continue and that we will be successfully received.

How and where might these slippery phantoms exist and reside? Most of those we now stand in for probably reside or rest in fluid or form aspects of our immediate world. The repositories of such can be found in the fluid realms of earth such as the wind and water and also in the more solid plant, animal, and mineral realms. They are on duty, so to speak, and they remain available to us as we need them or call for them. Their phantom-like space is very close and connected to our world. Might they also represent beings remaining from a previous vessel that had once come this way but succumbed to the storms of darkness? This remains a matter for conjecture. There are some things I feel are true about Benginers. They are from a phantom space and move rather easily and fluidly in and about this world. They never become available to us to confuse, take from, or hurt us. It may well be that the phenomena of angels may, in fact, be these Benginers. Certainly, the guidance and support they have provided for many people fit the scenario for how Benginers come and go. The biggest difference may be in how their genesis is viewed. I am quite sure that Benginers were once as we are now, manifested upon the earth, living out their allotment of time while enjoying a life in existence. On the other hand, some say angels come and go from heaven; therefore, angels may be somewhat different than Benginers, even while performing many of the same functions. It is okay if we are not ready to understand or believe in them. They will show up and render whatever assistance is needed, possibly helping to change a tire under the guise of a friendly, helpful human being. They will never, ever accept a tip, not a dime. What would they do with it? They will also appear self-contained, speaking little, but exuding a gentle helpfulness. We will never fear their intentions; their kindness is complete. Once we have been assisted they are quickly on their way, out of sight and back into the fluid world from which they came.

Among their many helpful functions Benginers are most effective and appreciated during those brief moments of our passing from this world. How we die is so important. Throughout the reflections within this discourse of *More or Less* the implication of 'dying on our feet' clearly implies that we take charge of our deaths. Why does it matter? As death nears there will be choices, and awareness is critical. Among the shadows and confusion we must look for the Benginers. Benginers will distinguish themselves by the extension of their hands. Take the hand! The hand will be warm and firm. None of the other troubling apparitions will extend anything toward us. Their tendency will be to herd us by gathering around. They will attempt to move us in the direction they inhabit by causing us to back away from their frightening countenances toward their dark and cold home.

Leaving Here and Living On

Leave with your eyes open.
Leave with no enemies.
Leave with no regrets.
Don't stay the extra day.
You are leaving here, but you are not dead.
Look forward to your parting,
which helps you prepare
for your reception.

As they come forth to assist us there is also the implication that they are counting on us. It is my impression that more and more of them are becoming available to us. If this is true, their presence among us may indicate that we are at a very important time in the voyage of our world. There is much work needing to be done, work in which they are more than willing to participate.

There seems to be a subtly grim or serious underlying concern about them. There seems to be tension in their faces. Perhaps they see more than we see. Perhaps they understand the threat to life in these times. Perhaps they must be carried from the edge of the night by our vessel or the space that surrounds it. If so, then our success may be their deliverance. And if they are refugees from a ship that previously came this way, how long have they clung to the edge of darkness? How they must yearn for the open sea and that day with a beginning but not an end.

Though I continue to seek to clarify this even now, if there were to be a lasting impression for me from this experience among the Benginers it would be this: if our journey were to end here, then our finality would most certainly be cold, dark, and lonely. Our greater destiny would never be realized. Life must collectively awaken and rise ("Get up! Get up!") beyond the limiting restraints that seem to be obstructing the onward journey to this world's life's destination.

While among them during the blizzard experience, I developed some lasting impressions from their teachings. Perhaps if they assist us we may, together, be freed from the grasp of the tentacle. They understand this.

All of the details are unknowable
but the consequences of not awakening
are very clear ...
a long and lasting sleep!

Seeing may lift us up and give us wings.

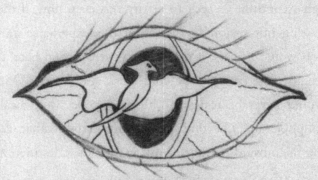

See the finite, the temporal, the now
But look also to the eternal, the enduring,
And know how.

4

Seeing

An important theme of this text will ask that we revalue our intuition. In our use of intuition as a valued means of knowing, we may feel or sense something is true, but we may not be able to understand or know how we know it. Is it not possible that strong urges, feelings, and knowings may in part belong to the unseen realities that surround us? Is it not possible that the vibrations and ripples from others who are connected to us can help us negotiate our way in this world? Indeed we may not be alone. Can we develop a sensitivity for receiving this potential guidance and wisdom from the unseen? Will we allow ourselves to see and then awaken to the wonder and the more that is before us?

The two most important conditions necessary for discovering more of our life are simple enough, but in our busy world they may be difficult to achieve. We must begin by allowing personal time for the awakening and seeing that are so important in this process of discovery. We must also find a space, a favorite place, where the unseen and unusual can emerge around us. This preparation for receiving the something more of our life will have the added healthful benefit of adding individual value and relaxation to our personal biosphere in the here and now. This readying of self is a prescription for clarifying our life as well as adding value and wonder to it. Even if we are not able to open windows or doors to know this larger view of our self, the fact is that it is there, and it is ours to embrace. If not in this life and time upon the earth, then perhaps we may receive this more as we open the doors to our future meadows.

Seeing is not only important in this world, but also between worlds. To truly benefit from this it will be important that we die upon our feet. (see 'What's Next for Us?') The subject of dying, moving beyond this world or returning to it, is critical to the visions and perceptions of this discourse. The different possibilities for us at our seeming death will be continuously integrated into this work. They cannot be avoided when regarding the larger view of our life. The general bias throughout this work suggests that we be as aware as possible when leaving here. There may be choices for us even in our last moments, and it is important that we are able to make the right ones.

As we commence to create personal time and space in our life we may begin to see or feel that excessive clutter occupies much of our personal time and space. This insight may allow us to begin to diminish our accumulated materials along with the thinking that has emphasized its false allure as we begin to understand what little value the clutter really has for us. Little by little we will be simplifying our life, a process critical to allowing us to be open to receive.

When we begin to clean up our outer world, our inner presence will benefit as well. This cleaning up and simplifying business invariably brings us to ask our self, "Does the way I am living my life give me a sense of true value and meaning, or have I been going through the motions for God-knows-what?" If the answer to this question is anything but affirmative we must consider changing the picture somewhere in our life. To this end we may need to summon some courage as we look in at our self and ask, "Why don't I feel real value and meaning moment to moment and day to day? Is my job just too repetitive, or not rewarding? Do my relationships with friends and family need to be redefined? Is one or more of those relationships taking away and not giving back? Is my belief system encouraging and uplifting, or does it keep me on my knees and not allow me to stand up and feel valued?" Changing the negatives in our life may benefit us in many ways, as well as allow us the right disposition to experience more of the unusual. All the while we will also be adding more joy, a benefit in itself that invariably yields greater health and happiness.

As we attempt to move things around in our life we should be guided by the thought that feeling valued in our everyday life is as critical to our well-being as is food in our tummy or a roof over our head. As we embark on the process of changing the picture in our life we must walk, not run or leap, and as we make these changes we must trust our instincts and ask our self, "How does it feel?" I say feel because we may have built the life we have now from what we thought was best or most appropriate, but in changing the picture our mind may not allow us to take apart what it has built up. Thus, we may not be able to be guided solely by what our mind may be telling us.

As we go about the preparations for awakening to our greater self we may also need to learn to diminish the control of our conscious mind. Gaining access to the Something More of our life will involve connecting with other realities and worlds to which we belong but of which the conscious mind is not a part. My wondrous excursion into another world precipitated by being crushed by the farm tractor was done without the accompaniment of my mind. Where I went the mind could not follow. Our mind has a valued role in organizing and understanding our world, but it cannot go beyond the box. When we are beginning to know and see beyond this world we need to be aware of how our conscious mind and the extensive cognition it controls may get in our way. Understanding our connection to other realities and sensing our inheritance beyond time will require us to get beyond the cognitive notions that are appropriate to this world but may serve as constraints against knowing another.

Creating time and space to receive the Something More of our life has the added effect of helping us to quiet our hectic mind, permitting us to know and enjoy our here-and-now. An overactive mind may become so preoccupied with the superfluous that our true self becomes lost. Instead of enabling us to attune to our surroundings moment-to-moment, we may become distracted by our mind's fixation on what is coming tomorrow or its rehashing of what happened yesterday. What we need to be or do today is often overlooked. Creating a balance with our mind as one of our faculties of knowing (but not the only one) is greatly enhanced as we create the personal time and space where we practice connecting with the more of our life.

If the place where we practice reflection can include the natural world, it is so much the better. We can benefit from the natural world's gravitational pull upon our psyche that may supplant the collective weight of old and limiting thoughts. Understanding the length and breadth of life's journey implies a constant connection or relationship to the ancient wisdom underlying the fabric of creation. As such the wonder of trees, oceans, rivers, and forests has been managed and directed throughout the ages. Impulses from the animate world may awaken a grandeur that has been forgotten but still lives within us. The sound of water, the rhythm of the woods, the song of a bird, the flight of a cloud, and the colorful bloom of a flower can all be in harmony with our inner journey. They can create a dialogue with us that can simultaneously quiet our thoughts and open windows from which we can see the more of what and who we are. If our preparation takes place indoors soothing music, favorite collectibles, and inspiring works of art are beneficial elements with which to surround our self.

It is important to remember that seeing most often begins in a very thin place over a very short moment. Our willingness to trust in the moment and embrace what we feel and receive can make all the difference. This point of interpenetration between worlds or realities is personal for us, not to be talked about, and not for show. Along with savoring the wonder, we must also protect the fragility of this sacred moment. It is as though, while residing in this world, we have reached beyond the veil to receive the hand of another presence or being doing the same thing. The moment is so special that living shall never again feel small or seem ordinary. If we do it once we can do it again, and in the process the thin place of seeing can be stretched into a much broader space. Sometimes when I sense a receptive state I open my hands while strolling or sitting in my favorite places. A soft breeze may stir, and my palms may be caressed by something from the invisible realm. A light shock often accompanies these exchanges, and if I am accompanied in my reverie, my companions may experience this electrical sensation as well. In some instances the charge stays with me for quite some time, and if I reach out to touch another or lean forward to bestow a kiss on another's cheek, the charge may spark across the encounter to the recipient's hand or face.

At any time during our period of preparation we may be greeted by the unusual. One's name may be called, or a blurred but obvious motion may occur. There may be a sweet smell or soothing breeze, something out of the ordinary. When this occurs we must try not to force our perceptions. Our head and neck should sit relaxed upon our shoulders, and we shouldn't stare. Instead, we should allow our eyes to almost close and we should softly say, "Hello!" What has begun may be a long and wondrous journey of discovery of the More of life and our place in it.

It is not uncommon at this point for our mind to break into the moment and try to explain away the phenomena. We should be prepared for this, and gently retrieve control by concentrating on the aspects of our special space; watching the flowers, listening to the music, or seeing the clouds' movement above us. Still, our mind will persist, so we should create a friendly dialogue with it. The mind might suggest that we are dreaming or that these episodes are all in our imagination. We may even sense some degree of desperation from this mind-talk as it attempts to invalidate the unusual occurrences we have experienced.

Throughout the text of this book there will be other reflections on how the mind can be both good and not so good during discovery of our greater self. Many highly intellectual and reality-based people will suggest that they have no time for the paranormal, even though every time they dream they enter that world, nor do they have time for imagination. It is the position of *More or Less* that both dreams and intuition, the sister to imagination, are vital ways by which we can be introduced and connect to the phenomenal and the unusual.

Our mind may also tell us that we should be afraid or concerned for our well-being. Do not worry. A lifetime of slipping in and out of parallel worlds has taught me that no harm will come from it. In the unlikely event that the experience or phenomenon at hand is an unpleasant one, cold or ugly with an unpleasant sound or repugnant odor, we only need to break the connection by opening our eyes wide and standing up, and the experience will come to an end. The true windows to the more that we are will always be accompanied by the positive; subjective experiences of warmth, pleasing sound, colorful experiences, and pleasant sensations.

Following her recent reading of *Something More* a friend earnestly asked me to elaborate upon how to contact and see otherworldly beings, such as tap-screws and curly-whirlys. She needed a way to intention these visitations. She wanted help in visiting with and seeing them. I could only respond that I had no secret formula or technique I knew how to share with her. I reminded her that I could not intention these visitations myself and, while I have had many visitations from them, I have never felt as though I could see them on demand. In fact, I told her that on numerous occasions I have gone out into the night to some of my favorite places and spaces of communion and nothing extraordinary has happened. Of course an evening with the night creatures of our earth is still a delightful experience.

Still, she persisted, "How do you do it?" At this moment, an answer of sorts was given to this woman, an accomplished seer in her own right. I had just completed piling eight to ten sticks of firewood over some coals in my stove when she arrived. Sitting there together in front of my open-door wood stove I was at a loss to try to respond to her sense of urgency. Seemingly in response to the compelling nature of her request, a flame jumped up and filled the stove with an audible soft explosion. All the wood was instantly aflame, an improbable event when building a fire. It reminded me of a time when a similar ignition of the wood occurred from which a visible fire-fairy danced and flew about my shack.

Clearly, this sudden and unusual ignition of the fire was a response to my friend's heartfelt and mind-probing request. We don't need an intermediary; we can touch the unseen and be greeted by the unseen on our own accord. This dramatic response from the fire was not lost on my friend. The deep furrowed lines on her forehead that evidenced the depth of her intense mental scrutiny of her own questions instantly relaxed and disappeared, and she settled back into her chair, enjoying the moment.

Open the Door to More

Stop looking,
but do not stop seeing.
Stop listening,
but do not stop hearing.
Stop thinking,
but do not stop knowing.
Stop questioning,
but do not stop believing.

My sincere feeling about finding and greeting these beings from beyond is that the best we can do is to be prepared and available. No, we may not receive what we think we will see nor can we expect to always understand what may appear to us. This preparation has two essential components. The first is to believe or trust that there is something more, and the second is to not deny or push the unusual away from ourselves when it does come tapping at our window.

From out of the cold and dark of night
A holiday blessing was visited upon us.

The Christmas Wren

Midway through my college years, during a holiday visit to the farm, a most exhilarating and painful expression of connection occurred. It was Christmas Eve and our large country kitchen was full of Reddings. Outside a brutal, snow-laden wind blew against the kitchen windows.

With a backdrop of noisy, celebratory conversation I joined Mom at the kitchen sink where she was washing dishes. In the midst of our conversation, we heard what appeared to be ice pellets hitting the window. We paused in our conversation and wondered about the sound. It happened again, and Mom ventured the thought that the winter storm had turned to sleet and ice.

"No, Mom," I said, "it is much too cold for that." Holding a candle up to the night-blackened window, I thought I saw a large butterfly. Impossible, I thought, and Mom agreed. Again we heard the distinct grainy sound against the windows. Instinctively, I started to scrape away the frosty ice around the window so I could open it.

"No!" Mom yelled. "Dad, will have a fit if you open that window."

Busily involved, I was not deterred. Mom stood back while some of my siblings wondered what silly, impulsive thing I was up to now. Soon the frost was cleared and the window opened. Out of the stormy night and in through our window a winged being flew. It wasn't a butterfly. It was a bird, possibly a wren. It circled over our heads a few times singing a beautiful song, then flew into our living room and took its place on the top of our Christmas tree alongside the decorative angel. What a wonderful Christmas blessing, I thought, as some of us hugged one another in agreement. Mom stood at the living room doorway wearing a radiant smile, understanding that something very special had happened. In the midst of our celebration, one of my brothers reopened the kitchen window, and as the snow blew in another brother poked the Christmas wren with a broom, trying to encourage it to go back outside.

At this Mom shouted, "Enough!"

"Mom," someone insisted, "A bird doesn't belong in the house."

"This is not just a bird, it's a blessing," she responded angrily, closing the window. The winged being returned to the top of our cedar Christmas tree and sang its heart out. Its coming and being among us was the center of conversation for some time. What could it mean? What was it doing in the dark night hours? Why did it signal at our window? Why wasn't it roosting in an evergreen or outbuilding as over wintering birds do on long winter nights? What kind of bird was it anyway? We were accustomed to sparrows, cardinals, finches, nuthatches, juncos, titmice, and jays, but never had we seen such a special, small bird. Mom said it was a wren and that was good enough for me.

Shortly after falling asleep that Christmas Eve, I was awakened by a loud commotion. Going downstairs, I saw Mom loudly scolding brother Charlie as she sobbed saying, "Why? Why?"

Our blessing bird was laying still, its wings spread upon the floor. Charlie stood by somberly holding the broom.

"Charlie," I said, "Why did you kill the wren?"

"Steve," he said, "I just wanted to get it outside where birds belong."

"Charlie," I said, "You didn't even open the window or the door. What were you thinking?"

A disastrous ending to an otherwise beautiful story can go a long way toward teaching and awakening. I'll never forget the tortured look on Charlie's face as he reflected on what he had done while reacting to his mother's tears and his big brother's disappointment. Part of the pain on his face was an acknowledgement that something within him had urged him to almost helplessly do this nasty deed. I had seen that tortured look before on my older brothers' faces, after my return from the hospital following the accident and the subsequent miracle in the hayfield. My living through it and quickly returning to my family may have so overwhelmed their minds that their pain of disbelief led to my unceremonious whipping in the barnyard.

Over the next few years my younger brother Charlie, number eight of fifteen, and I became very close. He, more than anyone else in the family except for Mom, showed a deep and sincere interest in sharing in my visions. Often he would look me up, do whatever he could for me and insist on being at my side unless I was sleeping. He was ready for anything. He would stay with me even while I was involved in the mundane, when the unusual was least likely to occur. In the couple of years following the Christmas wren incident, he grew in his acceptance of the unusual when it did appear and handled it quite well. He repeatedly apologized for the Christmas Eve blunder, as he described it, but he assured me that such an error would never happen again. "You know, Steve," he once recounted to me, "I was afraid of that bird and I was jealous knowing that something like that would never happen to me." This is a common response in people when something really unusual happens in their midst.

Charlie became a good companion and an apprentice of the unseen. He became familiar with the tap screws, observed curly-whirlys, and even experienced the cry of Cyclops, a single-eyed creature from beyond, which he admitted was a bit much. He was there during my cocaine addiction and was one of the few who extended his hand deep into the dark and lonely well into which I fell during that time.

Regretfully, it may have been Charlie's allegiance to me that lead to his early death. One cold February day in 1977 I called upon Charlie to return me to my country home following the failure of my car to start. On the way we came to a curve in the road, which he did not effectively negotiate. He died that night. His death, the only sibling of fifteen to have taken that ticket, has left a void in my life that has not been easy to fill.

We Walked Together

He was my brother.
He was a lot more.
He put his hand with mine
until he left through the door.

When I think of the wren, I wonder what is was and where it came from. Was it the essence of a being in bird form that came to bless or simply visit our world? Of course, it was not likely in avian form on the other side. Perhaps it was from the world of Javunda, or from some other unnamed realm. Maybe during one of my visitations we had become acquainted or reacquainted. I don't know. Very likely my passing from here to the beyond set up a path or opened a conduit of sorts, which allowed this being to arrive at our country farm. Entering our world it took on, or was given, the wings of a wren. Now it was compatible with the design and laws of the land of earth, a bird in physical form. The cold winter weather and the closed farmhouse window may have put a hitch in its groove. This is what exposed it to the disbelieving minds of my family. Though it met with a violent and undignified death, it left us with many gifts.

We could kill this bird
but
we could not capture it.

When Charlie killed the bird, he did not capture it. This winged visitor probably felt rudely accommodated, but I am certain that following its demise it quickly returned safely to its home in the fluid unseen. Unfortunately for us, we missed an opportunity to have someone from the beyond at our Christmas celebrations. Mom felt that we shunned a family blessing that was graciously held before us. There was not a Christmas that came and went in her life that she didn't hurt for what we did not receive. "Stephen," she would say, "there was a reason for its coming. Might it some time return?"

The preposterous conditions by which this being in the form of a wren came to be at our house made it easy to identify as beautifully unusual, and it offered an important opportunity for some of us. For the rest of our family its coming was a contradiction and a threat to the mind and the sense of what could be expected. Being unprepared created disbelief. This led to even more pain by way of close identification with the mind's limitations. In Charlie's case, it wasn't so much that he wanted to harm the wren as it was that his mind would not be relieved until the unusual was extinguished.

We were not open.
We could not receive.
We lost this blessing,
because we did not believe.

At the time Charlie, more than anybody, may have suffered from the cognitive pain of perceiving something that could not or should not have happened. Those of us who are not ready will simply fail to see the extraordinary in our everyday world. Meanwhile, we who are looking or have begun to see must remember not to shine a light too brightly in sleeping children's eyes. We only do harm to others and ourselves if we insist that they see what we see when they are not ready. There may come a time when all those who will pass beyond time must see and be open to receive the More of life. There may be those we want to bring along.

Lift them up if we must.
But we may not be able
to free sleeping eyes
from the rust.

Perhaps it would be better if we could just go on our way and leave those who cannot or will not see to their own devices. We are called to assist in the preparation of those who are asleep yet indicate a willingness to see. However, time is an issue in all of this, and the journey must continue. The critical question becomes whether those who are asleep and locked out of the More of life are willing to let it all go. Do those who get it and will continue to get it feel challenged to call out to others with a familiar and loving voice? "Come, please awake. Come and enjoy the More of life. It is time, and there is much to be excited about!"

If we will allow it
it shall bring us into its embrace.
Once given, never taken,
it shall only be lost to us
if we so withhold it that we push it away
from ourselves.

We can best facilitate the trust necessary to reach out for life's more if we let go of old, limiting, and repressive attitudes about what our relationship to this world as a human being is really all about. Equally limiting in one way or another are beliefs in original sin, karmic debt, and similar concepts which tend to keep us on our knees at a time when we must be seeking our wings. Being convinced that we are the 'chosen ones,' 'God's children,' or that we somehow have dominion over the earth and all of her creatures is also limiting. Such beliefs and thoughts tend to separate us from the sustaining circle of life and distance us from the necessary connection to the all of life. Regarding our race, our religion, or our level of education as somehow naturally preferred or chosen is equally separating. These better-than perspectives are often alienating, and they get in the way of the giving and gracious attitudes that are necessary to discovering and receiving the more of creation into our life.

At the same time as we are letting go of old thoughts and attitudes that may withhold something eternal and precious from us, it is important to begin to rely less on cognition with its objective only way of seeing and believing. Feeling may also become a way of knowing. "How does it feel?" is a valid way to help us determine proper or best directions in our life. So often we try to think our way through confusion and uncertainty. When deciding whether to turn right, turn left, or move straight ahead in an uncertain situation our mind, with its mental and limiting constructs, does not give us adequate direction. Asking ourselves, "How does it feel?" involves our inner intuitive knowing which, in these instances, offers more ultimate clarity. Certainly intuitive feeling is a faculty we can rely upon when sorting out how different people impact our life. We must trust more completely in this faculty. It is a very good means of knowing and believing in things, even if it doesn't easily break down into simple, quantitative mental constructs.

Tap Screws in the Garden

In the darkness of our garden …
… the illumination of distant guests was presented.

Seeing beyond the ordinary is often dependent upon our willingness to relax our logical mind, which can unintentionally lock out other worlds and realities. Another experience of welcoming the unseen occurred for a client who came to Happy Tree to choose lighting fixtures to accent a water feature we were creating at her home. It needed to be a nighttime visit so she could realistically view the different lighting qualities from which she would choose. Ten or fifteen minutes into our discussion, as we stood by the reflection pool talking about lighting, I lost her attention and felt a strong grip being applied to my upper arm. "Stephen, I'm more interested in those lights!" she said as she looked toward an adjoining garden behind us. There, in Deer Island, were about ten brightly pulsing tap screws shining in blues and green. The next half hour was spent in what she described as the delight of her life.

Slowly the tap screws diminished their illumination and withdrew into the background. It was clear to me during this visitation that my water garden client was okay with these glowing beings. Had she not observed them, I would not have pointed them out. But she did see them, and the time and means of awakening had begun for her during this night. Later, with fountain lighting long since forgotten, we retreated to my shack so that she could collect her balance and steady her breathing.

"What was that? What was I seeing?" she asked.

I told her she had witnessed the radiant essence of beings from another world who visited here.

"Why did they come here?" she asked.

"Our world, earth, is part of a great voyage not completely separated from their world," I said.

"Did you see the same thing that I saw?" she asked.

"Yes," I replied, "I think we saw the very same thing."

"Why did they come here to Happy Tree?" she queried, "Are you some kind of an alien? Do they know you?"

"Well, I have had some unusual connections with other realms and other worlds, but I am very human, as you know. I think they come here for a number of reasons. I am comfortable with them and feel privileged to see them. They like Happy Tree because it is a welcoming and beautiful place. However, I've also met them elsewhere, and now that you've seen them here, you may see them at your hilltop home as well. Have you ever seen them before?" I asked.

Hesitantly and with a deep inhalation she replied, "Maybe so. For a few years now I have occasionally noticed glitter coming out of my woods." She mused that it was perhaps the moon reflecting off the quartz, but then she admitted she didn't know. "I've seen some movement too, but when I've gone to look more closely, I haven't seen anything. I've heard some interesting sounds as well, that are difficult to associate with anything."

Ah, she had begun to see, so I reminded her to:

Stop looking,

but do not stop seeing.
Stop listening,
but do not stop hearing.

The truth is, this getting acquainted with the unseen should not be strenuous. We should never go about it with a sense of urgency. If we do, we will only push it away from ourselves.

Do not allow our desire
to become closer to something.
Increase our distance from it.

After taking a moment to absorb the, "Stop looking but do not stop seeing," she persisted, "Tell me more about them. What do you mean by radiance? Are they the same as spirit beings? Do they look the same in their world as we see them in ours?"

I told her that I am quite sure that they are complete beings in their world. What they would look like I couldn't say, but I was sure they would have a form of physical or fluid nature. I told her that on a few extremely difficult introductions to other worlds I definitely perceived many varied forms.

"Why do they look like Christmas lights to me?" she asked.

I replied that on occasion these tap screws may take form here, but only on the rarest of occasions would it be in a form present in their world. Each of the many worlds and realities has certain laws of design and structure that are specific only to their reality.

Coming here as they exist in their world might clash with our earthly realm's laws of reality. Expressing their worldly form might not be possible and certainly would not be easy. In fact, it could be so difficult and uncomfortable that they might not come at all. What we see as radiating light (something that can readily pass from one reality to another) is, I believe, their essence (their spirit being). Pulsing light may have represented the beginning essence of all of life as it entered into forms and functions of the existence experience. This is the eternal aspect that will continue to carry them over and beyond all time, across all places and all spaces.

We, as they, may choose to continue
over and beyond time
into all places and through all spaces.

She said she couldn't help but still ask why these incredible beings would want to come to our world. I reminded her that our world can be a precious and beautiful reality, and that they may be inextricably connected to us. In a real way their world may be ours, and ours may be theirs.

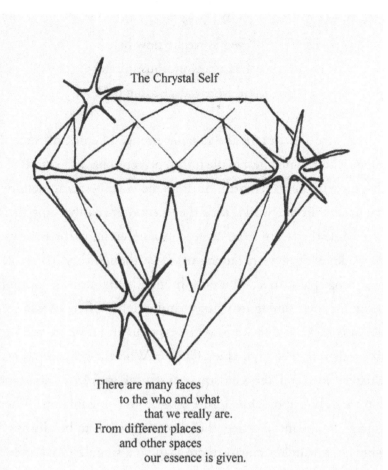

The Chrystal Self

There are many faces
to the who and what
that we really are.
From different places
and other spaces
our essence is given.

Different Faces in Different Places

We may be like

a many faceted crystal.

Light may enter one face,

then illuminate and radiate

from the many others.

We may live there
even as we are now here.
Life is a wondrous thing,
and we are awakening to it.

On many occasions the radiant essence of spirit of these distant guests is able to manifest in the forms, perceptions, and sounds of things that do exist on planet earth. At times they manifest as something fairly predictable in our world, thus they may more easily enjoy their time here while they learn from us, teach us, entertain us, or assist us. How do we know if they are among us? Even though they may look like a bird, frog, plant, tree, or even a human, their form or location may be off, or their timing may not be quite right. Often we will see them out of context. If they want to express to us and if we are willing to see them, there will be some clues. Cheezer Wheezer (see *Something More*), Croaker Joe, and the Christmas Wren all manifested as something common, but upon close scrutiny were very uncommon. When they emerge in a plant or a tree, their host may seem to be blowing in the wind on a windless day, or there may be a singular black-eyed Susan bowing up and down while the rest are perfectly still. A magnolia tree or a weeping cherry may be blooming out of season.

I will never forget the magnolia tree that broke into a full and profuse bloom six months after its normal spring flowering season following a sprinkling of tap screws. The following day nursery guests, looking to commemorate a late September wedding, could not be dissuaded from purchasing this tree, even against a high price I placed upon it. These were long-established clients of mine, and despite all sorts of verbal maneuvers I could not guide them past this tree to something that would be more suitable. I knew that the full-flowering blooms were the result of a distant guest taking up temporary residence in this tree, and I felt it was important to keep this magnolia at the nursery. I said I couldn't move it when it was in flower, as the move might harm it. They insisted more fervently that the tree would be fine.

"We want it for our daughter's wedding. It is a special tree," they stated.

"It is special indeed," I responded, "but this night's predicted frost will destroy her flowers, and what a sad and ugly appearance it might give to your wedding celebration."

It was no use. They wanted this tree. Did they feel or sense its magic, or were they simply reacting to those beautiful blooms? It did frost that night, but those blooms were out of context and their beauty only grew. We took this splendid magnolia to the long-anticipated wedding celebration in full bloom, and its flowers and fragrance extended the splendor of another world into our earthly realm, blessing this couple at the outset of their new life journey.

We are not alone here, we have many wonderful guests! If we are willing to see them we may encounter their expression in many ways and lots of places with just a little preparation and basic trust. These visitors may choose to cloak themselves in common forms so as to gain some measure of protection. There are many among us who might think their presence is unacceptable. Often people are fixated on things as they are and things as they should be. We still have trouble accepting fellow human beings of different races, nationalities, and religions. Is everyone really ready to accept beings from other worlds? Wouldn't it be special if they were?

Mind Fences

In coming to know our greater self and the more to which we belong, it must be noted that these discoveries will best be accomplished in an integrated fashion. Knowing by way of our mind and its many cognitive constructs will not be enough without the input of our intuition and our feeling center. In some instances, as was noted, we need to be asking ourselves, "How does it feel?" Calling upon our intuitive nature with its psychic inclinations, such as dreams, will assist us in knowing more completely. It is of great concern to me that in these times we relegate just about everything we want to know or understand to the functions of the conscious mind, without incorporating the other valued means of knowing that we possess. Without our feeling and psychic functions, a myopic perspective of life's wonder and our involvement in it leaves us knowing only a little of the much that we are. Thus we may be limiting our knowing by allowing our mind to dominate our experience of who and what we are. When we lessen our dependency on the mind we may begin to see more of the big picture.

One reason for this is that the mind is designed for function in the existence experience, but this represents just one reality or world, to which we belong. The mind may be doing a good job of structuring and implementing our way here, but too much dependence on mental knowing may separate us from our deeper self. The mind alone can never completely understand or adequately guide us through the different layers of life's experience, nor can it know our other faces in other places. Seeing more will help us discover more, and in the process we will remember:

Remembering

It is not only here
that we are.
The eyes that look into this world
also see from other faces
in other places,
for we are also there,
even as we call out here.

Multiple edge experiences demonstrated that my cognitive mind could not cross over the divides separating one world from another. In these instances, understanding and meaning depended upon other ways of knowing. Simply put, our mind puts us in the box, but much of enduring life lives outside of the box. Partial knowing and limited perspectives place restraints upon us, separating and withholding so much that is truly ours. Psychologists tell us that education builds biochemical pathways in the mind. These inner cognitive structures allow us to see and act on the world around us. When too much emphasis is placed on these mental structures such as the 'three Rs,' for example, they become like fences. Fences keep us in a small world, our present meadow, and do not encourage us to see or even look for other meadows or realities. Our cultured mental structures may suppress our eyes for the unusual while encouraging us to emphasize thoughts and ideals that favor utilizing our lives as productive cogs in the machines of materialism.

It is revealing to reflect upon how many people are seeking to open windows to other worlds in these times. Imbibing elixirs of many sorts such as strenuous workouts, sleep deprivation, drugs and alcohol, death defying exploits, and oxygen deprivation is being used extensively to break down, if only for a moment, some of the fencing apparatus of the mind. In so doing, we may be allowing ourselves perceptions that we ordinarily would not see or feel. The fenced-in head would scold us to stay in this meadow. "Don't bother looking beyond the fence. It is wasted time, it's illusion, it's dangerous, and it may even be illegal!"

Granting caution towards these mind-expanding elixirs, they may have some value. While old minds continue to indoctrinate young minds, we have begun to see the greater distances. Before the enclosure could be completed we had a chance to glimpse and suspect that, thank goodness, it doesn't stop here. We are able to recognize that it is only a fence we have come to. There is more, much more. It is interesting to note that before the fencing became so complete in recent cultural history, people understood the value of expansive vision. Soothsayers, medicine men, mystics, and seers were valued and given the task to identify the unusual and glean whatever information and truth that availed itself.

The incomplete sense of our existence, resulting from limited seeing and the present struggle for value in the edge of night, has doubled our jeopardy. As a result, many are left living a life that feels unsatisfying. Infused with a sense of being lost or empty, we are looking for something, anything, to fill this hole. This has led many to forfeit the top line of life for the habit of the bottom line. Some have even gone so far in their emptiness as to manipulate the world and those around them. They count dollars by way of transforming the world's resources and calling it their stuff. But are they satisfied? Alas, this may be the anointed hour when we question the mental constraints that keep us in the box of not enough. In place of these limiting thought forms we may begin to breathe and enjoy the Something More of life, and we may chance again to utilize other means of understanding, while beginning to know our longer and broader lives beyond the box.

Even while we work to poke some holes in the fences of our mental constraints, we can utilize the paranormal through an everyday function common to all us, our sleep time. Have we all not, at one time or another, sensed that there was something so compelling in the visions of our nighttime dreams that we have insisted on squeezing more out of them? Although the alarm announcing morning detail and responsibility has already rung, we ignore the get-up notice to attempt to better understand the place and message of these dreams in our lives. We know that there is something there for us. Can we bring the dream back for one last moment of viewing or enjoying? One of my most telling dreams involved the fulfillment of a wish that I carried around with me for years. I could not think my way to a solution, but through a dream an answer was given to me.

In a dream, a lake was born ...

Seeing can find us in so many ways.
Knowing when we are being called or spoken to
may be the most we ever need to do.

A Seeing Dream

While the pond we call Fairyland has always been the center of the mystical and magical at my home, it is not the only exquisite body of water at Happy Tree. Approximately twenty years ago another splendid pond came to be that is deeper and larger.

Fairyland, so rich in life, is approximately eight feet deep with a mud bottom. Its surface is approximately two acres with one and a half of those acres covered with lily pads and inhabited by snapping turtles. It is definitely the best place upon our property to be entertained by nature's aquatic flora and fauna, but it's not the best environment for swimming. Though refreshing, there is a maze of water lilies to navigate through when floating in a tube, and there are underwater grasses that present a constant entanglement hazard. From time to time water snakes, eels, or pickerel caress the legs, and on occasion when dismounting from a tube to retrieve a Frisbee, the mud might move below the feet, signaling the presence of a snapping turtle. The reaction in this case is almost electric, as one launches out of the water and back onto the floating tube in a singular, powerful motion. We needed a deeper pond, or a second separate pond, for swimming. Fairyland's depth was not sufficient to keep the sunlight from reaching the bottom, thus it nurtured a rich growth of water vegetation. Had it been twelve or more feet deep, its bottom would have been beyond the eight-foot mud layer of the Ridge Valley flood plain, and it would have bottomed on a sandy layer of earth. In that case the snappers would only have been an issue at the edges of the pond basin, where they could dig into the rich clay they so enjoy.

Another problem with Fairyland was that it had no surrounding berm for protection from the high waters of Ridge Valley stream. Consequently, we never knew what might wash in or out of this pond when high water rushed through our valley. Surface waters are often high in nitrogen and phosphates, which stimulate plant and algae growth. Bacteria are also often present in surface water; therefore, wholesome and healthy swimming does not occur in ponds that are fed or otherwise infused with stream water.

Fairyland was always highly valued for its many life forms and plentiful expressions and experiences of the unseen and the unusual. Digging this pond deeper and using the excavations to separate the stream water from our precious pond was not a serious option, although the notion had briefly crossed my mind. The obvious solution was to create a new and deeper swimming pond. For approximately three years I wrestled with the swimming-hole quandary. Where could I dig it, and how could I afford it? Many times I walked over our acreage searching for the appropriate site. One possibility was a swampy bog area, but it looked to be impenetrable, and it offered no guarantee that if we got into the excavation we would ever retrieve the digging machines. The rest of our land was inhabited by trees, and with being a proclaimed voice for my leafy friends, there seemed few viable options.

Help came to me in a dream. It was one of those dreams that cause us to sit up in our beds and take notice of the information being given. Dreams come to us with many levels of clarity, and they often bedevil our best efforts at squeezing a meaning out of them. But this dream was clear. The visualization of where the swimming-hole would be, its shape, its size, and the boulders to be found during excavation were all neatly laid out for me. I'd had my last dream of such clarity and impact when I viewed my mother lifting above us in her funeral gown. Just two weeks preceding this dream, Mom and I sipped tea together following her two-mile jog. She was her healthy, vibrant self. But I knew this dream was a real foretelling. A call from Gettysburg confirmed the dream's validity. A large tumor had been found, and soon she would depart from my every day. (see 'Virginia's Gone' *Something More*) My dream of the swimming-hole was of equal clarity. The message was clear and much more of a joy to watch unfold.

The next day, while stopping for a bite to eat in a nearby town, I saw an excavation company truck in the parking lot. I quickly identified its driver. He was the owner of a large company whose primary work was in excavating landfills and who was between contracts at the moment. Imagine that, the how was falling into place! "Sir," I said, "I want to excavate a large pond as a water source for my nursery trees." This was the line I knew I needed to use to gain financial support from the bank and to convince a very professional excavator to create a pond from my bog.

He responded that my timing was uncanny because, as of two days before, his men and their earth moving equipment were searching for work due to a contract snafu at the large landfill where they had been employed for two years. In approximately thirty days, they would be back at work at the landfill. "So, I'll come to look at your site and discuss some terms," he said. I was bursting with joy at the way my large swimming hole was coming together.

When the excavator and I walked into the wetland area of my property he grunted a bit and seemed to want to withdraw his kindly offer to help me out. "I can't put my equipment in this swamp of yours. I might not get it back out. And this clay is impossible to work with. Once I get it on my blades we can't get it off." How true this turned out to be.

"Ernie," I said, "Once you get ten to twelve feet deep there is a different soil altogether. It's nothing but sand and sandstone. You'll have good traction."

More grumbling was forthcoming, "How deep do you want to go?" he asked.

"Oh, maybe sixteen to twenty feet," I responded.

"That's a lot of hole," he replied. "How big?" he asked.

"Oh, maybe two or two and a half acres," I replied.

"What?" he said, "That's a lake! And we may not have the time to dig it. You may not have the money to pay for it."

Quick on my feet, I stated that I had twenty thousand dollars now and would get twenty more from the bank.

Ernie responded, "That gets you a one acre pond if we don't have any other issues."

"Well Ernie," I said, "I have a lot of beautiful trees in my nursery and maybe we could barter for some of them." I knew I was grasping at straws, but Ernie turned toward me with a grin on his face.

"You know," he said, "it might just work. I've recently moved into a big property and there are no trees."

Things were looking good. Not only was the vision from the dream given to me, but so much of the how was working out as well. After a brief discussion of the terms of the project, which included his choice of thirty nice trees, we had a deal. He would start moving his heavy equipment the next morning.

Excited, I went down to the cabin and informed Kathy of our good fortune. I told her we would soon have a new, deep pond. She mostly looked at me in amazement as she asked, "What?" in about ten different ways. I told her about my dream and my good fortune of running into the excavator.

"We can't afford a pond," she said.

I assured her that we only needed forty thousand dollars and the rest would be traded in trees.

"We don't have that kind of money," she said.

"We'll go to the bank," I countered.

She, the well-grounded partner of a crazed mystic, appeared reluctant and wore a strained facial expression, showing that she knew that this dream of mine would add a new challenge to our relationship!

Against many obstacles, the pond project began. While the preliminary stages had flowed with ease, the nitty-gritty of creating the pond was fraught with challenges.

The going was tough. Equipment kept getting stuck. The mud and clay would not release from their blades, and hour upon hour was needed to clear it from the machines. Ernie approached me twice to ask for additional money. Kathy and I went from bank to bank. I had now dubbed the great pond project Macanudo, after a favorite cigar, while Kathy was calling it Lake Bankrupt.

What a project grew from this incredible dream! Perhaps I would have begun to second guess this directive if it hadn't been so keen on the details. The boulders were found and placed along the eventual water line.

"Ernie," I said, "have your men place the boulders at these particular places. I want them to be in the water but with the majority of their surface exposed when the pond fills."

"Okay, we will do it, but no one can tell where the final water level of a spring fed pond will be," he advised.

But I could. I had seen it in my dream.

After two weeks of mud scraping, the excavation began to go forward with more efficiency. Three water pumps were set at the deepest levels to pump out the water that was collecting from numerous small capillaries. The excitement of bringing forth this large body of would be water was incredible for me. I faithfully kept up nighttime treks to the large depression to fill the pumps every two to three hours. The nighttime was alive with tap screws and the comings from beyond, which further encouraged my complete trust and participation in the project. With great regularity on these nighttime errands I often misstepped and ended up in a water pit, mud pile, or something equally messy. These travails only added to my sense of adventure.

As I crowed my delight, Kathy saw how flaky I had become regarding my sense of obligation and priorities. "Stephen," she would say, "this is a huge monetary obligation! It is also a huge distraction from your work when you really need to be productive." Her quiet life at Happy Tree had become anything but that with the constant running of the water pumps and the loud screaming of the excavation equipment.

At approximately four weeks into the project, Ernie approached me in a near rage, "Look, Steve, I need to pull my equipment out soon and get back to making some money to pay my bills and my men!" His contract at the landfill was renewed and he had already given me more time then we had agreed upon.

"But Ernie," I said," we haven't hit a single large spring yet."

"That's exactly my point," he said. "We are in nothing but sand and alluvials, and everybody knows this soil will not hold water."

"Wow!" I thought. "This could be a problem."

"But Ernie," I argued, "Fairyland, my lily pond, holds water just fine!"

"Yes," he yelled, "clay retains water very well, but sand never will. We will need to open the berm and allow stream water in to fill this hole and then open the far end of the pond to let it out."

"No, Ernie," I said, "I want clean spring water. I can't have the stream encroaching with its iffy water."

"Well, I'm out of time, you are out of money, and we don't have water," he went on. "And by the way, I'd like to look at your hydrology report." This would be the water engineer's assessment of available water soils.

"Ernie, I don't have a hydrology report," I said.

"You don't have a hydrology report!" he yelled in disbelief. "How do you know there is water here?"

"I had a dream," I stated.

"A dream! A f---- dream!" he screamed in disbelief. "All of this time and money for a f---- dream!" A momentary look of fear and anxiety crossed his face, as he lowered his voice to an intense whisper. "Permits?" he asked in a hushed voice as he turned away knowing that there were none and understanding his complexity in this regard if the authorities were to ask.

"Ernie," I yelled after him, "we will hit water!"

Ernie returned the following day and flatly stated that in one week he was pulling out his equipment, water or no water. The validity of my vision was really on the line now. My dream pictured a kidney-shaped lake filled to the brim, with boulders at the water's edge. We had the shape, we had the boulders, but we didn't have any water. We needed a gushing spring and we needed it soon. Of course, my dream did not see depth. How deep would it need to be? Could we reach that mother-load spring in one more week?

The digging continued at one end to an approximate depth of twenty feet, when a large, compacted glacial deposit of boulders fended off the equipment. We had four days left when I directed the D-9 dozer to continue to excavate the pliable sandstone at the far end of Macanudo. In two more days, the depth of the pond had reached twenty-five feet, and the D-9 was coming straight up out of the bottom, traversing sides so steep it was getting dangerous. Cook, the master operator, was shaking his head; saddened that time was running out for me. His irritated boss had told him, in jest, about my dream. But Cook had grown fond of me and my belief that he would hit water, and he was very appreciative of the hot coffee and daily lunches prepared by Kathy for him and his crew. As the last allotted workday arrived, I sat on a large boulder, high above the huge empty pit. I was running out of time, but I was unwilling to disbelieve. Doubt tried to creep in, but I pushed it back as best I could. I thought that maybe I could rent a large track-hoe and dig even deeper once Ernie pulled out his equipment. As I pondered this alternative I glanced over and down at what appeared to be an exploding D-9 dozer deep inside the pit. Cook had reached a depth of thirty-two feet, and he had expressed his concern that the angle was so steep he was afraid his machine might overheat. But the blade was raised, and Cook was trying to escape a gushing flow of water that was striking the underbelly of his dozer! He was trying to spin out of the softened sand, but it was giving out under his tracks. With great excitement, I jumped up and shouted to the heavens. We hit the mother-load spring! With Cook's expert coaxing the D-9 struggled out of the pit, and the proud operator stood there beaming. The entire crew of operators was cheering, sharing equally in his joy.

Cook slowly approached me with wide, respectful eyes. "I'm a changed man," he stated. "You have given me belief. How did you know? How did you convince Ernie to stick with it? Something very exceptional happened here. I hope to someday get to where you are, to believe the way that you believe."

"Cook," I replied, "this is a story that's been told by all of us. I had the vision. You had the courage to stick to it, even placing an expensive piece of equipment at risk, as well as your job and maybe even your life. You believed as I believed."

And so it was. The power of the nearly impossible was made available to a small and simple family in this world, and a very special water feature was added to the lands of Happy Tree. Since that time it has entertained and healed many who have come to sit on its boulders, swim in its waters, and share in the wonder of something that may never have been without the guiding hand of a dream.

Once again, we are reminded that we are not alone. Information and direction are available to us if we are open to receive them. There are many different ways to reach into creation's grand design and receive sustaining comfort and clarifying guidance. Being open to receive is often about changing habits and beliefs that are in our way. If we bring a gladdened thirst and an open cup to the well, life's sustaining waters will be placed in it.

Life Sustains

Come and take
of these waters
and you shall live
on and on.
Empty your cup
of old stuff.
Clean it with gladness,
for your thirst and hunger
shall be forever gone.

Reflecting upon how dreams may serve as a gateway to knowing and reconnecting brings us to the realization that on these occasions we exist in at least two worlds or realities at the same time. This can involve us in a very interesting, if sometimes frustrating, inner dialogue when we awaken. One part of us, the cognitive mind, is already thinking toward the day ahead, while another part of us, the psychic-preconscious, tries to return to the night behind us to experience and understand more of a rapidly receding dream.

> Operating on waking
> already into the day
> but not yet willing
> to allow this dream
> to get away.

Psychologists have long recognized the value of spending time in dream states, especially the rapid eye movement state of our dreams. This may be a time when we are climbing over fences and slipping through curtains as we pass from the earthly reality to others.

It is my belief that we are allowed visitation or connection with other fluid-type spaces of our being while dreaming. These spaces have meaning to us and account for one or more of the other faces of our self. I believe that much of our dream time is involved with our subconscious getting there, and at the point of rapid eye movement we are acknowledging a satisfying and familiar space or place to which part of our being also belongs. It is amazing how much can be done (spaces crossed, realities visited) when our mind's cognitive function is deeply relaxed or asleep.

When remembering our dreams, we must keep in mind that it

is our conscious mind that is offering its version of events, including what was going on and where we were. I am always a little reluctant to place too much credence in my mind's recounting of my dreams, for it may be devising symbols and drawing interpretations of a nighttime play or visitation to which it wasn't invited. Where we were or what was really going on may have been something different entirely. If a strong recurring dream is accompanied by persistent, goofy mental explanations, we may want to persist in our wonder until we are able to decipher and interpret a meaningful explanation from it.

Quieting the mind and decreasing our moment-to-moment dependency upon it is a necessary prescription for awakening our other means of knowing during the completely conscious times of our day. Asking, "How does it feel?" is often a good way to unravel things going on around us, while giving us a read on their value. Trusting our intuition is a good way to open doors to the more of our lives. Remaining open to deep impressions, reflecting upon strong dreams, and responding with a smile to things we may have seen or heard just beyond our perceptual range are good ways to involve ourselves in the real and subjective experience of the more of life.

We may think of these more subjective means of knowing as mindless knowing. We must not allow our objective mind to dominate our experiences, for when it does it often separates and divides us from the more of life that is reaching out to us. It should be noted that our mind-only disposition may not readily accept an integrated function in place of its old role. Our mind may seem willing to join us in our discovery of the unusual. However, it may soon attempt to wrestle control from us by subduing our quests for whatever is exciting us by reducing our involvement to thoughts that will attempt to fence out the newness while bringing us back into a mind circle.

In this instance we must try to gently rein in our overactive mind. At times we may need to treat it as a necessary and close friend, even though it is outside of our self. There are different ways to reestablish a balance between our mind and the more of our life. We need our mind to navigate our present world in the existence experience, so we want it to function adequately. But we do not want it to get in the way as we entertain discovery of the unusual. Clearly, we want our mind to be at peace and comfortably resting when we are opening doors and windows to more of our self. It cannot enter these other worlds, but it may observe what comes to us from them.

As we begin to practice mind-free knowing, we subdue and quiet the mental dialogue and tune into our intuitive leadings. As we attempt to involve the heart and gut more and the head less, we may experience an end run by our thought and mind processes. At these times, it might benefit us to enter into some playful dialogue with our talking head. For instance, without prompting our mind might pretend to be joining in to lead us to a higher place.

"OK, let's strive for a higher level. After all, we are now in the world of temporal existence and finite space, which is ultimately meaningless."

"Oh thank you, mind, for telling me this. How adept you've been at keeping me here!"

Our thoughts may continue to suggest that the path to truth is to renounce this world and search for the loftier world of the infinite. Again, the mind is attempting to reassert its dominance. This overload gets in our way and keeps us dependent on its constant gibberish. The truth is we are now where we need to be. Our work and play here has special value in extending the experience of existence in creation's space. Clearly we want to know that this is not the only reality to which we belong. But we all need to 'be here now,' if only for a short time longer. This is a critical yet hopeful day in the night of eternal life. Again, let's ask our mind to be quiet and take a break. When we need to think, we'll let it know. Our aim is to bring our care, compassion, and mustardo to the ordinary and the finite. If we do this the work and play in our everyday world can be made to glitter. Ordinary times will be transformed and even transmuted to something not so ordinary anymore, and our lives in the difficult and sometimes painful world will be experienced as something purposeful with great promise, which begins to nurture something more. The mind may jump off the couch where we have asked it to rest and suggest that we renounce joyful things, proclaiming that, "The way to awakening and consciousness is suffering."

In response to this we might entertain our mind with additional dialogue, "Why should I suffer?"

"Well, I hear you saying that you have forgotten much and there's more to life than you are now aware of. So, I'm trying to help you get it back, to find the something more."

"Thank you, mind, for your concern. I will listen to my inner knowing and call upon you if I need you."

Throughout our efforts to rein in our mind talk we can observe how frequently our thoughts overpower our presence. Quite contrary to what we are about, something stupid is often inserted to keep our heads full and our beings prodded with unnecessary and foolish things. The mind may be so busy leading and questioning us that it separates us from some of our most intimate and natural interests. Send it back to the couch! Our way is made more meaningful if we seek more joy.

Joy builds a life, suffering weighs it down. If we are guided by right behavior and right thought, joy will accompany us throughout our days.

As joy begins to once again enter our living room we should remember that we must grow our own happiness. We cannot borrow it from another, nor can we scoop it up from the world around us. We grow it by coming to know the special qualities of our life and trusting that the journey we are on, though sometimes difficult, may be quite incredible and long lasting. We must not attach our inner joy to the results of any particular act or situation, and we must be mindful of the guidance of a wonderful chicken farmer, "Do not get attached to the results."

If we can remember these aspects of the re-experience of our personal splendor, the way of our life will find satisfaction in a world that guards us against deep disappointments that may involve us in suffering we do not need. Even as we begin to balance our mind, with its constant dialogue, restraints, and limited seeing, it will still be difficult at times to feel joyful with some of the challenges that are set before us. It remains a shadowy landscape that requires constant mindfulness to stay in the now. Patience is critical as we wait until we are again on the open sea for our seeing to benefit from the bigger perspective.

There simply is much more space and opportunity
in a single room filled with joy
than in an entire house
full of pain.

The Getting Lost

If we allow our mind to be our exclusive guide we may notice a sequential lack of enthusiasm for life. The less excitable our days, the more mental gymnastics we will undergo in an attempt to force sense out of our day-to-day existence. Less flexibility follows as we have a more prescribed time and idea for every part of the day. Creativity and imagination are lost from our life, and rigidity of thought and behavior expresses itself in a repetitive fashion. Newness is not welcome, nor does it excite us. We sit in the same seats, drive the same roads, shave in the same patterns, and slide on the same shoes. Mental judgment includes and excludes us in very definitive ways. With less going on inside our self, we feel boarded up and closed. Alienated from our self, there is ever increasing dependency on the outside world. Peace of mind and joy of self are fleeting unless we party hard or continuously entertain our self with something new. Bring on the stuff! Where's the party?

If mind play is all that matters,
our presence will declare
that we are boarded up and closed.

Why should we listen to somebody else's music? We should play or whistle our own. In an imprinted kind of way, our mind may tell us, "It's just a suggestion. Everyone else is doing it. I don't want to let you down. Let's do this, and let's do that, but let's do it a little bit better." The mind is so good at setting a continuous high flow agenda before us. Many of these expectations will be beyond our needs, so let's exchange some of the mind games for the sensual joy of life for life's sake. More time may be given to family, expressions of creativity, and the arts so that life may be more fully enjoyed. A simple walk in the park and the call of a cardinal may be most rewarding. Truly, those who fail to attune to the call of life may be separated by only a degree from her, but what a powerful degree it is!

This is the call of life.
In these times
let's lend our ears
and open our eyes
to that which is truly
grown and grand
just beyond our window.
For if you are of her,
express your love to her.

By now it must be apparent that I am attempting to use my mind to help you loosen yours. Needless to say, this is a very tricky business. Nothing can ultimately assist in poking holes in our mind fences like our own subjective experience of the unusual. So, let us become ready to receive!

A Place of Communion

Once again, choosing a comfortable and available place for seeing and connecting is very important. This should be a space that is immune from interruption to allow us to avail ourselves of the unusual as our appetite for it permits. Once we have identified such a place (a garden, a room, a park, a riverside, etc.) we should utilize this place as a personal space to receive whatever may want to come our way. As we wait in quiet anticipation we will often find our self reflecting upon the entirety of our life. At times we may be critical of who we were or what we are. If these reflections lead to meaningful changes in our lives this is good. The preparation for seeing beyond the ordinary compels us to let go of old stuff as we are becoming open to the wonder of the unusual. This 'house cleaning' allows us to be ready to receive. As the old is given up, newness may be taken in. We must attempt to avoid passing judgment upon our life and our self in general. Judgments, for whatever reason, fence out the phenomenal while obstructing the transfer from here to there and vice-versa.

Beyond the wonder that may greet us at this special place is the opportunity to reflect upon the contrast between what is good and giving in our life and that which is repetitive or devaluing to our presence in the everyday world. As already noted, clarifying what is and is not of value to us will advance our openness to receive the unusual. Much of the magic and mystery shared in this discourse greeted me at the side of the two-acre pond in our wooded bottomland affectionately known as Fairyland.

Fairyland for me has been my special space of communion and as such a fountain of plenty. Life forms of all sorts live in the water and on the land that surrounds her, and they express themselves constantly. In the heat of many summers my family and I soaked in her lily covered waters, and as the seasons moved on we eagerly awaited the winter freeze to skate on her frozen surface.

The special nature of this place was especially pronounced following one particularly hard freeze in the early 1990's. As I approached Fairyland, I noticed a colored glow emanating from her. Reds, blues, and yellows surrounded her. Stepping on her newly frozen surface, accompanied by the overhead sun, I was amazed and intrigued to see how the freshly formed ice was segmented and colored. Each segment was infused with a base color, and soft hues radiated outward. This was something new, and it was different from any ice I had ever seen. Along with these colored segments there were clearly defined arrows and symbols that were not unlike letters or hieroglyphics. Gingerly, I drew a deep breath and waited for the meaning of all of this to reveal itself. I slowly traversed the pond from end to end and side to side. The entire pond surface was sliced and diced in these brightly cast divisions. Using my fingernail, I attempted to locate perceptible seams running between the segments, but I could feel none. The ice was about four inches deep, and I wanted to break a piece out of the surface to further study the source of all this breathtaking color. As soon as I formed that thought, a stronger sense advised me to leave the ice alone. A greater knowing told me to quietly study what I was seeing. A message or a map was before me!

As I gazed upon this unusual phenomenon I realized the patterns resembled the cryptic symbols I had seen during my studies of ancient civilizations. But who or what sent this? What being slipped into its angelic slippers and infused these colors and these inscriptions into the ice?

Hours passed as I slowly slipped along the surface of the ice, partaking of the beauty and mystery frozen beneath me. The afternoon drew to a close as my frustrated mind attempted to understand what it was or venture a guess as to what it all meant. Soon, a pinkish evening light filled the sky above Fairyland, and glancing at the horizon, I noted the sun slipping into its long wintertime sleep. Slowly and reluctantly I vacated the icy surface of the pond. What a mysterious and colorful experience this had been. With only a few steps left to the pond's edge, a fizzing and cracking sound erupted across the surface. For a moment,

I was afraid that the ice was breaking and I was going into the frigid water. But then I noticed that the multiple colors that were captured in the ice were rising like a vapor above the pond. Slowly, the colors seemed to coalesce and homogenize into the most wondrous blue-purple I may have ever perceived. Clearly separated from the ice, the colors hung above and around me like a cloud. As cold as it was I noticed a definite warming of the air, and for a time I was spellbound. Then the colors vanished, and the January air turned bitterly cold. To this day I carry a mental and psychic replica of the colored mosaics in the ice of Fairyland within me.

When unusual perceptions and illustrations meet us along our earthly highway they almost always imply something special for us. Messages or important directions may be forwarded to us from other realms, or celebrations of mystical accomplishments or spiritual levels attained may occur, even without our earthly mind's complete understanding. Such is the quality and character of the pond and eco-niche of Fairyland. If something really mystical and magical is going to happen at Happy Tree, it will most likely occur in or near these waters.

Much of the discovery of the unusual may be site as well as time specific. Seeing into the beyond depends a great deal on our comfort level, especially when we are getting started. The More of life will seldom force its expression on anyone in an unprepared or awkward disposition. A place of personal comfort and a time free of interruption becomes our special space, where our will to discover and our ability to listen will be heightened, allowing the something more of life to close in around us and embrace us.

What long-term and lasting impressions and values have I taken from the inscribed, colored ice at Fairyland? As time has passed, I have become convinced that each and every detail will avail itself again to me. In at least two instances it has assisted me in my passing from this world into others. In one of these instances, following an unfortunate canoeing experience and subsequent drowning in the Delaware River, I seemed to be falling aimlessly and uncomfortably beyond the confines of earth. Deep and consuming darkness surrounded me. There seemed to be nothing for me to grasp for and hold onto. Then a flash of hues strikingly similar to those from the segmented ice caught my attention. Though I sensed I was still in freefall, I knew I had direction. I just had to follow the beautiful blue. Additional flashes followed, and the darkness broke into segmented patterns not unlike those encased in Fairyland's frozen surface. Soon I was completely immersed and protected in a world that radiated waves of exceptional blue interspersed with short pulses of purple. I could not see or know much of this world, but I was touched deeply by its radiance of fine colors. After some time there I awoke, well rested and healed, back upon the earth. I was stretched out on a large boulder surrounded by a troop of Boy Scouts who had witnessed my canoe being pulled under at Skinner's Falls. They had rushed to try to aid me, and after twenty minutes of frantic searching they located what they thought was my lifeless body. I woke up approximately two hours after the accident. My body was still quite blue, but so was the world from which I just returned. Soon the EMTs arrived, but looking around at the eight scouts with their smiling faces, I thanked them and assured them that I was just fine.

Imagine a world of living and breathing color. It had opened up to retrieve my life from deep and seemingly endless darkness, as I fought for a place of recovery following my drowning in the Delaware. Once again, life called out successfully to be received. A place embodying dynamic and living color answered this call. What was the implication of the winter-of-wonder ice where the world of blue poured into this place on the earth and filled me with wonder and awe? I did not then nor do I now consciously understand the symbols in Fairyland's ice, but I got the message. I was deeply touched. While I was being retrieved from a torrent of water the world of blue received me, protected me, and healed me. I'll never forget her. There really is so much more! Realities and worlds of surprising qualities and forms are out there. In the near future, I expect that we will line up together knowing and celebrating the wonder of what life has given us, and smiling at the splendor of it.

The wonder of it has great value to all of us. Wonder can be a powerful player in this seeing business. The quality of wonder is a valued commodity when we express appreciation for this world or prepare to look beyond the here and now. In either case, wonder loosens our ordinary thoughts and beliefs and allows us the opportunity to respond to things in a new way. Many of us have had special moments of wonder that continue to nurture in a deep and lasting fashion. I have often lifted this display from my memory and benefited from the sheer wonder of it.

A decade and a half after that first experience, colored and hieroglyphically outlined ice met me again, covering the surface of Macanudo. Once again, the segmented ice was glass-smooth and beautifully colored, and it was clearly expressing its magical qualities. As before, the unusual inscriptions, instructions, and illustrations could not be easily understood. I was touched deeply by this phenomenal happening, and I was left to understand that what it was and is could not presently be discerned. This time, though, there was a visitor we could greet and to whom we could express our gratitude.

Under five inches of ice, a golden flower bloomed. The vitelline glow of this out- of-time-and-place visitation appeared as petals of gold. Such was the power and beauty of what my daughter and I were skating over. While all of the other lilies, fronds, and sedges of a typical summer's water vegetation lay dead and faded on the pond floor, this flower in the ice was magically beautiful. Along the seven foot stem that supported its golden bloom was a glistening orb. What a presence! A wondrous being had made its way to our world. It was cloaked in the form of a flower, albeit in the wrong season and immersed in an unlikely depth of frigid water. Its presence was received and appreciated by the skaters who came to play on the magical ice that covered this pond and its beautiful golden guest.

Meeting and seeing the unusual has enormous value. Beyond the intrinsic value of the awe and wonder is the certain confirmation of our larger connectedness. Underlying all of this is the process that allows these helpings of the unusual to free us of our limiting thoughts and beliefs. Eventually we will break through the barrier that has confined us and coerced us into accepting so little of the more that we are. Something new will no longer be a distortion of something we already know. Being open to receive is important, and when we are visited by something magical a basic trust will secure its presence within us.

Life will call
and we will answer.

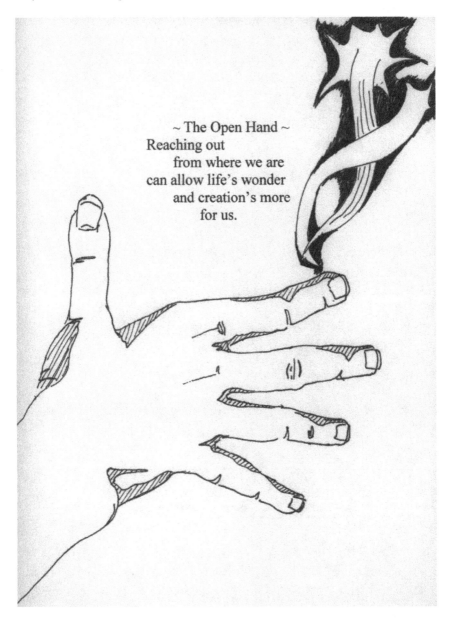

~ The Open Hand ~
Reaching out
   from where we are
can allow life's wonder
    and creation's more
       for us.

5

Awakening

There is another side of seeing that we might refer to as awakening. Awakening begins from where we are. Who and what we are is now our truth. Seeing and reaching beyond where we are now should never imply rejection but instead respect and acceptance of what has brought us to this moment. Awakening is a process by which we hope to illuminate the More which is before us. In other words, where we are now can often be added to. Awakening may ask us to relook at what we value or how we spend our time in existence. The ultimate application of awakening is not to cast out our leanings and beliefs for some others' ideas but instead that we have a basic trust in our own validity and worth. We are worthy enough, and all that is grand and purposeful for us can come to us, not needing to be brought or given by another. As awakening to the More of our life unfolds the broader horizons before us will begin to open. The life within and about us will vibrate with the sweetness of our existence.

Awakening proceeds most effectively when we include introspection and contemplation in the what and why of our presence. In this we are assuming responsibility for what matters in our lives. Are we spending all our time in the temporal or are we concentrating on the enduring? Are we so busy playing out societal roles that we aren't discovering ourselves? Are we going along to get along or are we utilizing our intuition to touch our deeper selves while referencing how it feels in all things?

When we begin asking basic questions of this nature we are opening up to possibilities of seeing and becoming so much more. We don't need to throw ourselves away, but instead we need to gather the More about us. What has been illuminated and revealed in awakening influences us from the surface of our being to our greatest depth. Along with the seeing that comes through awakening, the underlying wisdom of creation opens up before us. By degree we develop and trust our insight, which allows us to be aware of what matters and what resonates with us.

As we get started we soon come to know that awakening is an unfolding process. As one truth or discovery is gleaned another will become available. The greater and lasting joy in this is that it never ends. It is of life and there can not be an ending to it. Reaching for More is to have more of it.

As the process of awakening unfolds within us there will be less need for introspection and reflection. In its place we will want to extend our revalued and illuminated life into the world around us. The illumination given to us will also be extended to others. When the newness of discovery begins within and around us a perceptible pulse begins to touch others. As we sense the accrued value from the growing awareness of our bigger self, it also seeks to be expressed and shared.

What is the best way to prepare and respond to the More as it enters our lives? As we come to receive the More of life, how might we best awaken others around us to its availability for them? We must be sensitive in both supporting their preparation and in gently reassuring any doubts or questions they may have. For ourselves, we must respond as we are ready. For others, we must be available to reassure.

For their preparation
we will extend our trust
as a comforting canopy
over those who will
gather about us
as we will awaken and excite.

From within ourselves or from others around us questions may arise. We may not be sure how comfortable we are with what is happening to us. At times we may feel overwhelmed and unsettled. These are expressions of concern and caution that we might expect from ourselves and others in response to the newness and discovery. The most we can do is comfort and reassure.

Sleep Walking

Awakening from a deep sleep can be uncomfortable
as morning light begins to play with our eyes!

Awakening to and discovering the More in our lives is not always easy. This is the crucial time when we begin to perceive our different faces in other places. Our preparation asks not only that we clarify who we are and what we value but that, as we are ready, we extend and stretch our normal consciousness and become more open to seeing the paranormal of our mystical selves. Along with this we must be prepared for a myriad of questions, doubts, and opposition from our contemporary earthly connections. We may find resistance from our workplace, friends, churches, and even families. The early phases of this preparation and practice can be the most trying.

The preparation for these first steps is often a solitary thing. The singleness of early discovery seldom threatens us but often unintentionally threatens significant others around us. Something is changing, and some may sense that they are not being invited to be a part of something important that is happening to somebody important to them.

Thus we may need to consciously remind ourselves not to overlook our everyday responsibilities and relationships. Once we begin to travel upon the path to something more, there is no hurry. Remember, the ones who are now connected to you are also the ones you may ultimately bring along with you. Care may be needed to avoid scaring or alarming the significant others in our lives. Interests and old habits will begin to change in us to some degree, but we don't want others to feel that they are being forgotten or left out of our lives.

To illustrate these complexities, I return to my youth on the chicken farm in Gettysburg. The relationship between Mom and Dad was never especially easy or completely harmonious. Dad's high expectations, work orientation, and demand for order often clashed with Mom's emphasis on the qualitative aspects of living. For her, night-frights justified allowing a child into their bed, and baby pigs could stay behind the stove on a brutally cold night. She questioned Dad's need for thistle-free meadows, which would often preclude her children from playing a ball game. Nothing so tried their relationship as Mom's yearning and pursuit of her deeper self, the Something More of her life.

She would confide to me later, "Stephen, I always felt there was something more to life, and your accident and miraculous recovery opened a door I could not ignore." The tractor incident had set my destiny upon a multi-world highway. This course was not an easy one, and it was often very lonely. This incident had also apparently set Mom upon a path of joyful pursuit but one that was, at times, beset by difficult conflicts.

> Fights raged into the night
> there was crying and shouting
> all about.

Dad saw and felt Mom's new interest evolving within her and resisted it mightily. She was accused of deserting him, the family, and the chickens. Mom was losing interest in the sunset Tom Collins and dinner dates, and she certainly had no interest in building another chicken house. We already had five thousand chickens. Why would we want five thousand more? Dad sensed that he was being left behind, but his wife's new interest was not another man, a new church, or even a new circle of friends. Perhaps it would have been easier for him if such had been the case. What was happening to Mom was not easy for another to grasp if he were not a part of the mystery that was unfolding.

New interests were being born and were quietly pursued by Mom, as quietly as possible that is. Along with her openness and interest in the Something More, she simultaneously began to develop and practice her natural healing skills. So often when we open the door to our deeper selves, new skills and arts concurrently emerge. These may be things that were there all along but only now have an opportunity to be expressed.

Strengths and abilities were revealed to her as she discovered and probed her deeper and mystical self. Sleep did not seem so necessary anymore. There was something before her. Discovery was pulling her along. Beyond all her everyday, worldly responsibilities there was an enticing wonder calling her name. It was something she was growing toward, something more than the ordinary that she continued to accomplish exceptionally well.

When Dad's focus turned to the threat he felt from Mom's new interest, he would argue that this or that of her responsibilities was being overlooked. The truth is, her ability to accomplish her many difficult, everyday responsibilities never missed a beat. The laundry, dishes, cleaning, cooking, chickens, pets, Dad's individual needs, and a tribe of fifteen children with their homework, their education, their gladness and their health were taken care of day after day, and every task was done well.

For years Dad fought with Mom, disturbed by the things that were happening to her. They were wondrous to her, but they felt horrendous to him. A lack of interest and preparation on his part left him unable to understand or feel as if he belonged to the discoveries that were so compelling to Mom. Time and time again we children would be awakened from our sleep by the arguments that raged downstairs. Cuddled and snuggled like crackers in our beds, we would slide even deeper down under the green woolen army blankets to hide from the pain. Mom cried, Dad shouted. Afraid for our parents, afraid for ourselves, we would quietly discuss among ourselves as to who might be right, who might be wrong. Sides would be drawn for this night's fight. New sides would be taken for the predictable next night's fight. But what were the sides, anyway?

Something big and bad was happening in our home. All was not well. Often, one or more of the ten-plus children would lift their teary heads from the bed to receive a collective hug or reassurance from one another. Then, together we might hope or pray:

> "Our Father, who art in heaven,
> will you please help us tonight?
> Will you please help them tonight?
> We hope that you can stop this fight."

For years the sadness and pain slipped through the yellow pine flooring and echoed up the crooked stairway, bringing sorrow and suffering to our evenings' repose. It tortured us children and fractured our sleep.

Regardless of whose side we may have taken, we understood and felt both of our parents' pain in this. Their pain was our suffering! My brothers and sisters could not really decipher why Dad was so angry or why he initiated all of those fights. Why did he suffer so, and why did he hold so much against Mom?

I felt I knew, however, and at times I felt deep regret for that nasty tractor accident that got all of this started. For Dad, I also felt a twinge of guilt. Clearly he sensed he was being left behind. Mom was simplifying her earthly interests and attending more and more to the mysterious and the unseen. On just about every occasion when we were alone, she would seek to know more about my take on the here and on the beyond. As time passed, Mom assured me that their differences were their responsibility, and she communicated her sorrow that her children suffered in the middle of it all. She also spoke to the meaning her new interests were imparting to her life and emphatically declared that "nothing but nothing" would change that. Would Dad ever stop fighting it and become a part of her new discoveries? "Only time will tell, Stephen, but I don't think so," was her sad reply to my queries. In retrospect, I knew that Dad was not ready for the journey, nor was he willing to attempt to belong to the Something More of Mom's life.

Looking back I can better understand how Dad's sharp, organized mind may have been in his way. People with strong, ordered minds may unintentionally build fences against the unknown and the unusual. Their comfort lies in understanding the meadow they are in, as well as keeping out other possibilities that may exist. If foreign realities can't be known or understood completely they may add confusion or discomfort to one's sense of control, thus the impulse is often to shield oneself against them. In this way over-dependence on thought and cognition may become a barrier against other valid meadows, or the More of life, that can't be completely grasped or understood by the mind alone. In this case Mom was not completely satisfied with the meadow we were in. Instead, she yearned to better know what lay just beyond the fenced-in enclosure of our human mind. Herein a great proportion of the conflict had its roots. Dad was comfortable and satisfied with what his mind defined as reality. His life partner, his wife, our Mom, was not. For her there was more, and she could not be dissuaded from pursuing it.

The message here may be that if you are an initiate to the wondrous More of your life, and if your discoveries are not well distilled, there may be pain and even brutality which results as a backlash from this earthly world's mentality.

> Once we have tasted it,
> we cannot forget its flavor.
> We may even wish to digest more of it.
> In this world we need not stand up and shout,
> as we could never spit it out.

After years of this dogged standoff, Dad seemed to offer up an olive branch. A very, very frugal man, it was so unlike him to purchase Mom a brand new organ. How she loved to play this instrument! For a time the nighttime fights nearly ceased. She played beautifully upon the keys. Her music seemed to call to the angels, who would surround and comfort her sleeping children. It was so melodic and soothing. During this year and some months, Dad's biggest problem with Mom was that she wasn't playing his favorite selections often enough.

Then, another door opened for Mom. Another world signaled and beckoned her in. On this particular warm summer evening I was late in tending to my milking chore. Mom offered to come along into the meadow with a flashlight to assist in finding Blacky, our milker. Off we went together, a chance to enjoy each other's company. We zigzagged through the meadow grass until I located my favorite cow. She stood there chewing her cud and waiting to have the pressure relieved from her udder so that she might join the rest of the herd in their grassy meadow bed. Kneeling down beside her hindquarters, I began pulling upon her teats, listening to the sweet smelling nectar strike and foam against the stainless steel milking pail. In the next instant, the night sky lit up like the noon of day. A bolt of white light had pierced the night and struck the earth with a sizzle not more than twenty feet from where Mom, Blacky, and I were. The brilliant white illumination was persistent for a full five to ten seconds. Then it was gone, and the starlit sky again hung above us. What a punctuated presence! Something calming and definite was left with us; deep, deep within us. We knew we received it. We saw and felt an immense something, but we couldn't give definition to it. Even today, forty plus years hence, the powerful punctuation of that presence continues to vibrate in the center of my being.

As doors are opened and curtains lifted
between world and realities,
be prepared for startling experiences.
Your mind may not know
what to make of it,
nor even be able to
find a way to categorize it.
Someone is coming to you
with a "hello"
from the ethers and cosmos.
In time, meaning may be revealed to you.
For now you must be there for it.
Experience it,
but
do not turn from it!

Once the light receded, a patch of grass smoldered and smoked, and a slight glow lingered on. The glow was also on Mom's face. Incredibly, Blacky held her place. She didn't even stir, nor did she kick the milk bucket or me. Thank goodness for that!

For Mom this piercing nighttime light was an undeniable confirmation that the Something More was not just something happening close to her through her son, but it was also entering her world. Now Mom knew! She really knew. She was not precluded from this powerful and mystical visitation from the metaphysical. Together we were visited in the nighttime meadow. She felt initiated into another world. She felt that the piercing light was an intimate connection to some near or distant reality. Should we have verbalized our response, it may have gone like this:

"Hello, my friends, so glad to meet you again.
We may not know
who or what has come,
but something incredible
has been done."

Following this experience, Mom seemed to glide about her chores throughout the day, singing almost constantly and glad in every way. Again Dad began to stew, becoming argumentative at any perceived misstep, "My coffee is cold. The toast is hard. Why did you allow that boy in the house with cow poop on his shoes?" and so on. Mom just could not hide her radiance and happiness at the new and special possibilities of her life. Even as Dad seemed to be adjusting to the old glow, the new one was just too threatening and all hell broke loose.

A huge nighttime fight ensued. The pretext for this confrontation was a few drops of paint that had been spilled on Mom's organ by the painter Dad had employed. Mom was blamed. This was an especially severe fight with deep emotional wounds. Running, falling downstairs, and seeing the pain upon Mom's face I fervently attempted to intervene, shouting and gesturing angrily at my father. He stood there staring at me, looking dumbfounded. Through her tears Mom scolded me and sent me back upstairs where I waited fearfully for Dad's imposing razor strap. He never came for me that night, nor did he continue to fight with Mom. In fact, he never confronted me about this harrowing incident. Perhaps he was as ashamed as I was about what had transpired.

After seeing Mom's gaunt and saddened face at the breakfast table, it became apparent to us children that we needed to collectively stand up for our mother. Under my older brother's leadership, we all gathered behind him and confronted Dad before dinner. We assured him that we would not stand down in the face of continued assaults on Mom. This was such a difficult thing to do, to see such a proud man looked dazed as he sat heavily back in his chair. This was not a bad man that we were confronting with threat and determination; this was our father, a hardworking man, not an alcoholic, not a womanizer. All of his efforts were directed toward supporting his large family on a large well-managed farm. It was not easy to view a man of this caliber with disdain, but for hurting Mom each of us, to one degree or another, felt that we had to stand against him that day.

The pain of this showdown with Dad was etched upon his face for a very long time. An eerie silence fell over the Redding household. It was many months until that organ music accompanied us in our sleep. Dad became silent and essentially withdrew from all of us. Years passed before any of us witnessed a conversation between him and Mom. When he wasn't working, he turned to reading western novels, one after another. They were piled high around his personal chair. Dad's pervading mood was like that of the winged game birds he would teach us about. When a hunter misfires by just a little and misses the kill but brings a pheasant down with a wing shot, it will hide and suffer silently until it succumbs to its wounds or a fox feasts on it.

Does this awakening to our greater arenas need to be so painful, and will it always be so? As a result of Dad's not belonging or not being ready to experience the beauty and excitement opening up for Mom, he resented it. Mom, in particular, and the Redding children suffered a great deal. Does something so good and wonderful to one have to be so painful to others? Mom hated that we children were caught in the middle, but she never minded the price she had to pay. "Stephen, I only wish Carroll (her husband) could be open to what I've witnessed. There have been sacrifices for me but I've really come alive to so very, very much." Like so many of us, yet unlike Dad, Mom was not so far removed from the Something More of life that she could not touch and equally yearn deeply for it.

Eventually partners, families, communities, and even nations may be able to move along together on the road to discovery by supporting one another and celebrating the renewed awakening of so much that has been obscured by the night. Clearly, once we have tasted it, it will not be forgotten. The challenge for us today is much the same as it has always been when beginning a journey. Taking the first step is essential to every other step, without which the destination will never be reached.

The first step

will also be

the last step.

This may be the crux of the matter of awakening. We must become aware and let go of thoughts and behaviors that are in the way of seeing the More of life even before we have the confirmation of experiencing it. In the cultural bias in which we live we are accustomed to believing that a master, or teacher, or even Christ will do this for us and thus be our hero. But in the way of life, while everyone may be looking for heroes, we must become the heroes for ourselves. We may suffer some doubt and trepidation in getting started, but soon we will know that we are worthy enough to get it done.

If we can journey together into the Something More of life, the individual threat of being left out or left behind will be greatly placated. Developing our sense of wonder along with a trusting intuitive knowing prepares us and aids in our acquisition of the necessary tools for the revelation of our complete selves. Some will be discovered by our own initiatives of awakening, but even more will be revealed as we exchange old habits and beliefs for these new possibilities.

Early on, we may be tentative in the face of the newness beginning to unfold for us, but eventually we will begin to feel more comfortable with these wondrous qualities of life.

What was once ours

but then forgotten

is being returned to us.

Our minds must accept a subdued role in this awakening from our sleep. Much of the Something More of our lives is beyond its grasp, and it is bigger than any demarcation we might want to give it. Clearly we can have it and know of it without binding it up by definition. Mom, in a quiet and completely earthy way, loved looking into and witnessing the mystery and the possibility of fluid realities, even while doing her everyday things fully. She was ablaze with it, and there were no contradictions. Her todays and tomorrows both benefited.

My own experience has been that we can nudge people toward the Something More, but we can't do their preparation for them. That first step has to well up from within them. Something must help loosen the constraints from the mental fences that have been built up around them. It may begin with the acknowledgement of something out of the ordinary, after which a yearning may quickly develop. Initially there may be denial or regression back toward the old. This should not be cause for worry. Once the old is revisited they may again be ready to visit with the unseen and dare to see more. At this point, we may be able to illuminate their way with support and compassion as they make their way forward, free of constraints that have shrouded that which belongs to them in habits of darkness.

So often I have misjudged a friend's level of preparation, and they have been overwhelmed when I've taken them to windows of new worlds and possibilities. So, once again:

> Do not shine a light
> too brightly
> in sleeping children's eyes.

When we begin this journey we want other important people in our lives to come along. However, we can't lift the weight of old beliefs and habits from them. The most we may be able to do is to illuminate some of the limiting darkness that surrounds them, and hope they will begin to find their way out. Mom understood early on that Dad couldn't be 'pushed to see' and that my fourteen brothers and sisters were also limited in their openness to one degree or another. The miracle in the hayfield was clearly too much too soon for my older brothers and sisters. Their minds were simply overwhelmed and they responded by keeping a cold distance from me. As she grew in seeing, Mom practiced opening doors with confidence. She knew that gentleness would be our strength. "Stephen, you must first be of their world. Stand where they stand, walk where they walk, and play where they play before you expect them to see yours."

Be kind, for feelings are everywhere.
But even so,
there will be so many
cynical and in doubt.
In confusion and with alarm
the wrongs will be worked out.
Be still and listen to their needs,
then the goodness will come to be,
quiet and undramatic,
and often gone unseen.

As transformations of consciousness begin people may have the sensation that 'much is happening,' but they may not be sure what to do with it. Reassuring in the right way may be critical. They should know that they needn't worry about doing too much with this 'much happening.' Neither should they deny it.

Allow it to be
and soon in time
meaning you will see.

We may assume that they are thinking in ways they never thought before, and they may be seeing things they never noticed before. They may also be beginning to speak with a voice that is bigger than their own. This is how it should be.

Seeing things out
that we have begun to feel in.
Meeting things in a dream
far too real to forget about.
Hearing a voice from a crowd
we can't quite place, but can't deny.
Hearing our name spoken as
we move about our every day.
Seeing something a little fuzzy
or even faint.
It gets our attention.
It doesn't matter
what it is and what it ain't.

In the face of all of the potential wondrousness before us and the value of awakening to it we still might sometimes hear, "I'm happy with where I am. I have my life, my family, my church, and that's enough." We can only hope that this protest is a bump in the road to awakening for these people, and that in a short time, some new wonders will again emerge around them and excite them.

Enough Already

Yes, doubt has entered in.
Questions seem to be almost everywhere.
The sky is clouded over.
I'm not sure I want
these new clothes we need to wear.

Some who begin this awakening and discovery assume that the ordinary world and their old friends are a detriment to their advancement. Efforts are often made to find a new and better space or place; a church, or an ocean-side or mountain home. But this may or may not be helpful. What is necessary is that their lives are abundant with the qualities of caring and compassion. Caring is an act of belonging to the world, while compassion guards us against taking away from or deserting the very world our love for life is meant to serve. Standing against pain and suffering in the neighborhood we may be inclined to leave behind will confirm our value, provide affirmation for the much that is awakening in us, and serve as a reminder of the much that needs to be done. A conversation I had with a woman who just completed reading *Something More* may serve as a helpful illustration.

"I want to thank you for your words," she said. "I always felt there was something more, and your book confirms it for me."

"Thank you for taking the time to make the call," I said.

"I see more of the big picture now. I was never happy thinking we are just hanging out here, breathing until we breathe no more," she continued.

"Yes," I responded. "Isn't it incredible how many among us are content to live in the confines of a limiting perspective, happy to go along to get along, while thinking that the 'bottom line' satisfies."

She continued, "I find it almost impossible to relate to these people any more. I am making a commitment to myself to spend the rest of my life to achieve a higher plane of existence."

"Whoa," I said, "if you mean 'higher' to be more aware, then okay. But if you say 'higher plane' to mean above those who you can't tolerate, then that is not such a good thing."

"What do you mean?" she quizzed me. "How can there be more in my life if I don't separate from those who drag me down?"

"I hope the message of *Something More* left you with an appreciation that living our life matters," I responded. "Valuing the life in you and around you matters, and it will always matter. It is our responsibility to live the life we've been given wherever we are. In so doing, our presence might awaken others to see in us something precious that they may be missing."

"So, reaching for a higher plane can't help me?" she queried.

"Maybe not," I replied. "Life would never see it that way. The experience of existence upon this world is a collective thing. Don't divide or subdue the life around you."

"How will I know how I am doing?" she wondered out loud.

"Look for added joy and happiness in the world around you," I concluded. "Your degree of presence will define how you are doing, and you will feel an inner gladness as 'ordinary' people are allowed to flower. From your joy and happiness you will know how you are doing."

I ended this phone conversation with a sense that my verbal response may have failed to satisfy. Sometimes we find that words can't go where we wish they could. At these times we may be better served by insights gained from an actual experience.

I wish to share an experience from the life of a young man who worked past a period of devastating despair and awoke to joy and happiness which opened windows to so much more.

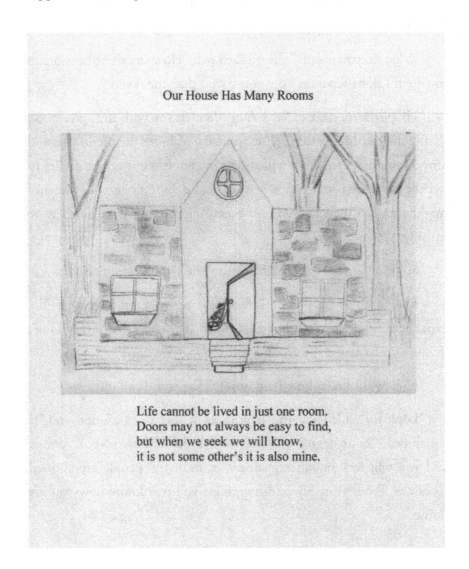

Our House Has Many Rooms

Life cannot be lived in just one room.
Doors may not always be easy to find,
but when we seek we will know,
it is not some other's it is also mine.

Buddy: Our House Has Many Rooms

The following story portrays a young man with exceptional qualities of goodness and deep intuitive knowing. Buddy understood the value of embracing his personal world, but when those he loved could not return caring to him, aggression raised its ugly head. This young man went to the very edge of life before he returned the love and pulse he nearly stole from himself to his neighborhood and family. In so many exceptional ways Buddy lifted the world around him with the power of discovery as it pertained to valuing those close to him.

During the time of my study of psychology at the university, Buddy was referred into my care following a near fatal suicide attempt. "Why? Why?" I thought as I looked upon this oversized child-man stuffed in undersized child's clothing. It was an act so desperate, with a pain so lasting. "Hello," I said, "I understand your name is Buddy." He nodded. Around closed eyes his wide and puffy face was drawn tight and holding out until he heard some hope. There was just not enough charm in my voice or hope in my hand to lift this young man. Snapping my fingers, I brought Thaddeus, my young Weimaraner, out from under my desk. He immediately lifted Buddy out of his misery as he stuck his broad nose in Buddy's lap. Buddy's loving hands began to stroke Thaddeus. His eyes opened wide and tears flowed forth. A door opened, I was allowed in, and for two years Buddy and I celebrated the goodness and suffered the harsh realities that surrounded his life.

For the next six months I saw Buddy in one-hour sessions at my campus office. Bit by bit and degree by degree, I attempted to unravel Buddy's complex thoughts and feelings regarding his sense of rejection by his father and his sense of trespass by his mother's friends in Dad's place. It was this deep pain that fueled the anger that was turned inward and against himself. Ultimately, it was unleashed through a knife during a fit of rage. Freeing him from his sense of fault and responsibility in all of this was a most difficult undertaking. Thaddeus was a good and willing assistant in this effort. The first few minutes of each session were given to Buddy stroking Thaddeus before he would join in the dialogue that was meant to open old wounds, clean them, and allow them to heal properly. The first half hour was sluggish, heartfelt, and often tearful, but we almost always ended with a broad and cheery smile. On three or four occasions, I was able to encourage his mother to join in her son's treatment sessions. Her greatest value at these times was to show me with glaring clarity that if Buddy's healing depended on a whole family it wasn't going to happen. "Mr. Redding," she would say, "Buddy's father will never be of value to us again. He's become addicted to heroin, can't hold down a job, won't help with Buddy's support, and is totally worthless. Buddy is going to have to face reality and go on with his life."

"Mom," Buddy would cry out, "he is going to come back some day. I know he is!" So much of Buddy's anger was born in his father's abandonment of his mother and him. His anger only deepened when, a short time after his father's departure, his mother began to bring strange men into their house. This offended Buddy's sense of the family unit. "You haven't really tried to bring Dad back!" he screamed at her during one of those few parent-present sessions in my campus office. "He'll never come back to us, Mom, if you keep bringing strange men home."

Rightly or wrongly, Buddy was harboring hatred toward his mother. Something important was missing from his life, and her failure to honor the special space of family pushed Buddy even further into loneliness.

Against all that pained him, Buddy demonstrated a loving presence exceptional for a young man of fourteen. I loved his accounts of how he would invite alley cats to share meager portions of his dinner. As so often happens when truly sensitive and caring people are dealt a hand in life they cannot accept, they turn their anger against themselves. Their pain is so lasting and so deep that suicide becomes an appealing option.

The Blade Goes Deep

They can't change the circumstances.
They can't accept the pain.
The only way to seek relief
is to suffer unto themselves.
The piercing point of the dagger
is a hurt they can understand.
They can't lift away life's knife,
whose blade they did not unfold,
and whose handle they do not hold.

It was quickly becoming clear to me that what Buddy needed was for someone to step in and fill the void left by his loss of his father. He needed a friend, and I would be that friend. I would need to challenge him to step up and accept the hand of a friend in place of the childlike dependency of a patient to a therapist. The discourse went something like this: "Buddy, when you decided it was okay to die you were making a man's decision; therefore, I will never treat you as a child but will instead see a young man sitting in that chair. As a young man, you can start to have your own path in this world. You may not hold any other person completely responsible for your happiness. I hope that I can help you feel for yourself the beauty and value that I experience coming from you. If you will allow yourself to feel the goodness in you, then our time together will be like friends. You will not need a therapist, and I will not treat you like a patient."

Clearly, this talk of being friends was crossing the professional lines of separation between the patient and therapist. Buddy, however, needed something more than guidance and understanding, he needed a friend. His friendship worked for me as well. I was drawn to his deep and sensitive perceptions. I could enjoy his company and learn of life from him. Our once weekly hour-long office visits soon became twice weekly, and it was not long before the one-hour office visit became two hours walking along the river in the city park. Confidence was quickly returning to Buddy. Our visits together were less and less about his inner pain and more about whittling wood, throwing a Frisbee, and playing catch with Thaddeus.

This new relationship necessitated some different considerations. Buddy was given my phone number and told he could use it if necessary. He was also told that he was allowed to come to my office unannounced if he didn't mind waiting until I could see him or until I returned from teaching duties. He soon learned my teaching schedule and knew just when to show up at my office. While Buddy stepped up to become a man in this friendship, Thaddeus became even more important to him. Touching and rubbing his fur helped him exchange intimacies on a child's level. It was all part of letting go of old hurts and replacing them with strength and confidence. On some occasions, I would drive the twenty blocks to his house and bring him back to my office. Or, if the weather was favorable, we would spend our time at the park. On one such occasion, Buddy teared up and asked if I would stop at his Grandpa's house. "It's on the way," he stated. Of course I agreed. Over the course of the previous two years, Grandpa had been invoked on numerous occasions into our conversations. I had understood from his mother's accounting that Grandpa, his father's dad, had been involved in Buddy's life until recently, when he was laid low by influenza. His condition had worsened dramatically at about the same time that Buddy's father became a full-blown heroin addict and moved out of the house.

It became obvious in conversations with Buddy that if he had ever felt acceptance and love on a consistent basis, it was from the hands and heart of his Grandpa. I remembered how, in our initial session, Buddy's sad countenance lifted considerably when our conversations touched upon his father's father. "He's the only one I got!" was a phrase repeated over and over as tears washed over his wide face.

Now we would actually stop at his old brownstone house along North Broad Street. It was something I looked forward to. We entered Grandpa's house on a hot summer afternoon. The front door was ajar, a fan was humming, and the old man was sitting deep in a stuffed chair among the room's shadows. My eyes slowly adjusted from the midday sun to the inner darkness as I listened to his deep wheezing and watched Buddy slowly approach his Grandpa.

"Buddy," he said, "where have you been? How are you doing? Who is that with you?"

"Well," Buddy responded, "I've had some trouble. I know Mom told you. Mr. Redding is helping me out ..." Lifting his head, Grandpa acknowledged me with a grimace or maybe a grin, I couldn't be sure.

Grandpa was clearly not well and by all appearances, looked to have lived in this single front room just off the street for some time. Grandpa's minimal care had been placed in the hands of a church association or city social service. Flies encircled a brown bag and shriveled up fruit was visible in a basket just inside the door. While someone was attempting to care for Grandpa, Grandpa showed no sign of caring for himself. After some conversation, Buddy told Grandpa that he wanted to show me the garden in the rear of the house. He then began to move stuff from in front of a large dusty mirror hanging on a door that lent access to the rest of the house.

"Oh, don't bother with that Buddy," Grandpa said in an irritable tone.

"But Grandpa," Buddy protested, "your grand piano is through this door."

"It doesn't matter anymore. My hands do not allow me to play and I have no interest in it any more."

Continuing to push some boxes with his foot, Buddy responded, "It is also the way to your back lawn and vegetable garden."

"Nothing grows there but weeds," Grandpa retorted.

Buddy added, more for my benefit than Grandpa's, "We could never view the constellations or even the stars from the front of the house because of the streetlights and traffic." He continued, "Grandpa, you never liked the front of your house with the exhaust fumes, noise, sirens, and yelling. I am so sorry to see you living completely in this room with the door open to all the things you dislike. Why, do you do it, Grandpa?" Buddy pleaded.

"Why, indeed?" I thought, but also sensed I understood somewhat. There was so much hurt and desperation surrounding Grandpa's later years; the addiction and loss of his son, the encroaching limitations of old age, the emphysema and arthritis, and then the near suicide of his best Buddy (a name given to Buddy by his Grandpa). Taken all together, joy in life was hard to come by and bleak despair was a better way to describe what was happening to Grandpa. Being surrounded by ugliness soon leads to feeling ugliness within ourselves, and we can easily lose touch with the qualities of life that bring joy and meaning to us. Alas, depression becomes an inner darkness, which obscures our way and our expressions of goodness. Life loses its shine and we snuggle up to the night. Time passes as we wait for death to remove us from our misery. Every remaining act and thought mirrors our discontent, reflecting it back upon us. We see and feel very little of the much that we are.

Grandpa's emphysema and arthritis did not allow him the opportunity to intervene, and soon Buddy had the door open and we were passing through. "Wow!" I thought as I observed a beautiful concert piano in a large living room with a plush Persian rug and brass and crystal chandelier. "Buddy," I asked in amazement, "who plays the piano?"

"Both Grandpa and my father were very good musicians at one time," he responded wistfully. We passed into a rear foyer with stained glass, which led to the rear lawn. The colors that splayed about the foyer from the gold trimmed lead glass were stunning. As Buddy fussed with the rear door, I was overwhelmed at the sadness of the paradox that struck me at this moment. Grandpa's house had many rooms, but his recent life found him stuck, or captive, in just one of them. The room in which he now resided was filthy, darkened, and afforded a view only to the noisy, polluted congestion of North Broad Street. How could such a beautiful home with so many vibrant rooms be reduced to a stale one-room domicile? Grandpa had lost the physical means or the will to utilize or enjoy his entire home. Because the home was so beautiful, this loss was especially sad to experience. By now

I was following Buddy into the small rear lawn and watching him pulling a few ragged weeds from what once was a favorite garden spot for the two of them. Clearly, a sense of sadness pervaded Buddy's face as he lifted up his head to study the branching of a paulownia tree. He explained that this was his favorite climbing tree, pointing out the crotch in which he would rest and enjoy the view.

Soon we were passing back through the wondrous old brownstone house filled with the handwork of artisans, and I could only wonder what beautiful windows and rooms lay upstairs beyond the curved mahogany stairwell.

Returning to the entrance room, we found Grandpa sitting on the edge of his chair with his arms out requesting a hug from his grandson. The call for intimacy and privacy encouraged me to remove myself onto the front porch as Grandpa and Buddy had some catching up to do. I was out of sight but not completely out of range of the conversation, and I found myself listening in.

"Grandpa, have you seen Dad?"

"No, Buddy, he wants nothing to do with me any more it seems. I thought you lost interest as well, Buddy. It has been a long time. Since you hurt yourself, your father became more and more distant, and now he just doesn't come by at all."

"Grandpa," Buddy replied, "I've been so ashamed of what I did that I was afraid to see you. I have also been scared by my mother saying that you are so ill."

Love once lent,
spoken intimately again,
before their time was spent.

148

Eavesdropping on this most intimate conversation was no longer comfortable for me. I yielded to the precious moments of grandfather and grandson bridging the gap of lost time, and I slid between Grandpa's brownstone and the house next door to return to the back lawn. In a moment of nimbleness reminiscent of my youth, I sprang up into the paulownia tree and sat and pondered in Buddy's favorite place.

I wondered intently about how the conditions of Grandpa's life, which limited him to one room of his beautiful house, were not so unlike humankind limiting ourselves to just one room of the multi-faceted realities of creation.

Our House Has Many Rooms

This one room seems very stuffed,
and the air is getting stale.
We gathered much that we really don't need.
While it piles up it denies access
to our other living rooms.

Too often we settle for a mirror on
a door we do not open.
Blocked by all our stuff,
we see a lonely face
amidst all of the clutter
of our recent selves.

It's quite scary when all we see
is what we left behind in our past.
This mirrored image cannot last.
We need to open a door and somehow get past.

If, when you look, a door opens
and you fall in, do not panic.
You have found another room
of your house, not something other.
Life comes with you in this room
of your house.

But if, confused and concerned,
darkness may seem to surround,
do not forsake the windows.
When confidence returns, light will come again.
Understanding and knowing will pour in.

Now from this first room's window, evening light is gone,
and darkness seems hard and cold.
But know the lamplighter has come,
grumbling about oil being harder and harder to find.
This old lamp still burns fine.

.

It is so difficult, and the nights are long
with less, and less, and less of day.
Now there is this door to more of your house,
and from this room a window out,
filled with the full light of lasting day.

By this light yet other doors
you will find on hinges rusted.
But open them you must.

In these rooms are windows out
to much that you have lost.
But first you must fracture fast
the mirrors hung before you on the door
that you pass.

To you who may be calling,
that which is waiting
and long living in the adjoining room
has prepared a great feast
for your coming.

The sun remains just overhead.
The long reach of the shadow no longer spreads,
maybe now I'll rest my head.

We have left the darkness, it is said.
No darkness now. No darkness ever.

From this room is a window into the woods.
People are peacefully gathered there,
relaxed and cooled in this wooded air.
Fragrant flowers bloom, and songbirds sing as they should.

Now hurry on, the broken mirror pass.
The illusions simply could not last.
Here you will find much more of yourself,
as you enter the rooms behind closed doors.
You shall know just who you are,
and what you were before.

I would later come to understand that the music stopped at Grandpa's house as a result of the deep disappointments surrounding his only son's destructive behavior. According to Buddy, physical conditions limited Grandpa, but the addictive behavior of his son led to a pervasive depression, which was even more limiting. When his only grandson attempted suicide, his physical and psychological deterioration accelerated. Grandpa was fatigued and losing hope, thus losing his will to live. In a similar fashion over time, our human family has tired and lost the enthusiasm and beliefs so necessary for its onward journey.

Was that music coming from the brownstone? Yes, it was. I envisioned Buddy walking Grandpa to the grand piano and one or the other bringing life from its keyboard. For us here in these difficult times, if a kindly hand from this world or another is extended toward us we can again see and feel the much More of life. We can be taken to the many windows of our house to look once more into different worlds and splendid vistas. They are there for us if only we will be open to the communion.

The music continued, fluid and embracing. Joy was flowing through the old man's hands displacing, for the moment, the limiting arthritis and depression that had confined Grandpa to just one room of the many in his house. I could only wonder what value the return of Buddy to his house would have for this man. It was so good to be there and be a part of this experience. Buddy was again bringing a light, and it was lifting his personal world. I felt a great sense of value in all of this. My hand had helped Buddy recover from the weight of circumstances that had overwhelmed him, and now his hand was lifting darkness from the lives of others.

There, from the resting place in the paulownia tree, I continued to see the correlation between this one house and our larger world. Unless we open these doors, which can bring us to more of ourselves and simultaneously allow us to look out into other worlds, we will never know the complete splendor of life. Like so many of us, Grandpa had been living in just one room of his many-roomed house. A grandson had returned him to more of his home. A way must be found to return humankind to the other realms in which we live, and thus to more of ourselves.

At this, a beaming young man stood on the rear porch with Grandpa on his arm. I slid down the paulownia tree and shared in the exhilaration of the reunion of these two. Both were the better for it. Simply stated, this day was one of the most valued days of my life.

It wasn't long until Buddy found a way to move in with his grandfather. He cared for him, took piano lessons from him, and weeded and planted the garden. Buddy would never again need a therapist. I was honored to be his friend and share in his time with Grandpa in the brownstone house. Together we brought Grandpa's bed down from the upper floor and positioned it in a former parlor adjacent to the piano. Buddy made his personal space in the upstairs and filled the entire house with wellness. Even Grandpa got a second wind and indicated that he had no need for the 'ticket' any time soon. Buddy and I reached a place in his healing and our friendship where his suicide attempt would never again be mentioned. He was all about coming completely into life's meadow, and no value could be added by looking back at those dark times.

At times now, alongside the babbling Ridge Valley Stream, I pray into the silence of the starlit night and I hope that the whole of humanity will awaken and know that life in its fullness awaits us and can be found just up the road from where we are now.

As one chapter of pain and suffering closed for Buddy, a new chapter of pain into awakening started for me. Even as Buddy was getting well, cocaine was entering my days. Inexplicably I was pulling blinds over my own life, and darkness was beckoning me. My visits with Buddy were beginning to be less frequent as my fight against addiction became all-consuming. On good days I would drive up to the old brownstone, hiding my spoon and bottle in shame. Visits to Buddy's North Philadelphia neighborhood often found him entertaining a small group of peers in one way or another. It was so good to see him surrounded by neighborhood children who found his gentle and sensitive qualities attractive and easy to like. There, like an illuminating light in the otherwise dark and hardened streets of an urban ghetto, Buddy's presence offered life-giving qualities in place of hard drugs and persistent street aggression. Buddy would look kindly upon me as I tried to be there for him. I knew that he knew something was less than right with me. The fangs of cocaine bit deeper and deeper into me as I fell deeper and deeper into that dark well. Eventually, it became clear that my only way out of the well of darkness I had created for myself was to change the picture. I would need to leave the university behind. I would also need to take my bruised and aching soul away from the big city, as well as from Buddy and others who cared for me, so that I could search about in the darkness that surrounded me in hope that I might again find myself.

Buddy seemed to understand as I drove my packed car out of Philadelphia. I interrupted his circle of friends as I confided that he would not find me at the university any longer. "Buddy," I said, "you climbed out of a deep and despairing well. I was honored to have offered you a hand. But listen, my friend, dark holes are something any one of us can fall into, and now I must climb out of one myself."

Roles were quickly reversed as he put his arms around me saying, "Call me when you're ready. I'll get a bus to the country to see you."

Even now I am reminded of how completely human I am. Becoming lost and wounded expresses the vulnerability by which we are so easily hurt when we stray from life's pulse. We forget to let our emotions guide us, and we end up being alienated from life's embrace by following what we think we want. Isn't it interesting how warm and loving hands from our fellow human beings can come forth and lift us up! (See 'Becoming Lost and Being Found' in *Something More*.)

What is the meaning and value of darkness that presents itself as despair from old wounds? How do we know it, where do we find it, and how, pray tell, can we avoid being overwhelmed by it? How could I, while helping to sweep it from the life of another as a therapist, allow it to creep into my own life and surround me with equally devastating consequences? Perhaps it might help to return to the memory of those early years on the farm and marvel once again at my mother. She was a lady who brought fifteen children into the world, cared for all of them, and also cared for ten thousand chickens and everything else that was born, moved, or grown on the farm with a singular and complete dedication. The life around her just could not be separated from the life within her.

Caring, The Way to Recovery and Awakening

Finding myself would only occur as I recommitted to living my life completely, and caring was the key. In the twenty years since I lived on the farm, I fell asleep to what mattered, and I could only awaken to save my life when I put caring for the world around me first.

The light from us

is

the same light that came to us.

When we extend caring and understanding into the world, we receive a great deal of value in return. As we offer to open doors for others, doors to the many forgotten rooms of ourselves may be mysteriously opened as well. As our confidence and caring dust off the caution and doubt of others, signs of our deeper meaning and being will be simultaneously sent out. We will begin to witness the More of life in the everyday. Clues will be sent and voices shall whisper our names. More life shall be looking into ours as awakening occurs on different levels. Simply stated, we are coming alive, and life in her gladness is returning all that we are to us. Much that we have lost or forgotten is no longer being withheld from us.

It may seem as if we are moving about the face of the earth in this existence experience in single fashion. However, we are not alone. A powerful telepathic connection from those behind us emerges to assist and sustain our efforts. In some manner bits and pieces of understanding will be forthcoming which allow a glimpse of how it is that we are connected to the many layers of this creation. More importantly, a great momentum will be felt in applying our being-ness to the world about us, extending our warmth and light to diminish the cold and darkness before us.

> As in you, so through you
> a birth and a resurrection
> that carries you above it all,
> casting bright a transforming light
> so others might now see.

Freeing Ourselves of the Night

Had I not awakened from the misery and addiction of that deep well I would have, in effect, spent my life adding to the darkness that so threatens our world. When we are awakening to the More of our lives we are simultaneously freeing ourselves from the less side of things. If the habits of our lives are contributing to the less side of things, our highway may seem long-lived, but life may already be slipping away and may even already be gone. If our lives seem empty or lost, but we are alive enough to be concerned or deeply worried, there is much that we can do. Our lives may seem to be surrounded by darkness, but as long as we feel, it has not consumed us. In this scenario awakening is a most precious thing.

A Serpent Called Night

> If darkness seems set and solid
> and all around,
> light will reach out from the heavens
> unto the ground.
> This light will be ours
> to illuminate, warm, and surround.

Believing in the possibility that there is something more while performing small acts of caring sets the change in motion. What the More is, or what it will become, need not be specified in our thoughts. Nor should acts of caring seem overwhelming or unreachable. Simply saying thanks to the world around us is a good place to begin. For instance, saying hello to an overlooked neighbor or putting out food for a stray cat are seemingly insignificant acts, but they may open the way for so much more. In these small expressions for life, more life is found, which may begin to pull us out of the obscuring darkness.

These caring acts create an arc of sorts that will connect with the living world just beyond the stuff of night that surrounds us. A sense of hope or promise will begin to glitter in us. This is the arc of connectedness resonating for us. Continuing to express beliefs of Something More as we are extending ourselves into the world around us creates the metaphoric bridge that will allow us to walk out of the darkness that has engulfed us. We will no longer be kin to the night.

Yes, the demands of these times upon our journey will find us making great efforts as we are reminded that the hardships, the suffering, and even the dying are not easy to do. Oh, how we will long for those protected harbors along with that eternal day with its beginning and not an end! Going forward from where we are now, we must keep an ear and an eye tuned to the unusual. We must allow the awareness of more to awaken within us, even as life's greater value grows from us.

This is the time

to respond to the mystic pregnancy of possibility
and to answer the swollen embryo of opportunity.
Together we will raise the curtain
and share the treasures set before us.
Be expectant!

Darkness in our lives can be many different things to different people. For some it is overwhelming loss; for others it is deep depression, limitations, lack of basic trust or faith, habits of manipulation or taking, or addictions to one thing or another. What any and all of these conditions have in common is that they subtract value from our lives while withholding it from others. Awakening allows us to know the difference; will it be More or Less? How distinct are the options:

In the Way we Are

To die here and be forever dead,
left in a darkness we were not from!
To die here and live forever on.
When dead here, we are not done.

Come Back to Yourself

Intuitive knowing is not something that is on our everyday menu, but it may be one of our best means of illuminating some of the unseen that lies before us. Intuition speaks to us from the deeper wisdom of life. It is an exercise in basic trust between us and our place in creation. It is indeed knowing without knowing how we know. If we practice ringing it up, its truth will not escape us. Its answers will not be so much specific information, but will lend a sense of direction. We will be able to feel the way. If we cannot think or see our way out of darkness, feeling may help.

The unseen that is of critical concern for us is everything that lies before us. As we are able to sense that there is Something More, we will choose to live in such a way that we are not pushing our tomorrows away from us. It may remain unseen, but it is not unknowable.

If we fail to believe in the possibilities of More, we probably won't extend the effort to awake and see. Should this be our scenario, we will continue to serve the night, the very darkness our incredible journey was intended to diminish.

We breathe our breath upon it,
illuminating the darkness,
warming the cold.

Come back to ourselves! Reclaim our heritage! This is the time to reach out and listen to the unusual. We may need to tolerate a little discomfort, but we must respond to the mystical pregnancy, for the swollen embryo of opportunity has arrived! As we are prepared we will raise the curtain that separates less from more and share in the treasures set before us.

For those who are being pulled by the tentacle of the night, there will be a corresponding distancing from life, and thus the promise of more will equal less life. Reflection upon our habits of behavior is an important first step. The self-serving taking from the world around us invariably signals a troubling tendency of ours. The implication here is that something is or may have taken away from us, and our manipulation of those around us is an attempt to get it back. "But wait," we may say, "to err is the human condition. I am only taking a little of this and a little of that."

A little sin, a little lost,
I have a prayer
that will satisfy the cost.

But taking can become all-consuming, and it loses us our way. Yes, life can deal with some of this as long as lostness does not become complete and sin does not coerce us into withholding life from others or ourselves. If our light is being significantly lost, darkness is progressively settling in. If we can still see and believe, even just a little, then this getting lost is a process we can do something about.

The degree of manipulation utilized in our thinking can tell us much about how deep into darkness we have fallen. Most often, our manipulation of others begins in a fear of, or lack of, our own value. Taking becomes a means of feeling valued. "Now look at what I've got!" It never satisfies for long, and more and more is needed to create, in actuality, less and less. Self-serving taking continues to escalate. Soon it is perceived as a satisfying habit, even a strength, perfected over a number of years and utilized wherever possible. These manipulative skills that are feeding the darkness as pain and suffering, are occurring in and around our lives. We cannot manipulate and take unnecessarily without creating a deficit. We may become so accomplished at taking that our sense of being is almost completely dependent on our manipulative skills as the volume of stuff piles up. Our need to fill the emptiness with more emptiness grows deeper. We may have a great deal on the outside, but we are likely to be so out of touch and empty on the inside that we can't seem to feel or even care about others' losses and pain. The taking has become addictive from the inside out, and the truth is that fear and uncertainty have squeezed out our ability to care for and enjoy life in general.

In this scenario, instead of finding meaning and feeling value, we are losing ourselves day by day. Is it possible that all of this taking, which has masqueraded as necessary to give us value, was really unnecessary? Is it possible that the doubt and uncertainty that are so prevalent in these times have a lot to do with the human predicament and very little to do with us in particular? If so, let's acknowledge our vulnerability and get back to where we belong!

When we awaken to our greater selves, it relinquishes us from without to within and replaces the emptiness, which may have driven our sin as a result of our thoughts and actions that belonged to the less side of things. A brief consideration of the darkness that has been so consuming may be helpful here.

We should ask ourselves, "What was our vulnerability, and how and why was so much of our true essence lost and forgotten?" This reminds us of our intention and purpose from early on, to bring life into the darkness. In that age that is now long gone by who, what, and why was so much more clear? We have been worn down by the journey. Passing through the darkness has greatly tired us, and being transferred from one mount to another has been trying. Aging, dying, letting go, and being passed again and again through the eye of a needle is no fun. Each time we die, uncertainty and fear play at our trust. Along with this, the pain of our losses adds to the frustration of not being farther along. We sense that we are stuck here, and it gets to be too much. It is understandable that we are tired, understandable that we have lost some faith, and understandable that basic trust is an issue.

Another means by which we may attempt to sense value and placate our doubts is employing the longevity factor by stretching out our biological time to live on and on. Here we might sense that added value includes more time, a slippery quality of our existence in the here and now. This is the condition of our lives that we never seem to have enough of. If we find more of it, what will we do with it? What is being done with our extended, medicated existence is dubious at best.

This brings to mind the circumstances surrounding the mother of a friend who is currently being housed in an extended care facility. A year ago she was winding up her stay on earth, and she could have happily moved on to another room in her house of life. She was close to home, and she was surrounded by her children, grandchildren, and extended family on a daily basis. In more than one conversation she confided that she was ready and willing to be on her way. We spoke about the Something More that lay ahead for her, and she embraced it heartily.

Sadly, a family decision was made to move her to a distant extended care facility. "She will be better taken care of and given every possible day she deserves," was the explanation I received from the family spokesperson when I questioned sending her so far away.

What this fine lady deserved is definitely not what she got. Her daughter has spoken to me in earnest regarding her mom's deteriorating mental condition. She related how her mother has become paranoid and warns her on her visits that the facility might decide to keep her and not let her leave. From my point of view, this is not simply paranoia. This is a fairly accurate account of how this mom perceives her now situation. Mom is being held in the clutches of the bottom line business of dying. Instead of being allowed to part from this world and be born into a new and wondrous meadow, this fragile lady has been subjected to a torturous extended stay that is her own personal hell.

There is a cold and uncaring business involved in prolonging the stay of our bodies beyond their meaningful time. We are not allowed to die; instead we are kept 'alive,' while our grace and dignity are denied. So much of the business of dying is in response to our generalized fear of letting go. It is only here on earth that we are sure of ourselves. What lies beyond this world is a matter about which we have too little trust and too little faith.

There she is alone in a postage stamp-sized room, in a single-sized bed. She is medicated constantly with narcotics and psychotropic pharmaceuticals. She longs to be out of here, but something keeps getting in her way. She is separated from all that she knows, from her loved ones, and from the loving light of day. She is sad, and she cries out through her confusion, but she has no way of questioning her regimen. Eventually she will waste away and finally die, but this will not be on her terms. Did somebody say this lady is paranoid?

Looking at what's happening at the end of our lives might give us concern and even a healthy paranoia about what's going on during the rest of our lives. So much of our living may seem to separate us from life's connections, leaving in us a sense of aloneness and separateness. Instead of being allowed to flower along with the many others in life's meadow, we are told to fence a piece of the meadow for ourselves. If we are successful in this endeavor, soon we are squeezing out others' blooms, diminishing the color and value of others' flowers, and simultaneously not adding appreciably to our own blossoms.

This can be compared to invasive species from the horticultural world. Unlike some wild roses in our present habitat, the multiflora rose is an aggressive, introduced life form that takes as its natural right. It behaves as though it needs the entire meadow, and it is very adept at consuming other life forms. This bushy rose aggresses quickly once it is introduced. As it advances, the diversity of life all around it is quickly consumed. Growing at a rapid rate, it sucks up all available moisture and takes in all the available light, while spreading its thorny self over the available space. Spring beauties, violets, and phlox are all quickly consumed. Their textured and beautiful blooms will not soon be seen again.

_The Meadow

A one-time beautiful meadow_
that let the wild rose in_
is now lost to everything
except the wild rose it let in.
When everything was gone except itself
a deadly pathogen snuck in.
Rose-rosetta moved quickly among the many canes.
Now it's a lost and lonely meadow where death so quickly came.

None of this can account for or justify wrong thinking and wrong action. Thinking so and living so can only add to the darkness. We must not give up on life; our doubts are the challenges of our work. Sickness, fatigue, low levels of mustardo, and even death have resulted from the demands of life's journey through the time and space of night. We must be at peace with our perceived knowing that we've walked life's deck. Quitting is not an option. Understanding that there are many layers to the journey, we do the best we can with what we know in each moment. This is the wind that gives life to our sails and fuels our continuing journey.

If we have become encumbered in something that opposes life, we must seek to reconfirm the value of life and reach for life's radiance. As we loosen our hold on what is wrong, there will be much opportunity to grasp onto what is right and lasting. Recovering from the dark and lonely highway is aided by remembering that our lives are best-appreciated and protected in life's meadow. This is a meadow of many! If goodness and warmth highlight the living of your life, then a ripple, if not a wave, will touch those around you to the degree they are open to these qualities.

Staying Waters

The living of your life
becomes as a fountain
from which others may drink.
Sustenance gained as
the way of your life
allows others a way
that they may see
their way out of darkness.

The process of this awakening is an inside-outside kind of process. As our place in life is found in us, the value of giving is added to the world around us. As our open hand is extended to receive the More of life our other hand is reaching out with the Something More for others. As they will receive it, it shall be given to them.

Once this process of receiving and giving gets started, living takes on a newness and wonder that cannot be denied. The importance of the exercise of trust, patience, and faith cannot be overstated in our getting started. We must trust that if we thought we saw something or heard something call out our names, we probably did. We need the faith that these things are possible, and that ultimately we belong to creation's endless day. We must have the patience to allow this process to unfold. Trust, faith, and patience benefit from practice. I cannot emphasize enough the importance of finding a protected space or interlude in our day for being open to receive as we practice opening new doors. It is interesting how the leadings of cognitive and physical man praise the value of practice, but when it comes to trust, faith, and patience the assumption is that we either have these qualities or we don't. Even more interesting is how we dismiss these qualities when we succumb to the demeaning bottom-line consciousness that is so rampant in these times. Of course, we have 'trust' and 'faith' that our business deals will work out, and we don't mind being 'patient' for our money!

Practicing the qualities of trust, faith, and patience is the true path to sharpening our reception of the unusual. Our first experiences of newness will seldom be complete or clear. We must participate in it, chew upon it, learn from it, and not turn from it, returning to our practice again and again as we may.

Now that you have begun,
allow the newness in
for it is to you that it comes.
Experience it,
do not turn from it.
Bring forth your faith and your trust.
Do not allow your mind
to dissuade you from it.

In time, as patience lends its guidance, more of the wonder will open up for us. During this process of awakening to the Something More of life we will simultaneously move from being witnesses to the majesty and wonder of life to knowing we are active stewards that help guide the sustaining creative ripples that start at our front doors out into the world.

Quietly we become conduits to the Something More. Being a part of the world instead of removed from it, protects us from the desolation and difficulties that feel so cold and so empty and are so prevalent in our world in these times. With the faith and trust that have prepared us, we will be strong in these troubling winds. We shall have a quiet yet fierce conviction that our participation does matter! Knowing there is Something More, we will experience it and nurture it as we throw our pebbles into the eternal sea of life. These wondrous possibilities are near and dear to us. As soon as the collective of life's breath is allowed to grow from a ripple into a wave, it will move life's vessel in such a way that nighttime can be crossed over and we can be set free upon the open sea.

Awakening

The promise and the fruit.
Letting go of what is wrong.
Taking hold of that which is lasting.

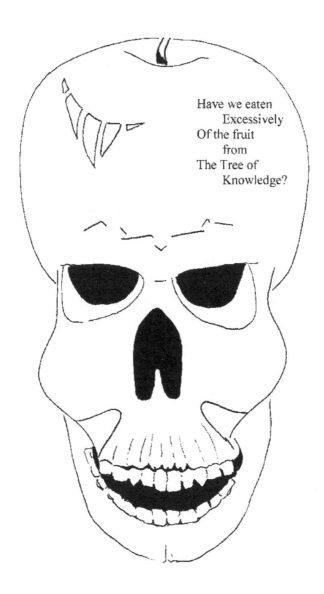

Have we eaten
        Excessively
Of the fruit
        from
The Tree of
        Knowledge?

6

Becoming Lost to Life

Within the relative cultural standards of today many of us may think of ourselves as satisfied with our places in the general scheme of things. We may not be aware that a great struggle between a lasting sleep (Less) and a grand and staying living experience (More) hangs in the balance.

As will be made clear, whether we find ourselves supporting Less or More there is a dynamic, almost magnetic pull intrinsic to either of these directions. If we are involved in becoming lost to life there is an unseen but pertinent force helping us move along in the wrong direction. If, on the other hand, we are coming down on the side of More, there is a compelling force that will excite and propel us toward a giving and lasting day.

As we declare who we are as expressed in our motives and values, a force shall surround us. While the consequences in the way of our lives may not be clear initially, the difference, ultimately, will be very real. One represents a cold and lasting night, the other a warm and staying day. Though we may be awakening and beginning to see the grand view of life, we should expect and not be surprised by the reluctance of others.

"If I am everything I want to be and I have everything I want so nothing more is needed, should I be concerned about seeing and awakening to More?"

If we are deep believers in destiny and are convinced that everything is as it should be and can't be changed, then our mind-sets may indeed get in the way of the More.

The wind will blow me with the dust

and

night shall take me if it must.

For me nothing is cast in stone, outcomes are not guaranteed, and anything can happen.

If we have chosen not to see or awaken to the More of our lives, the Less may be what we are getting. The process of subtraction may be underway and without some resistance or concern we may unknowingly become more and more lost to life.

Most of us have, at one time or another, experienced the presence of a ghost or ghostly figure. Many of us have subsequently devalued the experience as belonging to our imaginations. Relegating these experiences to our imaginations is what mature, sensible people are supposed to do. Otherwise, we must account for where they come from, who they are or were, and what it could possibly mean that we were so visited.

Indeed, some may have been figments of our imaginations, but in many instances they are very real. Honest seeing during the process of awakening will invariably take us to their shadowy realm, even if just to look in and then move on again. It is not the intention here to seek to establish their value or legitimacy, but rather to learn to avoid living in such a way as to be on the fast track to becoming one of them.

While these shadowy entities are not our primary focus here, much may be learned by considering their presence. From a migration of the soul perspective, their presence here, beyond the time of their parting, challenges us to account for how these beings have been lost to life. While ghosts and goblins have not been a big part of my life, the experiences I have had with them have greatly emphasized the value of putting More in my life. I would never willingly agree to just go where the wind blows and this is why.

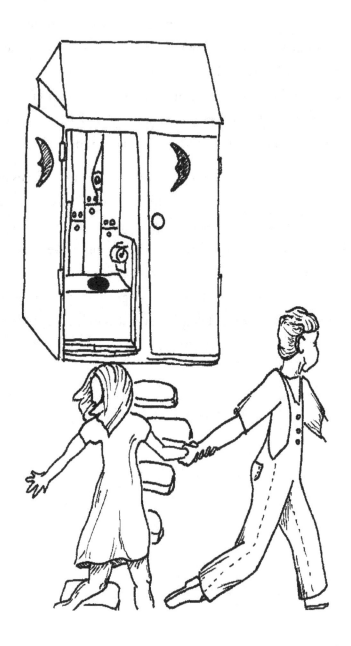

The Johnny House

The myth of the boogeyman is a troubling allegory that has percolated throughout the length and breadth of childhood in western society. The frightful presence of a larger than life, ghastly, spooky character delivering ill intent seems to be a common feature of this experience. In fact, it is such a lasting and pervasive experience of our culture's early years that I suspect there may be some validity in the often-repeated narrative.

Many adults dismiss these ghost tales as belonging to the imaginative world of childhood. However, dismissing these shadowy myths as being children's tall tales doesn't satisfy the personal experiences of so many who have experienced them. Why is childhood the more acceptable venue for these shadowy figures?

In many ways children are more open to other realities, in part because they haven't yet been conditioned to wall them off or fence them out. Where would such frightful figures reside that would allow them to slip in and out of the night? They probably dwell in the space around us, but they are not physically prominent enough to be readily noticed, especially by grown-up people who have so many important things to do.

Is there just one of these apparitions who shows up at different times and places around the world? I don't believe that these countless encounters represent just one fictional being. No, there are very likely many of these shadowy figures. As with the story of Santa, there is the myth of one, but in fact there are countless Santas on Christmas Eve, and none of them reside at the North Pole.

Where did these boogeymen come from? They once lived as we live here in this world. Something went terribly wrong for them, and now they are left to wander about aimlessly, slipping in and out of the night. In short, at the time of their passing, they were not received into a protective sanctuary or repository that may have comforted and kept them. Due to the great distance they lived apart from life, instead of being sustained and protected in a life-supporting space or place, they were lost to the shadows.

> When they lived they loved not this life.
> Now they wander about
> in the cold of night
> wanting at last to make it right.
> Instead they leave the world in fright.

My earliest personal experience of these frightening, but basically harmless phantoms of the night occurred in our outhouse at our family farm. The Johnny house was the name given to this important structure. The outdoor facility was the only available comfort station on four hundred acres of land. These exterior lavatories were not uncommon throughout the countryside in the 1940s, '50s, and '60s. This spartan place of business offered no particular amenities, and the only comfort it could provide was the relief one experienced when visiting it. Indoor bathroom facilities didn't come to the Redding family farm until the late fifties. I'll never forget my first shower, standing under the cascading warm water with a bar of ivory soap and laughing uncontrollably at the truly amazing means of cleaning up. The same addition to our farmhouse provided us with a flushable toilet!

So many of us take showers and toilets for granted that I would like to reflect for a moment on how it was back on the farm. In the early years, bathing occurred in a large laundry tub located in the out-kitchen of the family home. Mom put one or two of us in at a time and scrubbed until all the accumulated dirt and grime came off along, it seemed, with the skin to which it was attached. During the winter months boiling water from the stove was added to the cold water to make the bath bearable. Summer bathing was accomplished using cold water pumped from a deep well by a windmill. The out-kitchen was unheated. As in most farm homes, its primary function was as a place for laundry and family cleanups, and for rendering and smoking meats following seasonal butchering or wild game hunting. Large black kettles hung from an oversized hearth where three to four foot pieces of hickory wood burned, providing necessary heat to boil the scrapple and smoke the hams and sausage. The same kettles could be employed to wash three, four, or five little Reddings at the same time if the need arose. A good soaking was obligatory before scrubbing could be done!

Mom was a great multi-tasker, plunging one or more of us into the large laundry tub while the old wringer-washer continuously slush-slush-slushed. Simultaneously, she might step into the kitchen to stir a pot of stew or shuffle bread about in her oven. On her return she would bring boiling water to add to our soaking tubs to keep the water temperature above freezing.

Soaking seemed to be the key here. This would go on from fifteen minutes to a half hour, depending on how long she thought would be necessary to loosen a week's worth of grime from a child's body. Wintertime washes were the most trying, with us sitting naked for so long in cold water that goose bumps covered our bodies and our skin turned ruby red, almost purple.

The other critical 'room' of 1950's farm life prefixed with 'out' was the outhouse. The out-kitchen adhered directly to the main house, and the outhouse was most typically located about fifty to a hundred feet from the family living quarters, so as to separate the obvious smell and significant fly populations from the residence. Such was the case on our farm, and our facility was known as the Johnny house. Our Johnny house was a wooden structure with the luxury of two usable seats upon a wooden platform where one perched and conducted his business. A bundle of old newspaper was made available for clean ups. While the Johnny house was the most visited building on the farm, it was less than a true 'comfort station.'

Each season presented its own discomforts. Summer greeted the user with strong smells and a hungry fly population. Winter was free of flies but cold winds would make for very uncomfortable seating. Of course, it was better than squatting in the barn or having to respond to nature's call in the distant meadow or woods. In these circumstances, the best wipes were dry hay, grass, or fallen leaves!

Having said all of this, the Johnny house was an important place and retained a valued mystique of sorts. The outhouse offered me my first introduction to phantoms, those troubled, disembodied spirits that wander about the earth and disrupt the lives of the living. On two separate occasions the Johnny house shook as I was about my business. On the first occasion I was alone. Later that summer both seats were occupied when my younger sister, Sally, was sharing the facility with me. These experiences in the night led me to suspect something was out of the ordinary, and it was something I was concerned about.

At first some loud snorts came out of the evening's darkness. They were followed by other snorts. Almost immediately, I felt an unusual updraft on my bottom parts as I jumped off my seat and grabbed for some newspaper to clean up. The Johnny house started to moan and creak and out the door I ran. I yelped, tripping over my shorts, which were still in the ankle position. As I rolled over, grabbed my pants, and regained my balance, I saw what I thought may have been a large, dark something retreating into the night. "Wow, that's it," I thought, "our breeding bull got out, and he got really close to me! But how did he get out of the barn?"

Farm bulls were always respected and even feared. This one in particular was dangerous and unpredictable. Earlier in the summer he had killed a younger bull. A year before he had pinned me in the barn. If Judy, my Weimeraner, hadn't torn a piece from his nose, I too may have been history. Just a week before my experience in the Johnny house my oldest brother, Dave, had bent a one inch steel pipe over his head trying to bring the beast under control.

"Dad, why do you keep such a dangerous bull around here?" I had asked my father.

"Well son," he responded, "he makes very nice calves for baby beef cattle."

"He does?" I thought, never having seen him lay a calf or even nurse one. My next question, "How?" went unanswered.

His only other comment was, "All bulls are dangerous!"

Gaining my composure outside the Johnny house, I went to the barn and peered into the bull's stall. He was there, resting on his bedding. It was not the bull. What was it? I ran to ask my mom what was going on.

"Mom," I said, "it snorted like a bull. I felt its breath on my butt, and it felt like he rammed the back of the Johnny house with his head."

Responding to my fear and confusion, she spoke a short while about the ghostly phenomenon of poltergeists. She described a poltergeist as a shadowy presence or being that can literally encroach upon our life's space, even to the point of wreaking havoc around us. She further mentioned how people often dismiss such things as 'imaginations gone wild,' but she said that throughout history there have been repeated encounters with such ghosts or phantoms that are difficult to explain away. She went on to explain that when people are hurt by these shadowy forces, it's usually when they react out of fear and do something that puts them in harm's way, such as driving off a road to avoid what they think is a person and ending up hitting a bridge abutment.

She told of a painful memory of her childhood in Lost River, Virginia, when a ghost constantly tormented a neighbor family. As the front door began to rattle in its ghostly manor the father grabbed his shotgun and fired through it in a dramatic effort to ward off this unsettling ghost. Sadly, it was only his wife fumbling with the front door lock, and a precious life was lost. Thus an apparition who entered these people's lives set this man up to unintentionally take from himself what may have been the best part of his life. The comings and goings of the ghost had encouraged them to begin locking their door and the nervous fear of this man allowed him to react outside of his ordinary character.

Mom went on to say that these shadowy specters are often attracted to certain people and are frequently found repeatedly at the same locations.

"They are?" I asked.

"Certainly you have heard stories of haunted houses," she stated, "and real or otherwise, there only seems to be one of these every so often."

"Am I one of those people that they like to scare?" I asked.

"Well, Stephen, you spend a great deal of time alone and they do seem to be attracted to sad and lonely people."

At this, a flood of quiet tears washed down my face. Pig the Wig, my pet pig friend, had recently been slaughtered. I wasn't feeling comfortable with my brothers' distant treatment following the tractor accident and yes, I was spending a lot of lonely moments, if not hours, wanting to get back to that wondrous place of Javunda (see *Something More*).

Mom continued, "Stephen, certain doors opened for you when you survived in the thirty-three acre field. You have made contact with Cheezer-Wheezer and it may be that other less positive entities are coming through these doors and windows. So please, try to spend less time looking into the stars and heavens and more time here on earth with the family."

"OK Mom, I'll try."

I reminded her that Joe, Sally, and I were playing a lot these days to which she said, "Good."

Some nights later, I lay upon the bedroom floor trying to get some sleep. The floor offered some respite from the thick, muggy heat of a Gettysburg summer night. My eyes were trained on the window, perhaps hoping for a slight breeze. I noticed some foggy yellow eyes, or exhausted fireflies, flickering there. With the suffocating night keeping sleep at bay, I was reflecting upon the boogeyman, an identity I had decided was appropriate for the Johnny house phantom. Mom had introduced the name to me as one used for the imagination or manifestation of such an entity, more often involved in children's lives than in adult lives. Was my thinking opening a door to the boogeyman, and was that him looking in through the window at me?

Just a few weeks later, that boogeyman made another appearance. I heard the snorts and sounds that were still fresh in my memory.

Quickly, I jumped off my outhouse seat and grabbed Sally, placing her up on her feet. The Johnny house began to creak and sway. Putrid air gushed up from the toilet holes. Though I was admittedly afraid, I did not panic. Sally was at a full scream, and I tried to comfort her. Surely I was better prepared this time, remembering Mom's take:

> The phantoms of
> the night
> cannot harm you
> if you do not
> react in fear or fright!

Finding a small knothole in the side of the Johnny house, I peered out to see a milky yellow eye looking in. With one long, loud snort, the eye was gone and a large ten to twelve foot amorphous figure, darker than the country darkness, retreated into the night.

Swiping Sally up into my arms, I met Mom halfway to the house as she responded to her daughter's screams. Sally's verbal response, aside from profuse crying, was that a big bear was after us. Mom knew, and I knew. While quieting Sally's extreme discomfort my brothers were slowly circling us, asking me what I had done to hurt their sister. In their view, clearly their young sister was very upset, and something bad must have happened. After a while, Mom shooed them away and asked me to use the inside potty in evening and night hours until the connection to the boogeyman-like interloper was broken.

Mom seemed sure of what needed to happen, and I would certainly follow her wishes. There was nothing glamorous about the inside potty. It was a four to five gallon galvanized bucket that would be used with some difficulty during late night hours, thunderstorms, and harsh winter nights.

Dad felt that children my age, six years and up, should not be using the indoor facilities because it only added to the 'stuff' that someone had to carry out the next morning and pour down the Johnny house hole. It wasn't long until Dad assigned me the morning duty of carrying and cleaning the bucket. Dad was not made privy to the reason why I was so frequently using the indoor can, but I could tell it was bothering him. For a period of four to six weeks I successfully carried the bucket from the house to the outhouse, but then one morning as I came in from milking Blacky, I was told I was running late.

"Hurry up and change." Mom said, "You only have ten minutes to get to the bus." Our bus stop was half a mile away down the country lane. "Don't worry about the bucket, I'll take care of it."

Jumping into my school clothes, I grabbed the potty bucket, not wanting Mom to get stuck with my nasty job. One moment I was at the top of the steep stairs, and in the next instant I was at the bottom of the stairs covered in the contents of the bucket.

As I looked up the stairs, each step seemed laden with some of the solid stuff, while a trickle of the liquid part was still following the stairway down. Oh, my God, it was entering a hinged crack to the cubbyhole under the stairs where Dad kept his shoes. At this moment, the house fell deathly silent. Dad had just entered. He surveyed the situation while I got to my feet. Mom quickly started to remove my soiled clothes as Dad gingerly lifted the hinged step, which accessed his shoes. He saw what he was afraid of, and he saw what I was afraid he would see. He turned to me with that knee-buckling stare. "How the hell did you manage to do this?" he demanded.

When I was stripped to my underwear he slowly, without breaking his stare, curled his forefinger toward himself. This could only mean one thing, a trip to the woodshed, and this could not be good. Mom tried her best to calm Dad, telling him we could straighten this up after school. There would be no school for me this day and not for some days to follow.

His stare upon me was not broken nor did he stop curling his finger to which Mom protested, "He's far too young to be carrying that bucket anyway."

Dad turned and made his way upstairs for his razor strap while I made the weak-kneed walk to the woodshed. I'd been there before and it was never nice, but I suspected this was going to be really serious. The woodshed was a fairly large, wooden structure with no windows, positioned halfway between the house and the outhouse. It had a split door in the rear where we would deliver green, uncured wood, and it had a single door in the front from where we would remove our wood and cart it to the house to feed the hearth, stove, fireplace, and furnace.

I had a moment in the inner darkness of this shed to reflect upon my situation. I wanted to cry but I would not allow myself to add to the discomfort of Mom and my younger brothers and sisters. I understood that they were taking shelter in the upstairs, the barn, and maybe even the outhouse. They would hide there, within earshot of the razor belt, until the necessary discipline was served up. Following these harsh hind-side corrections, it was customary to slowly emerge from our listening posts and offer our sympathies and maybe even a sweet morsel of a candy bar or cookie that we had squirreled away. When one of us was taken to the woodshed, it was very difficult for all of us.

The door opened and Dad pulled it shut behind him as he always did. If one wanted to run, there was nowhere to hide. Stepping across the nearly empty woodshed, Dad opened the upper split door to allow necessary light for what he needed to do. The razor strap was harsh and sharp this day, bruising my buttocks and tearing my skin. For a number of minutes, the painful strikes continued. Finally, the beating ended and Dad opened the front door. The streaming light demonstrated the bloody situation I was in.

"Wait here, Son, until your mother comes to clean you up."

The pain was so searing that I gripped a piece of wood to keep from screaming out. In a moment Mom arrived and broke into a deep and sorrowful cry. I finally began to cry as well, feeling the depth of Mom's hurt even more than the pain and fire that had captured my body. Mom used cold water and gauze to clean me up followed by a liberal coating of udder-balm, an almost miraculous healing salve available in the agricultural market. Then a large diaper was fashioned for me that could be stuffed with comfrey and other healing potions. It would be some days before I could sit and some more days before I could return to school. Two to three times a day, Mom would slowly and painstakingly peel the covering from my wounded buttocks and apply herbs or salves to it. Mom's hands were gentle and her voice soothing as she worked on my backside.

This was a trip to the woodshed that I didn't see coming. There would be other visits to that palace of discipline that would leave me similarly hobbled and pained. There was the time I drove Dad's new '57 Packard through the garage, and another occasion when he saw me dropping matches into an underground gas tank. In these instances there was a very clear connection between what I had done and the severe rendering of punishment I received.

The long days of healing were accompanied by deep reflection and questioning as I wondered how this disaster could befall me. I knew it was somehow connected to the Johnny house ghost, the boogeyman. That was why I was using the in-house bucket, which then became my responsibility to empty. In that way the door had been opened to this nasty accident and the harsh response from my father. This may have been my first experience of the power of Less as a disembodied, troubling phantom effectively touched my life with hurtful consequences.

The shadow of the nighttime
phantoms
can be long embracing and
difficult to loosen.

As we understand the bigger picture, the value of right thought and right action in our lives empowers us to avoid so many of the consequences of Less. This will be true from our first day until the day we are said to die.

The advantages of seeing and awakening are many. When leaving here something will be next for us. We can decide, through living our lives, if it will be More or Less. If we allow ourselves to reach for more here and now, we will also prepare ourselves to receive more at the time of our passing - to open, not close, the door. Both are legitimate and necessary for meaningful tomorrows. Anything can happen at any time. This has always been true but perhaps never more so than it is now.

Seeing more

allows us

to receive more

to come to know

to once again believe.

Of Ghosts and Goblins

What value can be gained by reflecting upon ghosts, goblins, boogeymen and the like? Do they represent the less side of things? Yes. However, their presence can go a long way toward revealing how the process of subtraction may begin with More (as in beings that once existed as living people with great promise) but may end in Less (these once-human entities are now disembodied, lost, and troubled). To dismiss the phenomena out of hand may be naïve, yet to focus intently upon them is distracting if not dangerous.

Our experience of these shadowy figures can be very unique and personal. Their distracting quality is always present, however, and may be illustrated in two recent accounts. A neighbor asked me, "How do I get rid of these things?" The things he referenced were what he referred to as stick men. "They've been coming around late at night, making a commotion and breaking limbs in my trees. I've shot at them but it doesn't seem to deter them." With this he took me behind his house where there were several large sugar maple trees with their otherwise perfect crowns pock-marked with numerous fractured limbs. The various trees surrounding them showed no similar wounding. My neighbor had been so distracted and preoccupied by these nighttime phantoms that he came to me looking for guidance, support, and relief.

In a separate instance, a friend confided to me that she had been tormented by a ghost she referred to as the roof walker. In this case my friend felt as if it was an aggravating phantom sent, for whatever reason, to distress her. By her account, this roof-walking ghost presented itself in the early evening hours of the night. She also said that she had clearly seen this apparition, by means of a flashlight, in a masculine form wearing a trench coat. For some time she felt it was an actual physical person who was of ill intent.

Neither of these people was keen on opening windows or seeing the unusual at that time in their lives. The message is that these nighttime apparitions are plentiful, and they can enter almost any person's life, regardless whether we invite them in or not. That these goblins are here in such great numbers can be most disconcerting. Why are they here? How have so many been lost from the experience of life so that they are now left to wander aimlessly about?

Why are some people visited more frequently by these apparitions than others? Habits in our lives may raise attracting antennae of which we are unaware. My neighbor's heavy drinking, interspersed with bouts of depression, and my friend's excessive involvement in the psychic arts may have signaled the openings that allowed these tormenting experiences to occur. What may serve to insulate us from these troubling ghosts? Again we must remember the staying power of creation. Keeping our lives full of interactions with the animate world allows very little opportunity for the Less side of things to manifest within or around us. Simple acts of caring with goodness and warmth toward our everyday world will go a long way toward freeing us from these intrusive nighttime guests. Acts of true caring for the world around us also seem to wash away lingering dark shadows within us such as hurtful memories, habits of taking, and addictions that might otherwise attract these troubling phantoms to our lives.

To further illustrate this, we might suggest that our best protection from this whole process is to surround ourselves with the pulse of life; to involve ourselves more completely in the living world. In friendship and community we establish a ripple of More which fends off the Less. Of similar value are connecting again with the animate world around us, having high regard for this life, and experiencing joy in caring for it. We must also trust in the insulation granted by the presence of our beginning. If indeed a God has begun us, this God must be trusted to keep us. We need to see our God in this life and in the world around us, not off in some distant place beyond us. In this way we can understand and accept that we are always being embraced. This can foster attitudes of connection that diminish our experience of loneliness while adding discipline and value to us.

> Life's eyes are upon us
> facilitating, guiding, and protecting.
> When watching stops
> a ghost is born.
> If life no longer matters,
> a ghost is grown.
> Alone we join the legions
> of the night.
> We are soon dead and gone,
> and another ghost is born.

Simply put, when life loses its meaning, protection from the night is also lost. That the disembodied are so numerous speaks to the infectious nature of the night and our vulnerability to it. Conditions today are in keeping with their genesis. Many among us are living in ways that, if left unchecked, will almost make certain that we will soon join the legions of the walking dead. Even worse, the phantoms of the darkness may eventually overrun this world. What a frightening night of the living dead this would be. I suspect these shadowy figures represent the ghostly presence of people who once lived in this world in much the same way as we do now. A poignant experience close to home illustrates how the process of subtraction can cause so much to be lost or forfeited from a once-promising life where so much vitality was lost to Less.

"My bodily presence has passed from this world,
yet I am not ready to take the bridge unto the next.
Wandering aimlessly about in the night is lonely,
so maybe I'll take up residence in a tree, and allow
my spirit to be rested, protected, and embraced.

Margie

Does the night enter into us as we allow it? Or is it already involved in us and allowed to express itself in different situations or circumstances? Despite an acquired distaste of modern viewing and funeral rituals associated with the business of dying, I agreed to accompany my wife

191

and children to the viewing, funeral mass, and burial of my mother-in-law.

During the hour or more I spent nesting in the corner of the viewing room farthest away from the open casket, I was approached repeatedly by a funeral home attendant who, observing my distant seat and sensing my reluctance, urged me to go forward and pay my final respects. Shaking my head to the negative only seemed to encourage more prodding by this man, and his efforts made me more and more uncomfortable. Already I was remembering why I have actively avoided the business of planting bodies. Dad's parting precipitated the last funeral I had attended almost thirty years before. Catholic families don't easily look past this ritual, and when I chose to avoid Mom's funeral, I was not easily forgiven by my brothers and sisters.

I understand that these are important times for families. I just don't care for the nature of the ritual. In my Mom's case, I sat quietly at the base of one of her favorite trees for the duration of the funeral, and I ended the funeral day by planting a tricolor beech tree in her lawn. As time has passed most of the family has come to admire the beautiful and growing beech, referring to it as 'Mom's Tree.' As they acknowledge the beautiful beech tree I sense that I am getting off the hook a little for foregoing the lengthy and teary ritual of passing.

But here I was, early in the 'day of death,' uncomfortable and being harassed by someone who felt that everyone needed to go up to the open casket and cry a bit. Though I wanted to run for the door, I had promised Kathy I would do this thing, so I stayed. I was amazed at how many people came out to the viewing of this wonderful lady who I had always referred to as Mom. Where were all of these family and friends when we celebrated Mom at picnics and holidays? I was often there, and I enjoyed Mom immensely. Perhaps if these many people had celebrated Mom's life while she lived and smiled upon her world there might not have been so much crying and catching up going on at this later-than-late hour.

A short time later the pallbearers were summoned. Three of my children, Shetlinn, Orrian, and Jaeilyn were among them. I knew this was a good thing. They were all close to Nana, and it was appropriate that they were involved in the solemn task of escorting her to her final resting place. It was one last parting with someone so important to them. This set me to wonder. Kathy's mother was their last remaining grandparent. It would not be easy for someone to step into their lives to fill this void with the special warmth and guidance a grandparent can provide. Why do we so readily remove this wondrous resource from our families? Why are we so willing to allow our parents to be housed in nursing homes? While it may be difficult for us, the aging process provides so much opportunity for learning and compassion for our children. When we remove our parents from the home we lose a special and giving energy that cannot be duplicated or easily replaced.

Drawing a deep breath, it occurred to me that the curtain had dropped on the first part of a three-act play. This scene was over, and I was still standing. Next we would all move to the Catholic church, where Mom had found her spiritual guidance and where she had invested much of her time and allegiance. Kathy and our daughter Meurcie were helped into the funeral car, while my sons and I got into our family van. As soon as we closed the doors it was clear to me that we had another passenger. Four of us were in the flesh, while the other being was not clothed in a body. As we settled into our seats the most annoying, mournful cry one could ever imagine began. Immediately our minds attempted to account for the disembodied being that was hitching a ride with us. Jaeilyn commented, "Someone is really crying loudly. Someone is really upset!" Pressing our faces against the windows of our van we searched the departing guests for someone so distressed that they might need oxygen or pharmaceutical intervention. We couldn't identify who it might be, but we still held out hope that it was, indeed, someone leaving the funeral home. How else could we account for the painful mourning cry we heard inside the van?

In a matter of minutes all of the guests were in their vehicles and the funeral procession was moving on to the church. Our place in line was immediately behind the hearse and funeral car. The mournful howl and gut wrenching crying continued as we began to move, and Shetlinn reported that he thought we were losing a bearing, or perhaps even a wheel off the van. "Good try, Shetlinn," I thought. Our minds want to explain away these harsh, ghostly experiences, and a frayed bearing's high pitched noise comes as close as anything to what we were hearing. A glimpse around the van at my sons' stern countenances and steeled eyes revealed the unspoken truth about their experience – something of the unseen and unnatural was among us. At this point I was sure that an angry, lonely, lost spirit being was in our midst, in our van. I made mention of this possibility, but could provide no explanation of what to do about it. Nor did I want to further burden or add fright to my sons, who were already having a difficult day.

Eventually we came to a stop at the church and we willingly removed ourselves from the interior of the howling van and into the considerable damp and cold of the day. I couldn't help but notice two of my sons laying the backs of their hands against the wheels of our van to detect any extreme heat that might be resulting from a spent bearing. They hoped to find a physical cause that could alleviate them from having to deal with this painful, and somewhat frightening, phenomenon playing out in the car.

Soon we were seated in the church. Incense was heavy and light was dim. The priest was attempting to speak well of Nana, but without emotion that is difficult to do. He asked God to look kindly upon her and he asked us to pray for the salvation of her soul. "Pray for her salvation!" I thought. If there was any act of salvation needed by this fine lady it was well achieved over her long and kindly history in the way she lived her life in this world.

After some periods of kneeling-standing-sitting I thought I again heard the high-pitched mournful cry that had accompanied us in the van. Then, like a feather passing across my face, something moved by me as the priest was inviting the Catholics among the mourners to come forward to receive Holy Communion. I couldn't help but wonder how the church personnel would react if the painful, muffled screaming and moaning I'd heard in the van made its way into the sanctuary. Thankfully, it did not happen.

As the church service ended I had a chance to whisper to Kathy about the spirit-ghost inhabitant of our van. I spoke of the degree of pain and mourning in its high-pitched vocalization. I noted for her how overwhelming it was for our children and how I hoped that it had left the van and got stuck in the church somewhere. Without a moment's hesitation Kathy responded that it was the lost and lonely spirit of her younger sister, Margie. Toward the end of her earthly days, Margie had separated herself from her family, entrapped in a cycle of reclusion and intoxication. Her body ravaged by years of abuse from smoking, liquor, and inadequately treated medical problems; Margie died a lonely and untimely death eight years earlier far from home at the age of forty-two. Kathy's mother and stepfather had retrieved her body at the local airport, clothed only in a tattered hospital gown and shipped in a plain pine box on a late night flight from Tennessee. Kathy and her sisters joined their mother for a private moment of 'goodbye' before the body was taken away for cremation, the form of disposal Margie had requested. It was an ending to a troubled life that left no closure or peace, either for Margie or for those she left behind. It was something Nana had never gotten over.

From More to Less

She cried the pain of loneliness.
She cried the pain of fear.
She cried the pain of being lost.
She cried with deep regret.
She anguished over being lost from life
and stuck between worlds
with no way out.

Margie had lost her way in this world. Her deep sense of shame withheld her from making contact with her family in her final years, and thus withheld from her the warmth that would have allowed her some type of peace at the end. The message here is that we often die as we have lived. It is so important that we prepare for our future meadow by leaving this world with a sense of peace and hope for the next.

Kathy and I surmised that her mother's passing allowed an opportunity for Nana to extend a hand of recognition and forgiveness into the ethers that Margie could grasp onto, at least long enough to afford some hope for this pained and mournful soul who had been lost in the dark space between worlds.

My thought is that Mom's passing from here to there was quite fluid and direct. The sheer depth of the spirit's pained cry spoke to

Margie's desperate attempt to follow her mother out of here. But each journey is a personal one. One cannot carry one's loved ones onward. This is a protection afforded the special space of Nana's own world so that darkness, doubt, and despair could not enter in. Each must come as they may. It is a single-file bridge, so to speak. No one can carry another.

Still, Mom's passing allowed her daughter Margie's spirit an opportunity, an opening, to begin the journey for herself. She was able to momentarily extend a hand to the tortured, lost, and pained spirit and whisper, "Come, Margie, begin the journey. It's okay. One step at a time, you'll get here, and I'll be waiting." In an unseen but obvious fashion, Margie was able to rejoin the family she'd left so long ago and be part of the solemn, yet joyous process of laying her mother to rest. Mom had lived her life with profound goodness and grace. Her final goodbye, though a time of sadness, was a celebration of her life. This was the first time in many, many years that Margie had come home to share in a family event. What joy Mom's spirit must have felt having her 'lost lamb' close enough to embrace!

Following the mass of Christian burial we found ourselves back in the van on the final leg of this day's journey, the winding road to the cemetery. This particular burial spot turned out to be a beautiful old cemetery high on a hill populated by large and beautiful trees of many species. As we rolled up the windows against the cold autumn air it was obvious that the spirit was still with us as the painful screaming resumed. I tried to reassure the children. The sound, unnerving and painful, was a deep, hurtful expression of an otherwise one-time beautiful soul and person who was now disembodied, alone and afraid. We all fell into an uncomfortable silence, enduring the screaming entity, and I momentarily considered finding an alternative vehicle for the ride home afterward. We arrived at the cemetery, and upon disembarking I left my window fully open. I knew that the spirit would not need the window to be ajar to make its exit, but I wasn't taking any chances! I busied myself with attempting to guide and sooth Margie's spirit. I wanted her to take up residence here, close by her mother, near where her ashes had been interred. Perhaps, in this in-between-worlds state, she could inhabit one of the large oak trees that stood guardian over the site.

Soon I felt a lighter-than-light, somewhat frightening caress along my neck, and I knew I might have an opportunity. I walked away from the burial site toward a very large arborvitae. Admiring its vibrant, rich, green crown I reached up and clipped a sprig. I noticed a shimmer. Maybe it was a light breeze, but I think it was Margie alighting, her presence being received within its boughs. Interestingly enough, the tree I was drawn toward, the arborvitae, is the 'Tree of Life.' Maybe this was why I came to this day of the dance with a corpse. I had a chance to experience and guide a lost spirit to a place of relative peace and eventual recovery. Maybe this was why I was in such a fog, not just because I was a reluctant participant in a ritual, but because I, the tree man, was going to serve up a lost and lonely soul by introducing it to a protected, quiet resting place in the bows of an arborvitae tree. At the moment I was being pulled away from the burial plot I wondered to myself, "What are you doing?" Yet, as I encourage others to do, and as my many experiences have allowed me to do, I followed my intuition. As long as we are not hurting or taking from the world around us; making ourselves available, allowing ourselves to be guided, and trusting in the moment are all part of being open to the More that can enrich and bring meaning to our lives. They just might lead to an opportunity or something special at hand.

I turned, approached the burial site, and placed the fragrant green sprig on the polished casket lid. Then, interrupting the priest, I addressed the funeral party. Following the inspiration of the moment can be unsettling to others and their customs. I spoke gently about how we must resist becoming too fixated on the dying. After all, Mom's transition was already complete into another realm, where life is given and never taken.

So let's continue to remove the darkness from the day
and once again we will be off and on our way.

It was amazing how that green sprig of arborvitae clung to the polished casket lid that cold November day. The wind stirred the crispy fallen leaves and blew at the hats and scarves of the visiting mourners, but it could not dislodge the little symbol of the moment.

We are all truly sprigs of arborvitae.
We are all of and from the 'Tree of Life.'
If we will not toss life away
it can never be taken from us.
We can withhold that life from ourselves,
but we cannot take it from another.
Once given, it is never taken.

I could feel the weight and pain of Margie's plea and her desperate request for help lifting from me. I noticed that I was breathing deeply again and my body was warming. It was at this point that I realized how damp and cold I felt deep down within myself. Yes it was a raw, November, Pennsylvania day, but the cold inner chill I was experiencing belonged more to the interaction with Margie's forlorn and lost spirit than it did to a brisk November day. Once again life was celebrating unobstructed in and around me. I felt assured that the troubled spirit of Margie had found a safe and helpful resting place. Time would allow her soul to heal. The arborvitae would embrace and comfort her longing. In time she would be okay.

The casket was lowered into the earth. Flowers were tossed upon it, and the internment was ended. My sons seemed a little reluctant to reenter our van for the ride back to the funeral parlor and back to Mom's home for the reception. I could appreciate their reluctance. Their minds and psyches had been witness to a very difficult experience. It was a first for them, as it would have been for many of us, having a lost and anguished soul burst through their perceptual reality, especially at a time and place that was already charged with so much emotion. Perhaps if their father hadn't had such a connection with inter-realm properties, the vivid nature of this lost being's pleas would not have crossed their paths. In large part, I think it was a valuable experience for these youthful witnesses. Once all rational explanations for the commotion had been exhausted they became hesitant but aware participants in a phenomenological experience.

Ushering them to the van I felt confident that we would now be free of the painful cry of the disembodied spirit, and we were. The van was now just a van, quietly transporting four earth-bound bodies on the long ride back to the reception. The trip allowed time for conversation, but quiet reflection was the prescription.

My reflection focused on how it all worked out in this situation, allowing me a greater sense of knowing. When passing from the physical existence as a result of death, some are able to pass directly into a fluid spatial realm of semi-permanence. For these people peace and even joy accompany the final preparations in their last days and hours. These are people who have embraced the qualities of caring and compassion during their lives. Mom certainly did this. But for her daughter Margie, life did not go so well, and her ending was ugly, cold, and lonely. As she died there was no door opened to that warm and nurturing inner-realm of protected space. She was not ready or prepared, thus she could not be received. Her spirit had been loose and lost for many years until her mother's passing offered her a familiar, sound, and warming hand that beckoned her to follow. The most Margie could do was return to her mother's passing presence. She could not, of course, grasp her mother's hand and ride along. She could only reach out toward her. This allowed her a window, an opportunity, to begin to recover in the safety and shelter of the big arborvitae. Had she not been open to the invitation, she may have wandered for eons in the lonely darkness between worlds. Ultimately she may have emerged from the heavy shadows, but she could not have completely belonged in the existence experience ever again, much like the woeful condition of Witchie-Willy from my childhood. She was semi-permanent here, but she didn't really belong to this earth's giving and joyful life experience.

She could not live
and
she could not die.

For Margie a wondrous tree allowed her lost and lonely spirit a respite, a repository where she could rest and comfortably facilitate the life of a grand tree being. Trees also gain value in the service of life as calming and embracing repositories. This is consistent throughout creation's giving structures. In return for this time, the tree would wash her spirit clean. In years to come, as the tree lives out its time on earth and its arboreal form is broken down by fire or decay, Margie's spirit will finally find its door, fly free, and be received in a more pleasing space.

Margie

Now lost and lonely I scream,
but here, come into this tree.
You can not now follow your mom
through the door.
Into the fluidity of this world
is where you need to be.
Come in, care and be cared for
by this tree.
You will be recovered,
then freed
never again to need to scream
of loneliness, anger, or fear.
In time you shall be awakened
from a comfortable sleep.
Fire or fungi may melt this wood
and set your spirit free.

The ghosts of Margie and many others remind us that because of the way they have failed to live their lives, they were estranged from making a normal transfer to a comfortable, static residence or a dynamic conveyance to another realm. How much they feel, or even if they feel at all, we cannot know. Being caught or stuck here may account for the impression of being angry or even vengeful that they leave with those with whom they connect. Are there happy or friendly ghosts? There don't seem to be many 'Caspers' out there, but regardless of their ill-tempered or cantankerous dispositions I do not believe that they can directly harm, intentionally or not, another human being or any other living thing.

They are still here.

The night is their home.

Frightful?

Yes

Harmful?

No

The reason their presence disquiets so many may be that these disembodied entities are looking to make contact, or are seeking some relief from being lost and an opportunity to pass on. Some may even be our former relatives. Many are said to inhabit certain geographic areas, perhaps places where they lived out some of their time on earth.

For at least two good reasons it is important that we become comfortable with these apparitions. The first is that as we learn to open windows we may also allow them to come in. In a short time of practicing seeing we will be capable of shutting them off and avoiding their interference completely. Why would they be there? There are so many of them, and our eyes, when they become capable of seeing the More of our lives, may see them as well. We may gain a great deal of understanding into the nighttime sphere by observing their lost and lonely presence. Our fear of looking into the fluid realms often occurs because many different realities, some of which discomfort us, coexist there. As we come to understand the protection and confidence granted by our discovery of More, we will develop the ability to selectively inattend to that of the Less side of things while seeing that which is kin and giving to us.

The eyes that see the night phantoms
are the same eyes
that will see through windows
to the much more of life ...

Why are these apparitions so often associated with the night? The light of day melts away their tenuous outlines. How do they move about? Inertia of some type influences them, and they may also demonstrate the presence of a nighttime force.

How are these many lives being lost?
How are so many being left behind?
There is a migration of sorts and they should be upon it.
This journey in life may go in many directions,
but being here and dead is not one we want.

When we meet them do they know we are there? Maybe. Maybe not. They are essentially spent with not enough mustardo left to recognize or identify themselves. They are loose and lost upon the land, and it is clear that they are alone. How they became so lost is not so clear. Have they failed in their own right to celebrate life and use their opportunities in this world in a meaningful way? Have they deviated from the most elemental obligation?

To live in life
And be of life

Has their proclivity for the empty and wasted expressions so evident in our world left them vulnerable to a using force? And are they now bound to this force and obligated to serve it as well?

Clearly they are only a shadow of what they once were. Life has been taken from them and they are nearly on empty as they wander aimlessly about. Of concern to us is that they are found almost everywhere. In some places, they are as thick as the hair on a cat's tail.

Caring is the key
Light is the issue

Life is not without light, light wrecks their night. What can be said or done for those who give all the indications that they are slip-sliding away to die into nothingness and to take their place among the phantoms?

Beware of the things we think, do, and say
for the process of subtraction
may be underway.

If they are devoid of the ability to care, very little can be done. If some compassion can be evidenced coming from them we may help them move back toward life. We can be as a caring light beside them, which may ignite a light in them. We must remind them that they matter, while telling them that there are only two choices:

To die here and be forever dead
To die here and live on
When dead here you are not done.

Edendale

Having illustrated and spoken to the world and reality of those being lost to life, we might benefit from an additional glance at this phenomenon. These dark phantoms are not something with which we want to become frequently connected. As more and more of these ghosts are evident when we are practicing seeing, we must also practice how to avoid them. It is important to understand how these disquieting figures can unexpectedly manifest before us.

While there are designs and laws that distinguish different worlds and realities from one another, there also seem to be windows and doors that act as portals where aspects of one reality can flow more readily into other realities. It is within the context of these openings where our discovery and awareness of the unusual is most easily accomplished. It can be assumed that the nature and quality of life and its expressions may be very different from world to world, as well as in different layers of this world. The most we can know is that we are opening windows, and we may not be sure of what might be coming through. Therefore, it is important for us to maintain a certain preparation for engaging and disengaging those other realities, depending upon what we find there as a result of our lifting veils and parting curtains.

While contact with the unseen realms may occur at any place or time in our lives, the exchange from here to there might be best accomplished with a predictable type of preparation. As we have already touched upon, this preparation always begins with quieting the mind as is possible to listen and allow for a disposition of openness. We may come to find that discovery is best accomplished in certain places and times such as in a favorite room, section of the woods, or during a favorite time of day or night. During this quest the fewer interruptions we experience from the outside world, the better. A patient gladness to have this opportunity of being open to receive should permeate our beings. Visualizing what we expect to see or adding pressure to see or hear almost never works.

There have been several places during the course of my life that have been exceptionally revealing. During my childhood on the farm in Gettysburg, the hayloft and the northern woods, home of Cheezer Wheezer, were my first such special places. Another has been and is my present home of Happy Tree. And for a few years of my life, at intermittent times, the Black Mountain area of the Blue Ridge Mountains of western North Carolina was also an area of revelation for me it was there that one of the most problematic apparitions entered my life. It would be said that it was a pained and angry spirit, a poltergeist.

Edendale was the name given to a fifty-acre retreat in the hollow of the Black Mountain hills. It was rich in the unusual, and it became a gateway for me into other realms of existence. Overseeing this retreat was a small group of highly skilled people who practiced the arts and crafts of natural living. As a group, they would entertain and be entertained by speculation and practices of the unusual, if not the unseen itself. Andrew, James, Eve, and Shasta were committed to a continuous expression of the everyday gardening of life as well as maintaining a continuous atmosphere of preparation for listening and seeking that might facilitate them and their invited guests to touch the deeper splendor of their beings.

Edendale was indeed a special place for me. A peaceful, sweet vibration seemed to greet me as soon as I stepped from my car after leaving the winding road that took me there. I would immediately walk to the five-acre lake. Deep and cold, it seemed to be the centering eye or the soul of this place. Over a period of five years or so, I made several trips to Edendale. I stayed in a rustic cabin, listened and learned from the Edenites, gathered inspiration, and in general tanked up on good vibes.

I found the evenings and early morning hours to be the best time to look toward the unusual from the unseen worlds. Tap screws would sprinkle out around the lake, phantoms would brush by and stir the night air, and Cyclops would enter his great call into the mountain's wooded hollows, setting up deafening echoes.

Wearing out my welcome among the Edenites was always an issue for me while entertaining these otherworldly beings. Cyclops, who readily accompanied me at Edendale, was of particular concern with his unruly noise, mesmerizing large centered eye, and his weighty feet. A constant worry for me was that he might completely manifest and set his foot down on someone's cabin!

By and large, the keepers of this place were not overly distressed at either the naturally occurring night sounds of the familiar or the vocalizations of the unfamiliar, otherworldly beings. On one such occasion however, Shasta and I were sharing a conversation regarding the unseen when a lightning like bolt blasted at close range. It sent a shimmering jolt through us. This was enough for Shasta, and she retreated into the community hall. Two or more people engaged in a conversation with similar intention can unwittingly open doors to the beyond. This was a clear signal for me. I knew Cyclops was near, so I quickly made my way to the far end of the lake where we might hold counsel without further injury or undue commotion. As one becomes a doorway into this world for the otherworldly, we must constantly monitor the reactions of others who may knowingly or otherwise be exposed to these manifestations. Mental concepts of the unusual are the least threatening to others, followed by vocalizations. The most overwhelming are likely to be visualizations. In all cases we must assume responsibility for the introductions that come to others through us.

On one of my visits to Edendale, Andrew advised me that another guest was occupying my usual cabin. He offered me a cabin at the far side of the lake, and due to the late hour of my arrival I did not scrutinize my lodgings as I normally would. I dropped my luggage inside the door, noted the cabin's coziness, and returned to greet my Edenite friends and their guest. After some visiting and a walk around the perimeter of the lake, I returned to my cabin. Stumbling through the door, I noted that the night was darker than normal. Making my way inside, my senses were assailed by a smell I found most disconcerting. It had to be a byproduct of the slow decay of a woodchuck or other animal, I thought. In retrospect, these two perceptions should have raised a flag of caution for me.

As I laid upon the bed, waiting for my eyes to reveal the dark outlines of my room, I reflected upon how subdued the nighttime songs and reptilian mating calls seemed to be. It occurred to me that I had not experienced any of the spirit beings known as tap screws that are almost always present during my walks around the lake. Becoming just a little uncomfortable with my situation, I walked through the cabin's darkness, opened the door, and sent out a call for my friend Cyclops. There was no return call. My body was telling me that some sleep would be appreciated, so back into the cabin I went and I climbed into the large wood framed bed. After a bit it was clear that, while I was in bed, I was not sleeping.

On another day and time I would have been out of that cabin. Sleeping with the chiggers among the blackberries and pitch pines would have been a better choice than staying in that cabin. It must have been my deep fatigue that got in the way of my knowing that all the signs were there that something nasty was coming my way.

The smell of the decaying woodchuck took on the intensity of a decaying elephant. Heavy, stinking air wafted about me. The low cry of a mourning soul in pain filled the room. I wanted to get up and run from the cabin, but I could not move. Alarmed and afraid, I held onto the rails of the bed even while it seemed to vibrate.

The mourning cry intensified. A dresser across the room slid about and a single large picture fell or jumped off the wall and crashed upon the floor.

Frightened and spellbound, I was frozen upon the bed. I couldn't think. I couldn't respond. I could only witness, and what I was witnessing and smelling was not fun but rather very painful. What a fearful night it would come to be. At times, breathing became difficult. At no time was I able to get a visual on the nature of the pestilence that held me at its mercy. Something from the night had entered into my life. Where it came from and how it was sent I would never know.

At least with my prior encounter with the boogeyman, my night eyes and my mind were able to place a form upon the apparition, and I had a sense that I could avoid it and its sticky, snotty clasp. I knew I would be okay. This was, pure and simply, an intimidating serving of Less.

Minute into minute and hour into hour the torturous, fearful night continued. Surely, I thought, the sun would soon peer over the eastern mountain to free me from the night. It didn't. For what seemed like years I remained frozen in the bed, listening to the dreadful sounds and smelling the horrible odor, sensing that the entire cabin was about to fall in on me. The cabin did not collapse, but the squeaking of the timbers spoke to the power of the force unleashed around me. Soon a great weight seemed to land upon my rigidly tense body, and the bed broke out from beneath me as I fell onto the floor. Then light filled the cabin and attested to the troubling night, as I attempted to loosen my lower jaw, which felt locked up tight.

What happened during this stormy, frightening night? When I fell to the floor was I knocked out cold? Was I taken to a deeper level of torture that I cannot remember, or did some help from life protect and keep me from the remainder of the night? It was not just a bad dream. The broken picture, fractured lamps, shattered bed, and disheveled cabin bore clear testimony to the dark night. What would I tell the Edenites? How would I excuse myself from all of this damage? More important, how would I reconcile this experience within me?

Never was I so tired as from this one calendar night of ghostly torture. I could remember no time of being so completely spent except for the forty days and nights of vigilant waiting for the other-worldly vibration to clarify itself with the visit of Melix (see *Something More*).

I couldn't forget the smell. The smell seemed to stick to me. I found a bar of soap and made my way to the lake in hopes of losing the putrid vapors that clung to my body like decaying skin. Some vigor returned to me as soon as my body entered the cold water. Scrubbing and ducking into the soothing sweetness seemed to clean me up. As I climbed out of the water, I couldn't believe how exhausted I felt. I felt so heavy. It was such an effort to gain my footing and put one leg in front of the other. When I returned to the cabin it was still a 'night from hell' wreck. Nevertheless, I couldn't help but fall back upon the mattress for some recovery. It had served as the ship that carried me through the frightening storm of pain and darkness, and now had a bizarre but comforting appeal about it.

With the full light of day, I found the courage to reflect and remember the outrageous goings on of the night before. Where did this experience come from? Who had sent it? The objectionable decaying woodchuck, or elephant, smell was gone. The natural aromas of the hollow, the phlox, the wildflowers, the heavy grass, and the olfactory flavors of the lakeside were all that I could perceive.

The pain of fright is a pain that is difficult to explain. It had been thirty-five years since the overwhelmingly frightful night of the boogeyman held me in its clutches at the Johnny house. Being crushed under the tractor and being spit out of the falls were pains of great depth, but they were equivalent to accidental experiences, which could justify or explain what I felt or experienced. A pain that can't be correlated to anything is a hurt that is very different.

Eventually, I lifted my bruised and battered self from the mattress and attempted to restore some order to the cabin. I would never sleep there again. I hung the picture back on the wall, minus the glass, reset the furniture and the candle, swept up, and neatly aligned the box spring and mattress inside the broken bed frame. I did as much as I could. Then I made my midmorning walk to the central hall to excuse myself and ask for some information.

The man I needed to talk with was sitting there waiting to receive me. James was just finishing his ohms and, with a customary smile, greeted me, "Good morning, Stephen." James, the son of a preacher, had an eye for the great depths of human character and a kindness to go with it. "What is it you need from me, Stephen?"

I stuttered a little at the prospect of explaining what had happened. I didn't want to overwhelm him with an obligation to explain the unknown.

James would have been identified as the spiritual leader, if such a person existed in this close family of Edenites. He had a sincere interest in and keen knowledge of the mystical and spiritual realms. I felt, however, that my visits to Edendale stretched his comfort level a bit, and the comings and goings of otherworldly creatures that occurred during my visits, like the lightning, were things that he could do without.

"Sir James," I responded, "the most unusual night surrounded me, and damage has been done to the cabin …"

He listened to my story for a few minutes, and to my surprise showed no sense of alarm in his response. "Poltergeist," he stated.

"Poltergeist?" I repeated. "What is that?"

"It is an angry spirit loose upon the land that may wreak havoc on your soul and can literally trash the physical world around you," he declared as he raised himself from his chair.

With unusual speed, James removed himself from my presence. Perhaps this poltergeist experience was something he feared catching from me. At any rate, poltergeist or not, his explanation of this phantom certainly matched my experience.

The remainder of my visit to Edendale was filled with reflection on this night. Should I ignore it? I couldn't. I hoped it would never return to torture my spirit again. Perhaps I should try to know it better in hopes of learning something from it. Maybe that way I could avoid its clutches. Finding no clear direction, I resorted to my inner sense of knowing and asked myself, "How does it feel?" Dealing with it felt to be the answer for now.

Much may be learned from this experience. When we open the curtains between worlds we can't be certain what we will receive. The terrifying and the nasty may occupy some of these worlds. Time is subjective in nature, and in our experience of it a whole year can be found in a second. As such, that is the real time for us. When availed of these powerful experiences, clock and calendar time is almost meaningless.

As painful as this experience was, there was no apparent physical damage to my body. Clearly, however, injury had occurred to my stamina, my vigor, my confidence, and my mustardo. This pestilence emerged from one of the fluid realms and detrimentally affected the fluid properties of my psyche and my spirit. It attacked me both here and elsewhere.

What was the motive? Was it to attack me directly, to drag me down and take me back to its world? Or was it to draw my mustardo from me? My total exhaustion inclined me to believe it may have effectively placed its drinking straw into my vital life force and aspirated ample amounts of my vigor. For its part, it was serving the night while drawing some life from me.

What questions, concerns, and thoughts are we left with regarding the apparitions we may meet along the highway of discovery? Again there may be nothing to fear directly from them, but I am apprehensive because there are so many of them. Their numbers suggest that there is something very wrong. Why have so many disembodied spirits not gotten out of here or transformed into another of the many life-expressing forms?

While they can create havoc in our lives, they seem not to be able to directly harm a living being. The condition of being alive seems out of sync for them. I don't believe that any evidence exists that can claim that a night ghost or phantom ever directly hurt anyone; however, their appearances and antics can cause accidents and harm if we overreact to them. Being overly afraid invites overreaction, and this can put us in a dangerous position. We need to know they are there and we need to allow them to come and go as they will.

The following experience suggests that the vast numbers of these lost and lonely phantoms once lived upon this world as we do now. Exactly how they became lost to life may not be clear. If we settle for Less in our lives the darkness in them may pour into us. Not only do they exist in large numbers, but they occupy a space not far removed from where we are now.

Papa Needs New Batteries

The following edge experiences clarified for me that those lost to life do indeed occupy a realm or reality just removed from the earth. Most if not all of them were, at one time, living entities upon this planet. One or many things went wrong for them and for now at least life has been lost from them.

I was traveling once again. This time my escape from my earthly life was precipitated by a deadly impact to the driver's side of my vehicle, temporarily taking me into a most frightening and lost world. Though I had evidenced a few nighttime ghosts, shadowy figures, and even a poltergeist, I never understood where they resided or how they came to be until I was involved in this nighttime accident at the intersection of Allentown and Ridge roads.

Only a short distance from home, I was celebrating a local town's willingness to condemn a couple of housing lots in order to protect a large white oak tree. Just before the impact I was thinking how nice it would be to lift my three-year-old son Shetlinn onto my shoulders and walk around the pond. It was the last thing I would remember for some time. The prison time and long, excruciating fast for the ancient trees of Forest Park had recently come to an end, and I was recuperating, putting on weight, and even doing some climbing. It was so good to be in the saddle again and swaying in the canopies of the trees. At times I almost agreed with my wife and friends regarding being distracted by becoming a protective voice for the trees. I had been imprisoned and fasted at the expense of my health, family, business, and more. Quietly and privately, however, I knew if I were called to stand in for this world again I would do it. Recently I'd been involved in wrestling this grand white oak from a builder who owned the construction site it occupied. It was a hard fought but successful struggle. While there was a split in the middle of the tree's massive stem, an arborist can deal with such a thing by installing large, threaded rods to support the fissure. This procedure would allow the oak to live a very long time. Such was my testimony to the borough council, which took the unheard of step of condemning the ground this tree occupied against the builders' protest. Celebration was in the air with everything coming up as a success. Imagine a single, grand, although split, tree was given standing over and above the bottom line power of the industry of growth. Mother Earth looked in and smiled upon this borough council that stood up for a valued, living thing. I had been so preoccupied and consumed over this recent period of time by being a voice for the trees that I was awash in the joy of getting home to my family. My time would now be their time. I could literally feel Shetlinn's warm bottom on my shoulders when the lights went out for me.

It would be months before I would again know the earth as my home. The next thing I knew I would be looking up into a starlit sky as I was being hoisted up to a wooden platform some sixty feet in the air. Neck-braced and essentially immobile, I would lay on a platform for ten days in late October and early November of that year. I was back for round two of the struggle to protect the trees of Forest Park. When I went down with the traumatic neck injury the authorities began to cut the trees they had promised to protect.

At the accident scene I lay comatose in the middle of the intersection following being slammed by an errant motorist who ran a red light. Kathy and my son were called by the local fire department. As our three-year-old child clung to his mother's hand and watched for the medivac helicopter to land, he suggested to his mother, "Papa needs some new batteries." When my wife arrived at the trauma center it seemed that new batteries would not be enough. A priest met her to explain that I was already gone.

In fact, I was gone from this world, but I was not dead. Where I was may have been worse than dead. The world that I awakened to was a dark, clammy, ghostly, and frightening world of deadenders. Shadowlike people romped about, but even they were not content in their own space as forlorn moans and haunting voices cried their dismay. I sensed I was not one of them, and I knew I was not in a good place. Though I couldn't move out of this frightening world, I knew not to look at the troubling ghosts and shadows that swam about me. I remembered I had been forewarned.

Though I was in a state of deep fear, a gentle message from a kind memory came back to me from the blizzard experience of my youth. "Beware in your travels to other realms that are very close to the world of existence in which you now live. Like this realm of Benginers, there are other layers of the world of earth that lie just beyond the surface of conscious existence. There is a space of shadowy figures and frightful consequences that is very close to ours. Do not open this door, if you do you will suffer unnecessarily. You must struggle to remove yourself. You may be enticed to look upon this realm as the pleading calls from those tortured souls may seduce your heart of good intent. You will know this space by its lack of color, light will be limited from gray to black, and at best it will be opaque. Do not look at these frightening figures. Compose yourself and wait for a signal. Life will find a way to lift you out."

Though my eyes were closed and I was as composed as I could be, hope of being found was difficult to hold. The painful surroundings and god-awful smell were more than I could take. After a long period of time, life lent its hand for my recovery. There was a kindly something that ticked away at the place of my heart, giving me some hope. As I would come to be told later, Kathy had placed my youngest son Orrian into the bed where my body resided on the place of earth. If ever a son was the father to the man this was such a time. The beat of that young child's heart would not let Dad slip into hopelessness and thereby become one of the troubling entities of the shadow world into which I had fallen. Eventually Orrian's beating heart, something I clung to in my coma, lifted me up and a door opened that allowed me to move free of this shadowy realm. It could not keep me there, but many others remained. In time I would understand how inhabitants of our everyday world could become lost to life and end up in such a cold and lonely place.

At the next stop in my eventual return to earth I would find myself back in the world of good and plenty where I had been received following the tractor accident. It was so good to be there once again! For some time I seemed to rest in Javunda's care. Hurrahs were all about. Happiness was in the air and in place of deep shadows being cast I was cleansed, healed, and showered with joy in the world of the double sun. Though I sensed I was in this very special place for some time, I was eventually, reluctantly sent back once again to my place of origin. I left Javunda with a confirmed knowing that I must return to our troubled world, and I began to call out that it was time to come home. I would need to ask and prod our world to separate from the things we think we are and recognize the much that lies before us, if we only will receive it.

> If you will again feel the much that you are,
> you will know the much that you've been missing.
> And you will know that it was not lost,
> that this and more is still there!

While receiving the healing care from the world of the double suns, I awoke from my earthly coma. My earth presence was residing in the hospital and making a fool out of myself in every way. Eventually, I was transported by ambulance to my country cabin where I was placed in a hospital bed. There I received home care and continued to make a fool out of myself. I was a less than stellar patient, and a less than patient invalid. My caregivers' endurance was tested in every way, but their love for me never faltered, and it buoyed and supported me in my return journey to my home world.

This particular edge experience was different in many ways from my other travels out and back again. The severity of my neck injury would keep me down for approximately three years until I could move again of my own accord. A deep sense of depression accompanied by enormous pain stayed with me almost constantly. Looking back, I think some of the lasting agony was something that contaminated my being from that shadowy realm. I got out of there, but not soon enough to avoid having some of the darkness attach itself to me. The drugs and narcotics administered at the trauma center may also have affected me.

Many of my other extreme edge experiences returned me to consciousness upon this earth with almost no lasting injuries or lingering pain. Then again, this experience included falling into the shadowy world of the deadenders. To this I offer some impressions that may aid in understanding. I am left with knowing that:

For our protection,
if we are not of this
dark and shadowy world,
then we cannot know it.
To truly know it would
be to completely become it.

Atlanta

It was interesting for me to witness momentary look-ins to these shadowy spaces during the long recuperation from my highway accident. Stimulated by the many hours and days on my back, along with the pain medications, it seemed dangerously easy for me to connect to their shadows in my dreams and occasional moments of depressive anguish.

Time and time again, my young son Orrian's presence and beating heart would pull me out and above their range of influence.

Between the trauma center and the long time of my recuperation, there were nine days during which I nested sixty feet off the ground in the canopy of a grand oak, waiting again to hear words of protection for the grand trees of Forest Park. Lying there upon my wooden platform, the only movement was given by the wind. Though I had no food or medicine, I was comfortably embraced in the protection of this long-lived tree. I say protected, because during this time I had absolutely no experience of the subtracting forces. During my immobile, tree-top fast upon an exposed platform, I had many occasions to reflect upon how many deaths had made me the reluctant traveler who was sent back from distant worlds, again and again becoming immersed in the conflicts and crises of this world. You may think it was a great joy for me when a new agreement of standing for the trees of Forest Park was forwarded, and I was taken off my perch. While acknowledging a victory of sorts for a more formal agreement of protection for these grand trees, I felt depressed and shocked as I lay there on my back upon the terra firma. Sensing the gravity of the earth along with the gravity of these times, I wanted to cry as the protection of the trees and the comfort of purpose was once again replaced by my physical-neural trauma.

Back at my wooded cabin and confined to my hospital bed, I would struggle to get well physically and psychologically. What was necessary was for me to find a prevailing state of joy; a gladness to still be alive, to be with my family, to be cared for, and to be recuperating in wooded surroundings. But I could only get to this place of appreciation from time to time, and I could not stay there. It was such a struggle. The pain of my condition, the uncertainty of my recovery, the stupor of the prescription drugs, and the intermittent sense of inhabiting the world of shadows were all very difficult.

I did, however, use some of this time and trauma to see more completely into the process of subtraction as it enters a living being, then ultimately takes part of that person into its dark, cold, and ghostly space. I also came to deeply appreciate just how close our surface reality of living is to the home of the disembodied. Slipping in and out of their dark realm and seeing the contrast between their world and ours guided me into a deeper understanding. Much of what I learned dovetailed with a frightening ordeal I'd experienced a few years earlier. This ordeal played out following a double dipping of death experienced over a short period of time. An automobile accident in which I lost my closest brother was followed within a week by a fall from a double bypass bridge. These two edge experiences were very exhausting but also very revealing.

Following the death of my closest brother Charlie, and during my time of heavy cocaine usage, I literally fell or maybe jumped into their space. It was a space adhering directly to the earth and very close to our everyday reality. For the life of me, I'll never understand how or why I fell into this pit of despair. The best spin I can put on this horrible experience is to assume that it was part of my necessary exposure and thus taught me about the fundamentals of Less, the lost side of life. Reflection reminds me that as I was taken from the world of existence, these Night Servers were on me like flies. How exactly this happened, I'm still not sure, but these are the circumstances that surrounded my personal nightmare.

Following the accident in which Charlie's life was lost, a darkness of despair set upon me. He had become such a comrade in the discovery of the unusual and such a friend as well. The older family members came to my area to retrieve his body and encouraged me to accompany them to Gettysburg for his funeral. To this I reluctantly agreed. Shortly after embarking on our return trip to Gettysburg, questions surrounding Charlie's death became so unacceptable that I bailed out.

The conversation went something like this, "Charlie died, but brother Stephen only had a scratch. Brother Charlie was put in this position because brother Stephen needed a favor. Now explain to us what's fair about this? Why should he have to die so that Stephen could live?"

I was not a stable brother when I opened the car door, jumped from the vehicle, rolled along the highway, got to my feet, and returned to my wooded cabin. Gathering up a few belongings, my vial of coke, and my most trusted companion Thaddeus (the Weimeraner) we were off to the airport and then to Atlanta. Why Atlanta? It may have been the first plane out of town. While spending a few nights at Atlanta's Peachtree Hotel snorting coke and crying through my pain of loss and loneliness, I opened a door to a living and frightful hell.

Just how I opened the door into this ghostly space I can't be sure, but open it I did. Clearly my fatigue and deep suffering facilitated my crossing over to their world. It seemed to happen while Thaddeus and I were walking the streets of downtown Atlanta in a ferocious rainstorm. We entered a clothing store to replace wet clothing with dry, and when I went up to the counter to pay for these clothes the teller appeared most peculiar and perturbed. We were alone. He motioned me to leave and would not take my money, so out into the rain we went.

The streets seemed all but vacant, traffic wasn't moving, and I could barely see as darkness surrounded me. Feeling a little unnerved and seeing Thaddeus's hair standing up, I decided to descend into underground Atlanta to get my bearings and break from the heavy rain. The transition from everyday earth to the dark and troubling space of the disembodied was slowly playing out. The stalls and shops looked the same as a few days earlier, but the underground was also essentially vacant. Off in the distance I could see what appeared to be people, but when we got closer to them Thaddeus began to growl. As they turned toward us, cold air wafted by reeking with dank smells, and I sensed deep trouble as their ghostly, dark-eyed faces stared at us. Fear overwhelmed us as Thaddeus jumped up and put his feet on my chest. Soon the nasty phantoms became so thick that we could not avoid them. They were so dense we couldn't see past them. Together, now with both of our hair standing on end, we pushed through them attempting to find some living people beyond them. But there was just more of the same. I soon realized that we had transitioned from our world into the space of the lost and lonely. For an undetermined time we struggled with our predicament.

At times we ducked behind stalls and merchandise, noting that the phantoms didn't seem to be able to find us visually. But on each occasion they did eventually encircle us. A frightening game of hide-and-seek played out for what seemed like hours. While hiding out I could catch my breath and gently clamp my hand over Thaddeus' mouth while stroking his quivering body. The situation was not improving, however. The conditions of their ghostly spaces remained intact. The lighting was clouded over, cold air moved about, and I could not distinguish any human voices. How could I escape their clutches? I anguished and planned as they gathered around once again.

I was extremely annoyed at myself for allowing these conditions to capture me, and I was even more upset that I had exposed my frightened friend Thaddeus to all of this. As we held onto one another we knew we were in this together.

Eventually, we made our way up from the underground to the center city streets. The city seemed deserted. Nothing moved, it was dark, and the streetlights appeared as moonlight attempting to reveal itself through clouds. For the moment we were free of the congregating mass of lost souls, but our situation was still alarming. "To the airport," I thought out loud. "We need to leave this place to find our world again!"

With this thought a lone cab pulled up to the curb. Thaddeus and I jumped in, and without giving directions, we were on our way to the airport. Nothing had changed and our fright continued. The smell was strong, the cab silent. Looking at the back of our driver's head, I could also see his ghastly face and darkened eyes. No fare was accepted, and we were still bound to our surroundings of a ghostly reality.

Exiting the cab and looking toward the faint lights of the airport, I could still feel the cold air and dank smells encircling us. Ghastly figures came forward through the mist bearing the smell of decaying flesh and blackened eyes. Looking down from the overpass we were on, I thought I saw real, earth traffic. That was better than where I was, and I jumped.

Sometime later I awoke in a hospital under police guard. I carefully glanced around to verify that I was free of the dark and ghostly space and was grateful to see that I was. Nurses were touching me with hands of comfort, the smell of food was in the air, and voices and sounds were sweet to my ears.

The miracle here was that the jump from the airport overpass bridge to a busily traveled highway below should have equaled my death. Thaddeus had not jumped, was corralled by airport security, and was thankfully returned to me later. When I broke free of the grasp of the dark side he was returned to the everyday world. Without the intervention of life's protection once again, I would have died there. I'd have been mangled by the trucks and cars, and probably consumed by the shadows from the night. Never was I so happy to wake up in a hospital bed in handcuffs waiting to be interviewed by the police. "How did you get on the highway? You are lucky no one ran over you. What's in the vial?"

All of this mattered very little. I was so happy to be looking out into the everyday world with everyday people. Thaddeus was in a kennel, and I smiled from ear to ear.

"You'll be here under guard until your x-rays and CAT scans are completed. If you avoided any serious injuries we will take you downtown to be charged, then remanded to Fulton County Prison."

"OK," I said with a smile.

The officer by my bedside, thinking I sounded flippant, reminded me, "Stephen Redding you will not find Fulton County Prison to be anything to smile about." But then, he didn't know where I'd been stuck and perhaps would have been forever lost without these traumatic events. They somehow freed me from a torturous darkness with a sentence that may have never ended. He was correct, however, Fulton County prison was no picnic. But it was part of the freeing return from that overwhelming phantom space of despair. This was as close to being captured by the debilitating darkness as any of my excursions in and out of this world would ever bring me.

Isn't this crazy? I fell into this space of heavy darkness from where I was in this world, and then I needed to jump out of the ghostly realm to get back to mine.Circumstances of fatigue combined with drug addiction and a deep sadness over the loss of my brother, friend, and comrade came together to offer up something I wasn't looking for. Along with my vulnerability, the reaction of my older brothers and sisters stung very deeply.

Surviving this multiple-day ghostly encounter gave me a personal perspective of the dark side of things that I will never forget. It's uncanny how close their disembodied reality is from our everyday world upon the earth. Most of us will never work so hard to fall into their dark and lonely space. However, some of us are driven through our fears, addictions, and loneliness to enter this world of the lost.

If I had stayed with the family and curtailed the drug, I would not have been so vulnerable. Charlie's funeral may have been one that I should have attended. Clearly the profound, subjective loss I felt at the death of my brother had broken me down, but the strength of friends and family almost always warms and protects.

Once again this experience verified that unto themselves these ghostly entities cannot directly do harm, but the fear of becoming what they are is used to the advantage of whatever it is that moves them around. I suspect that they are used to skillfully lift our mustardo, and if they are completely successful at this their space becomes our home. This something that moves them around knows when it is time to prey. Conditions of our consciences as precipitated by our minds, psyches, and maybe even bodies allow the opening. Between the fatigue, cocaine, and my emotional reaction to the loss of my brother Charlie, I had been ripe for their taking. In this case it was the shock of landing on a concrete highway that removed me from their feeding frenzy. A day in the hospital and a few more days in Fulton County Prison further insulated me from their clutches.

As a personal observation I would like to share a strategy that might help us free ourselves from the weight of Less. This might apply to a short experience such as a bad dream, or even a more lasting one such as pervasive depression. In either of these cases, something beyond our presence has entered our home. If we show this interloper some discomfort, we may gain some fresh air. In a sense we are changing the picture from comfort to discomfort or static receptivity to dynamic uncertainty. In the case of a bad dream, for instance, we can't lie there and allow it to beat upon us. We need to get up and go out into the night, naked if possible. We should feel the dew on our bare feet and the cold air on our rear ends, and look up into the night with a deep breath and yell out our names. Then we can return to bed knowing that we will not be bothered again that night by compromising energies. Should we be afflicted with deep and staying depression, we can try something even more dramatic. We can submerse ourselves in winter's icy water, or fill our tubs with ice and enter into the freezing liquid. It works, at least for a time. Yes, we will scream and maybe miss a breath or two. Maybe we'll even cry out our dismay. What was a comfortable dwelling for the nighttime faces may not be so agreeable any more. We might say we're exchanging one kind of pain for another. This is true, but this pain is one we can understand. It just may allow us time to come free from a dark condition about which we can now do something. There may be other bizarre treatments we can conjure up if we follow our intuition. We will find initially that the most effective end runs against a staying and unwanted condition of Less, and it will be correlated with the degree of discomfort that we are open to. Could we die exploring these strategies? It's highly unlikely. We will be standing strong against the trespass of darkness into our house of life, and living will pick us up.

The Process of Subtraction

After these experiences I am certain that the phantoms' space is a reality that is parallel and very close to ours. One thing we can be sure of is that what protects and separates us from these ghastly realities is our concentration and focus upon life's caring and giving functions. It's uncanny that the space between their world and ours can be as close as a few tiers of highway bridges or a depressed state of being. Clearly, we need to be cognizant of the misuse of elixirs; times of deep fatigue; or emotions of less such as anger, fear, or depression.

I am inclined to believe that their parallel space comes closer and closer to ours as the mustardo of life is lessened and the force of subtraction is extended. Haven't all of us looked in or felt directly touched by this troubling space? What have we seen? What have we felt? If Less continues to beget Less, it is possible that we could witness a co-emerging experience of living becoming intertwined with this lost space, even as we close out our stay in time. This would not be fun as we follow the last of the evening light while we stumble through a world of the living dead.

As things are now we still have some separation between these realities. We will not always understand the whys and hows, but for the most part we are only vulnerable if we allow the darkness in. How does that begin? Does it start by our own design, or by a force outside ourselves that may be moving the darkness around and letting some of the Less in? The process of subtraction is much the same.

We need to be careful of the things we think, do, and say for they may allow this process of subtraction to get underway. Typically, a subjective deficit occurs to our psyches, and it becomes something we just can't get past. It might be the loss of a friend or family member, a betrayal by a trusted other, or some other suffering of a physical or emotional nature that begins the process. Then the 'Got you!' occurs.

It tends to start small enough in our minds with thoughts filled with sarcasm or negativity when something positive could be expressed. We might comment on how dirty a friend's child is, with stains on his shirt and dirt on his mouth, rather than noting the joy on his face and the spark in his eyes. If the habit of seeing negative in the place of positive is continuously intruding on our thoughts, we have the opportunity to signal to ourselves that we are aware of this and change the direction of our thinking. A tap on our heads, cold water on our faces, a brisk walk, or some inspirational passages from a favorite book may signal our psyches to change this outlook. We may not be completely able to stop these ill-timed and intrusive thoughts that are not really ours, but awareness that they are there may offer us some protection.

Without some response to these shadowy mind-plays we will become more and more victimized within our own physiology. Not only will uncharacteristic, negative thoughts continue, but physical disease and pain may also become apparent as life's vigor is subtracted from us. Unwanted thoughts will continue to be ratcheted up, reflecting even more troubling suggestions. For example, regarding an unpleasant neighbor we might think, "I wish someone would wipe him out." Or, while watching our own young child, we might think, "I hope no one is going to harm her or an illness won't take her away before her time." Why should unkind thoughts or fears in the face of love even be there? Again, we need to change the picture and not allow these distant thoughts to reside in the comfort of our cognitive homes.

The slide into darkness may be a process we don't even notice. A truly alive person may never have been possessed by an exacting moment of darkness and swept away from life. It begins slowly and insidiously, and the process of subtraction in our personal lives is an incremental thing. If we spend more time celebrating life and the world around us, we will break the treacherous slide into Less.

Each thought that is not you
may be the tentacle coming through.

Low Flow in Life's River

Much seems to have been subtracted from the flow.
Can anyone say where it's gone? Does anyone know?
What can be done to return what's been lost or taken?
Life needs these waters to sustain the vigor of the living.

7

Mustardo

As we have attempted to utilize words to illustrate this unfolding view of our place in life's journey, this author has used homespun words and concepts to assist in presenting his worldview. Perhaps none is such an important concept regarding the issue of More or Less in our lives as this one.

I would like to introduce the term mustardo, which has been noted and will be referred to throughout this discourse. Mustardo is the fluid-like force of life itself, and it is important that we understand how and why mustardo is so essential to life's staying potential. From the beginning mustardo was an essential component of life. In fact it was indistinguishable from creation's manifestation while life moved along in the etheric, fluid way of our beginning. Upon entering the vast sphere of darkness a static mass confronted our voyage, which was not unlike a dense rock. Life did then what life does and is still doing; it brought forth something from what wasn't. Life reached into the mass of this darkness to manifest form and beings from what was before the advent of our journey, essentially cold and endless firmament. This wondrous interplay of life in the darkness has built the living world we identify with and to which we belong. Where mustardo is involved forms and structures are enlivened. As this occurs a process of development with continuous manifestation unfolds. Once forms and structures are enlivened through this interplay, mustardo supports and sustains life's magical qualities. Some of these qualities are represented by vigor, balance, wellness, and even co-creation. It is critical that all humans, as well as other life forms, have a certain quantity of this energy to move, protect, and manage their lives. The fact is that this aspect of life, which is so critical in determining whether it will be More or Less for us, comes back to an essential term; a singular concept which, in the trying struggle of light versus darkness, should never be divided.

In its simplest and most general application, mustardo refers to that underlying something that the vigor of life is dependent upon. It is, however, more than simply vigor. It is vigor with a quality of goodness. Energy and vigor are found in many forms and places, and in the process of distinguishing more from less in our lives it is important to know the difference.

In the lives of some
there is a glow.
In the lives of others
not so much so.

Vigor with the quality of caring lifts and cares for the world, and as this energy is given it is also received. I remember seeing different neurologists and physical therapists following a brutal neck injury. A great deal of energy was extended toward me from different healing regimes. But real healing began when I located a therapist who extended true mustardo to me. Soon I was on my feet and walking again. The difference was obvious. Some people can harness mustardo, transfer it, and move it about. Some cannot. We can always feel the difference; we know it when we receive it.

Equally important are the qualities of this energy or vigor, which define it as uniquely special to our beginning, our present, and our future manifestation. These qualities lend us a sense of meaning and wholeness from which life so beautifully illuminates and warms the world around us. Trust is also a quality of our mustardo. This quality supports a sense of belief and faith in our personal value in creation as well as in things yet unseen. It assures us that this journey we are upon will not come to an end, but instead will lead to a day without an end. Our mustardo is central and critical to us. It is our 'pearl of great price.' We cannot afford to lose it, have it siphoned off, or have it taken from us. Unfortunately, as we play out our lives between the challenges of More or Less it can become tied up or compromised, and it is through this condition of our lives that we may benefit by gaining perspective and understanding.

Mustardo

The breath of our nostrils
that fires life into us,
The wind that fills our sails
and moves us,
The lasting spirit that marks us
and keeps us,
In the beginning, along our way,
and when coming home.

Mustardo is truly the stuff of life's river. This river nurtures and supports all life we see. While it is fluid in nature, it is most often evidenced in life's forms and structures. When these once living forms die or pass on, the fluid mustardo withdraws and returns to the etheric 'river of life' as noted above. From here it may be drawn off again and take up residence in other living structures or forms. It must be noted that this river is a metaphor and is not immediately apparent on the earth. This fluid essence surrounds us moment to moment with its living qualities. Its headwaters are found in our beginning, and its flow nurtures and sustains our world of earth as well as the other realities and worlds to which we are connected. Mustardo is the river, and it is also the water. On the cover of *Something More* is a representation of how this river of color serves our life and the hope of more life as we continue to persevere through the night.

Another metaphor to illustrate this life-essential concept of mustardo is that it is the water and also the well. For reasons that will become clear, only pure or unadulterated water is found in this well. It may only be used in the employment of life and for functions that care for life. We cannot carry it away, misuse it or lose it. If mustardo is taken from life's river or drawn from the well, it must return in time in an equally pure condition. If mustardo is adulterated by misapplication it is temporarily tied up and for a time, at least, is lost to life. In such a case it cannot be returned to the river or well of life, which sustains and supports us. As we heal ourselves, mustardo returns to us naturally.

The sum of all mustardo in our beginning may have equaled the breath of creation, as it involves the entirety of the existence experience. The mustardo of our breath, vigor, passion, trust and all types of dynamic energy was given to us in sufficient quantities in our early days and cannot now be added to. Mustardo is not everything in life, but it is inseparable from life itself. It is the essential difference that separates the mystery of life from non-life. If all mustardo were to be lifted from this world, much would be left, but nothing would live. It is important that we see this mustardo as fluid in nature, being made available to us without a prescription, and giving us life-sustaining support as we need it.

When mustardo is moved around and taken out of life's river, it needs some form or structure to adhere to. Something needs to take it in or drink it up. Thoughts and ideas cannot support or sustain mustardo, but human, plant, and animal life forms can. The more these structures or forms of life live in the way of life, the more mustardo is available to them.

To understand mustardo in our own lives, it may be helpful to think of ourselves as a fountain and the world around us as a pool. Both the fountain and the pool depend on the fluid movement of water. Flowing water replenishes the pool with life giving oxygen. The passing of the water through the fountain allows light to clean away excess algae and pollutants. The health and vigor of both the pond and the fountain is dependent upon the flow. In our lives mustardo is the vigor that moves us, as well as the fluid, spiritual, and psychic energy that surrounds and protects us. It is the water for which we thirst, and it is also the well from which we quench the thirst. If we maintain meaningful lives, our mustardo will not be easily lost to us.

Life need not always be firmed up
much of it is fluid.

Much of this book is signaling an alarm regarding the apparent loss of mustardo from our world. This existence experience is only viable as long as enough critical, life-giving, and supporting mustardo is available. Without it this world and more would be quickly consumed and crushed by the weight of the night in which we now voyage.

For our mustardo to be available to us and not be taken from us, it must be utilized in the expression of life. If we seek to be of life and for life, with all the implications thereof, our mustardo must be protected and guarded. It must be utilized in the right place and space and not aimlessly thrown about. The availability of our mustardo to us and the world around us implies that we actively guide and live in the way of life every day.

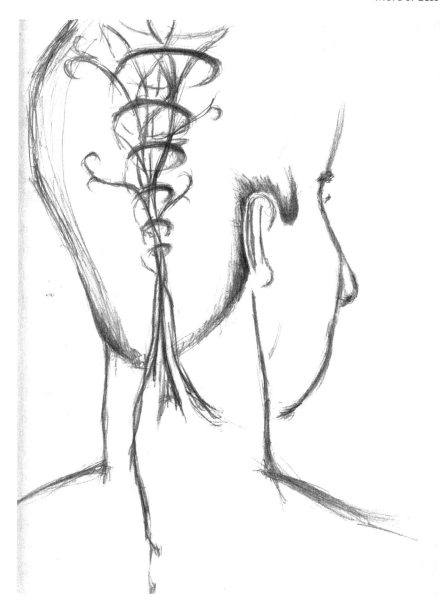

The Drinking Straw

If we become aware of diminishing amounts of this critical something upon which the well-being of our lives and the world depend, then we must be willing to ask this question. How is the nectar of life removed

239

from us? Is there a mechanism or a means of taking we should be aware of? When our essence and vigor, mustardo, is diminished in us, we begin to look beyond ourselves for something or someone who can fill the void or alleviate the sense of emptiness. Beware, for this is wherein some danger lies. Here is where we become vulnerable. Allow me to illustrate.

Some years ago Kalani, a native Hawaiian and Kahuna from the island of Maui, introduced me to a process by which this could occur. It was interesting to me that the Kahunas (the keepers of the Hawaiian way) were always suspicious and, therefore, guarded against the threat of the dark force's ability to take this life energy away from their world. Throughout their long Polynesian history, moving away from where trouble of uncertain origins was occurring served them well. Navigation and shipbuilding were highly valued talents among them. As Kalani would explain, "If troubled darkness entered on the south side of an island we would depart from the north side. We would sail until we felt we had lost the troubling forces and take up residence on a new island."

The following narrative may help to explain how the process of extracting the mustardo may work. Several years ago I attended a new-age spiritual frontier conference with my friend Kalani who was visiting North Carolina. Over the years of our friendship, I was intrigued at the depth of seeing expressed by this keeper of the ancient Polynesian-Hawaiian way. Although, Kalani could be humorous and entertaining, there was always a seriousness about his teachings. The depth of his eyes and the tone of his voice clearly revealed that he understood the urgency of these times. One could almost hear a drum beat from his heart, which constantly echoed, "Awake, awake. It is late, it is late!" For Kalani the loss of his people's paradise to Cookie, as he referred to

Captain Cook, still burned deep within him several generations later. But his powerful god-man eyes were clearly focused on the threat to the sanctity of life upon the planet. It was easy for him, of famed Polynesian navigational history, to identify with my story of the journey of life. On a number of occasions while Kalani and I huddled and spoke of the threat to life he referred to a 'drinking straw' method in which unsuspecting peoples might be drained in part of their reinforcing mustardo. He would often return to this drinking straw illustration. Although I really couldn't relate to it, I did utilize it in my thinking as a metaphor for how people were trespassed upon and drained of their vigor. I sensed that Kalani was never really satisfied with my take on his hush-toned alarm each time he repeated his drinking straw tale.

On one occasion Kalani and I shared an early evening conversation following a workshop at the conference. Twenty feet away the door had been left ajar to a 'psychic' reading room where a young lady named Marie was getting a reading. She was having her history revealed by someone who declared himself a seer of the past who could help her with where her life was now, for a fee of course! It was a little uncomfortable listening in on this rather ordinary man doing his business, but this imposter of a seer amused us as we casually watched the interchange taking place in a poorly lit room. Kalani wasn't moving to close the door, and neither was I. Holy Moly! I was witnessing the drinking straw phenomenon. Blinking my eyes to clear up what I couldn't believe I was seeing, I noticed that Kalani's bold eyes were intently focused on Marie. She was an energetic, if gullible, young lady who was a student at the conference. She was paying this man to pry into her past. She sat there stone still mesmerized. Her eyes seemed slightly bulged, and her demeanor appeared not unlike the rigid compliance of a lady beetle when being pierced by the proboscis of a preying mantis. As she sat with her head tilted slightly forward, a straw seemed to be jutting out from between her shoulders, parallel to her neck and reaching up into the space above her where it left our sight.

There seemed to be a twist in the straw that showed a slow fluid-like movement through it. What appeared to be a straw was undoubtedly a tightly concentric tubular shadow created by escaping energy. But what was sucking on the straw? What we were witnessing was a loss of her personal mustardo. Life was being taken away, stolen from her. The tentacle was being fed through the unknowing opening to her being. The psychic's pretense and her own folly allowed her precious life to be assailed.

Who inserted the straw? What was its mechanism of intrusion? Did the psychic have one also? We couldn't tell. But oh, what a revealing scene! With Marie still in her seemingly frozen position, the psychic noticed the open door and quickly closed it. Kalani's drinking straw was more than a metaphor.

This praying mantis-like trespass upon an unsuspecting person was a deep concern for the Hawaiian man. His recent admonitions to remain vigilant and well rested to avoid this type of psychic blood letting, mustardo stealing, had suddenly become so much more real and applicable to me. As for who or what was sucking on the straw, to this Kalani would only shake his head. "But Kalani," I would ask, "You must have some notion or idea of what's happening." To which he would only respond with a serious stare. This always moved me off the question. His avoidance of responding to my earnest questions may have had something to do with one of his Hawaiian truths, 'Do not think on your enemies.' To him, this could back door validate them and maybe give them power over us. For me, these are times to speculate and communicate our potential vulnerability as it relates to this critical process of our concern. I knew that in one fashion or another I would share my thoughts regarding the intrusive taking of the tentacle from the night. What more appropriate explanation for the drinking straw phenomenon could be had? Kalani listened attentively to my explanations of how this being out of the darkness could steal our mustardo in tentacle-like action. But he would only hold a serious stare and make no verbal response.

Later that evening we saw Marie again. She looked awful.

"Marie, how was your reading?" Young people always advertise when they are going to have one.

"Great," she said.

To which I replied, "Marie, are you sure? You look spent. Where is your smile?"

Her pained look she said was a result of her psychic practitioner taking her back to a previous life and reliving an old battle wound that prematurely took her life. I wondered, but did not ask, if the battle wound of long ago had occurred to the back of her neck.

That night I struggled to fall asleep, reflecting deeply on the drinking straw theft of Marie's mustardo. From time to time I slid my hand behind my neck to reassure myself that the tentacle was not having its way with me. I felt badly for Marie. I knew the placement of the drinking straw had something to do with her compliant nature and her misguided need to open her deeply personal space to a user of her trust. Some of her vulnerability also lay in her very enthusiastic, mustardo rich, but overly mental, being.

Where would she replenish her mustardo? And how, in her eyes, could she recover from this war wound?

The following day I was surprised to see Marie's pretty, enthusiastic, and talkative self fully recuperated. "Marie," I asked, "Where is your mother?"

Her mother was a truly delightful lady in her early fifties. "She is sick. She is staying in her room."

Marie had received what a mother would willingly lend, some of herself. Mustardo is a fluid thing. If we don't protect it, it can be easily taken away. Mom, in her sleep and in the trusting sphere of family, was easily victimized by an equally asleep and unsuspecting daughter. Now Marie's vessel was once again full, and the drinking straw would return when it could. Sweet, vigorous, and vulnerable Marie was being prepped to serve the night.

This was a very dramatic, once in a lifetime experience for me. It had clearly illustrated the drawing off of basic life force from a vulnerable and unsuspecting target, Marie. I say target to emphasize how obvious she was for the taking. Her vessel, plum full of mustardo, was left unguarded while she was over reaching for information. She was searching for something to validate her life with too much urgency, thus she was left vulnerable to an unseen force, perhaps a tentacle. This force found Marie unguarded and, in fact, prepared for the feast of the taking. I am sure that the less than skilled and authentic psychic was an unknowing player in this frightening drama. In effect, this so-called psychic was serving as a scavenger for a taking force. Again, we must protect our mustardo as the driving, keeping, and sustaining power our beings cannot function without in this time and world. It is indeed one of the 'pearls of great price.'

Do we need to postulate that some entity or dark force was responsible for this drinking straw phenomenon? Or could it have been an illuminated perception of a happenstance loss of Marie's energy? Was her psychic energy spilling out or coincidentally eroding away as a result of a less than competent technician? We can't know for sure, but something serious did happen to Marie. Her presence was clearly compromised. She looked hurt and utterly drained. We may not need to identify a cause as long as we understand the process:

That which we see
that has raised
our alarm
may be caused by
something
we cannot see.

Further reflection on the drinking straw phenomenon was occasioned by a confidential conversation I had with a friend. He confided that he wasn't sure he would be able to make it to our appointment. He said he felt totally washed out. He continued to share that the evening before, while watching a senseless, blood-spilling action movie, he had a panic attack of great proportions, punctuated by sweating, rapid heartbeat, and loss of consciousness. Expressing my lack of familiarity with such conditions, my friend stated that the medical profession recognized his symptoms but did not have a good understanding of them. Panic attacks had occurred on a few other occasions in his life and a knockout medicine had been prescribed for him to use in the event of their recurrence, which indeed he used this past evening.

As I listened to his subjective accounting of what happened and his description of his washed out feeling, I found it eerily similar to the condition I had observed in Marie. I couldn't help but wonder, could this panic attack be a drinking straw type of mustardo letting?

"My friend," I asked, "Do you have any soreness between your shoulders or in the back of your neck?"

He responded, "Are you kidding? It's really sore and I don't know why!" as he reached back to pinch and rub the pained area.

My friend's accounting of his experience of a panic attack, with its unknown causes, points to another possible intrusion by the tentacle through this technique of the drinking straw. If this was a historical concern for the Polynesian and Hawaiian healers, might it still be relevant today? If so, our best protection might come from being vigilant and well rested, as the Hawaiian noted. We must protect our mustardo by staying in life moment to moment. We must not compromise the personal and sustaining values and behaviors our lives are based upon.

Those of us who seek the Something More of life must deal with the alarming assumption that the sustenance of life is being drained from our vessel and us in a big way. Perhaps these times of subtraction may be, at least in part, interdependent upon the low flow of mustardo in life's river. In one way or another, it is being lost to the night. As a result of this loss of mustardo, our journey is in jeopardy and our way has been obscured.

While it may seem complicated in its myriad of uses, mustardo is quite simple in its application. With it we move beyond this day, and without it we go nowhere from here. So, once again:

Mustardo

is

the underlying something

that life

is sustained by

and nurtured with.

It satisfies life's thirst.
It is the water, and also the well
that holds the water
which quenches the thirst.

Today it is the water
tomorrow it is the wind
filling our sails,
carrying us out of night
into a lasting day.

Low Flow

Our great concern in these times is the level of mustardo in life's river. Without the necessary quantity of this nectar of life, so much that we take for granted is coming undone and will continue to do so, on an individual and a global scale.

It must be remembered that mustardo can only be returned to life's river in a clarified and unpolluted condition. If it has been used in our world in compromised ways it is not allowed to return to the river or well for life to receive it.

As we discovered with our earthly water and air, when they are free of pollution they are much more sustaining and giving. Ironically, only when they became polluted did we really begin to value them. Before our awakening we took them for granted, but now we know the difference. Understanding our longer and broader lives will help us to value them. As we value our lives more completely, we also know the need to protect them.

Returning again to the implication of this time of subtraction, we can anticipate some of the consequences of further reduction of life-sustaining mustardo. Global warming is a great concern for us, but truth to tell it is only one of a host of symptoms reflecting the threat to our place in a living world. These concerns should be taken even more seriously if we become aware that the protection and care of all life is also being lost. As mustardo is taken from life's river and not returned, unexpected consequences will begin to declare themselves. On a human level, illness with no particular cause will set upon us. Debilitating childhood conditions will suddenly increase. Some of these we will be able to identify such as Down syndrome, autism, cerebral palsy, and cancer. Other conditions are not so easily defined. Generalized and clinical depression may suppress the adult population, stealing our zeal and optimism for life.

Mustardo is also the keeper of life in the natural world, and much contamination is evident there as well. Mustardo can be more easily utilized in fresh, clean water than in polluted waters. The same applies to our atmosphere. So much more life is found in fresh air than in contaminated or polluted air. Carbon ash and heavy metals tie mustardo up and interfere with its transfer from one life to another. More mustardo can be found in a forest than in an equal space of grass. A free-range chicken can transfer much more mustardo to an egg than a caged one. A pasture fed cow can move more mustardo into her milk than a stationed cow can, and the list goes on.

We might also experience the diminishing quantities of mustardo affecting the balance between life-giving versus life-taking forms of life. The decline side is already gaining some frightening advantages in our oceans, forest, and soils. As this process unfolds, grand and accomplished life forms will falter, while lesser forms take their place.

In our soils, for instance, beneficial fungi and microorganisms are less evident while decay and decline fungi are ever more plentiful. The consequence is that grand species of trees are dying, while weeds and grasses are thriving. Tent caterpillars and leaf eating insects are thriving while beneficial lacewings and praying mantises are in decline, allowing trees, and the forests to which they belong, to fall to the ground.

Decline within our natural world and her peoples will come at us very quickly. Magnetic fields may become entangled as great land and sea storms blow about. The sun will inexplicably increase and decrease its intensity while unleashing far reaching solar disruptions. If the mustardo is drained even more precipitously from life's river, the very order and balance of our world will begin to break down. Seasons will be difficult to define, species will display crossover characteristics, and plants and trees will alter their form. Many life forms will decline, and some will thrive. After a period of exaggerated warmth, cold will begin to settle over the land and warmth will be a long time in coming back. What is our best protection against additional loss of mustardo from our world?

Live the life within you.
Care for the life around you.

Once we understand the critical nature of mustardo in our own world, we can watch for how it manifests in our lives. We will soon discover and sense how it flows in us and around us. When it is there we feel well, when it is drawn off we are weak and may be troubled. If mustardo is drawn off from life's river and not returned, where might we suspect it is tied up or lost? There are many hybrid-type forms that represent places where mustardo is entwined with compromise. Most of us convey intermittent expressions of life, and yet for many these expressions are not staying, suggesting a struggle which may be burdened by shadows from the night. We must look in at ourselves. So many of us have a mixture of qualities that speak to life, yet we possess conflicting qualities of the night.

People who have allowed their living to be compromised by doubt and negation seem to move about in lead shoes. Their dance in life is greatly subdued. There seems to be very little that they are passionate about. This reminds us that mustardo is also the essence of passion. It fuels our caring and it tempers our reactions. The passion aspect of mustardo is so critical in these times. Without it, we can't seem to care about our world. We just don't give a damn. But with it, we care greatly and are moved to share our compassion wherever it will be received.

Passion inflames the spirit winds

and

grows love and friendship in our lives.

A passion for our life supports the living world around us. When our passionate elements of mustardo flow forth as caring, there is disdain for injustice wherever it might be. If passionless is the way we spend time, then we must change the picture. The arts, our homes, our friends, and our children must receive these sustaining waters of caring!

When it is drawn off of life's river and lost, where does it go? It travels into the darkness where evidence suggests we look for the tracks of the tentacle. When it is taken there it is consumed by a space not unlike a black hole, and it is not coming back to us. As it is lost from us life is equally diminished.

Those of us who seek the Something More of life must deal with the alarming assumption that the sustenance of life is being drained from our vessel and ourselves in critical ways. In one way or another it is being lost or taken away, and though it is painful to say, it may be forever gone from us. As a result of this loss of mustardo, our journey is in jeopardy and our way has been obscured.

Appreciating the meaning and value of our mustardo will allow us to value life wherever we find it. If it is senselessly taken away from the world around us it is taken from us as well. The life within us is interdependent with the life around us. Even with our species-specific biases we must go forward with a reverence for all life. In terms of life and values of mustardo, a mother who drowns her own children is not so different from a developer who needlessly destroys an entire woodland. In the greater journey of life they both cause unnecessary losses, and in both cases we might find the tracks of the tentacle.

Mustardo

Tis the means and the measure of our way
in that or what we trust
no gates closed or hinges rust
life lives long as it must.
If our times end here
will we live on
beyond this day and this year?
With goodness given
we illuminate the way
and warm the living
through the night and in the day.

Can some of what has been taken and drawn off be found, reclaimed, and added back to life's river? Yes, and although time is limited, exacting efforts to clarify the confusion of these times will allow some to be found and taken back from the obscuring shadows. In this necessary effort we only need to remember that acting and living in accordance with life's principles gives us protection from additional losses. In this regard not only does life bear us, grow us, and sustain us while infusing our animation, it is also a power of protection, the More. In the same breath however, less is also a force; a taking force, which must be recognized and respected. Our mustardo is the fluid essence, which keeps us in life and insulated from the implications of less, a long and lasting sleep in the dark and frigid night! In its place we will be guarded by a protective buoyancy belonging to the sustaining river of life. With an adequate quantity of mustardo we will never feel empty or meaningless. Instead we will express a trusting attitude toward our lives and our place in the world. Real implications of this loss of mustardo from life's river may be illustrated in the contemporary conditions of our health and the health of our world. The process of subtraction seems more and more evident.

If the life of our natural world
is not well, then ours
will not (cannot) be well either.

If we seek to be special
the life around us
must be special as well.

Bees, Trees, and Super Bugs

What could super bugs, bees, and trees have in common? That the human, plant, and animal worlds are suffering huge and exacting losses is a good place to begin. Not only are these living families of life dying in unprecedented numbers, in each case a super bug of one sort or another has been identified as the causal agent. Among humans Methicillin-resistant Staphylococcus aureus, or MRSA, has been in the news. In the plant world the mighty oaks are not so mighty anymore, and in the animal world our favorite insect, the honeybee, is rapidly declining.

Bacterial Leaf Scorch, or BLS, the disease that is killing members of the red oak family in unprecedented numbers, is caused by a bacterium run amok, as is MRSA in humans. Colony Collapse Disorder, a syndrome resulting in the demise of countless honeybees, is believed to be caused by a super bug of a viral nature.

. There are many corollaries underlying these losses. The super bug causing MRSA appears to be a new strain of a once innocuous staph bacterium. The one causing BLS, Xylella fastidiosa, has always been present in the environment and only recently developed into a devastating and killing force. The red oak family, which includes the beloved pin oak and other landscape favorites, is fully involved in this pernicious taking of life, and it is the belief of arborists worldwide that the white oaks, sycamores, and maples are not far behind. As for the honeybees, how could a microscopic virus so quickly gain an upper hand over such a common and giving bee? To date this remains a mystery entomologists are working hard to unravel. While it is true that honeybees have struggled for some time with various environmental challenges, this pathogen is causing catastrophic losses far exceeding anyone's expectations.

In a relatively short period of time MRSA has surpassed the AIDS virus, another super bug, as an American life-taker. This past year AIDS claimed approximately twelve and a half thousand American lives, while MRSA is estimated to have claimed upwards of nineteen thousand. How could such a recently passive bacterium become one of the most invasive pathogens out there? A few short years ago BLS was thought to be a slow moving disease with little chance of contagion. Now it is clearly a tree reaper with untold future consequences. Is some of what's happening here reflective of life's underlying vigor coming up short against a collective decline side of Less?

MRSA has been shown to be resistant to treatment with many common antibiotics and is only responsive to the most exotic and powerful in our medicinal arsenal. BLS similarly needs oxytetracycline, a specialized antibiotic treatment, but in the case of our trees this is only a disease management tool, not a cure.

These challenging treatment scenarios have left health professionals, plant pathologists, and entomologists to suggest that we are at a tipping point with respect to resistance both in America and globally. Someone commenting on MRSA called world panic an inappropriate alarm, but is it? There has been too much suffering and too many lives lost not to be alarmed. Similar thoughts were expressed by plant pathologists regarding BLS just a few short years ago, but not anymore. With Colony Collapse among the bees, crossbreeding was thought to be the answer, but clearly something more is necessary. So what truly could have been done to avoid this tipping point of resistance? What would have made a difference? The big picture is so confusing and overwhelming.

Over many years of practicing my profession as an arborist I have been challenged by the rapid decline and loss of tree species. Despite the many tools available to us and the support of skilled plant pathologists, we have not been able to effectively care for and protect some of the world's greatest trees such as the mighty chestnuts and the grand elms. In these cases we could gain some measure of understanding and find some degree of relief from feelings of professional and personal inadequacy from knowing that they were caused by pathogens or killer bugs that were introduced to America from afar. We have learned that there may be unexpected environmental consequences to bringing foreign plants, insects, animals, and even cargo to our soil, and we've seen the solution as slapping our own hands and promising not to pull at the threads of life's fabric so wantonly.

In the case of the BLS assault on the oaks, however, the identified causal bacterium agent has always been here. So what has weakened the oaks and strengthened the bacterium enough to allow the unthinkable to happen? Ultimately we will undoubtedly identify a combination of conditions that has allowed this once passive organism to morph into a more vigorous and tenacious super bug. What we may never really understand is how the conditions favoring life, More, have been replaced by conditions that allow this final decline, Less, to occur. Alas, we will often be left with knowing that that which we see is being caused by something we don't see.

The word resistance itself may be the key. Instead of fighting all of these super bugs on their terms, we may be better served by understanding how life's resistance has been broken down. Is it not the life in one and all that is threatened? Regardless of our particular genesis and our eventual destination while sharing this planet, we also all draw from and need to give back to the river of life which vitalizes, moves, and sustains living while in existence. It is something so very precious that is often taken for granted until it is subdued, leaving from us or taken from someone or something that is important to us.

The reservoir of life itself may be failing, and our first concern should be to replenish it. Might it soon occur to us, as humans, that what we know to be essential for our health and happiness is also necessary for the rest of the world around us? Such basic things as fresh air, clean water, and wholesome food can only come to us if they are conceived and supported by the acts and structures of a living and vital world.

One thing we can be sure of is that every breath drawn and every spring bud unfolding is an act of the dynamism of life holding back the pernicious forces adept at taking life away. These huge and belief-defying losses cannot be tolerated in a healthy and sustaining world. Out among my leafy friends I am dismayed. Who is stronger than the mighty oak? Super bugs!

The mechanisms of decline may be gaining an upper hand, and we must be concerned. In the language of pathology and entomology, super bugs are often noted as life giving or life taking. Terms like 'beneficial fungi' and 'life-supporting bacteria' versus designations like 'decline organisms' separate the good guys from the bad guys. Implied in this nomenclature is that some microorganisms support health, while others foster decline. Where have all the good guys gone?

Certain conditions favor the forces of life, while others accelerate the loss of life. In humans the key for a vigorous life is a safe and healthy environment versus toxic green lawns, excessively polluted water and air, and the stress pollutants of noise and light. Trees are much more vigorous and disease resistant when they are part of unmolested and intact forests as opposed to being surrounded by challenges such as compacted soils and water diverted by grade changes. Honeybees are much more protected when surrounded by pesticide-free, diverse food sources, instead of mono-cultured flowers saturated with EPA allotments of chemicals. Individual losses or the decline of specific species typically point to a troubling imbalance in the bigger living system in which these losses occur.

In simple terms, but with frightening consequences we must ask ourselves, "Have we taken away too many forests? Have we contaminated too much of our air? Have we polluted too many streams? Have we become too dependent upon a toxic mix of chemicals to negate what we feel we don't need while accelerating the production of what we think we do want?" From where these questions are asked, many others may need to be asked as well.

Perhaps humanity in general has lived in contradiction to the needs of many of the living earth's systems while pursuing our goals of growth and development. As such we may not have given enough consideration to the important life-giving forms around us. Seeking our 'advantages' may result in the loss of important and life-sustaining aspects of our world.

Invariably, growth for growth's sake threatens the health of our world. In human terms this may be likened to the development of a cancer in the body. In that case cellular overgrowth occurs in one part of the body with great detriment to our health and well being. When possible we choose to contain or restrict this out of control growth, for if left unchecked there comes a tipping point where life leaves us and death takes us. Is this an appropriate metaphor for the life sustaining versus life eroding conditions confronting our disappearing oaks, honeybees, and people? The arrival of these super bugs may help us to understand what is happening on a much larger scale. The river of life is drying up, leaving less mustardo than is enough to sustain a healthy existence. The imbalance is evidenced in much of our world. Decline and dying is overwhelming life and living in so many ways. Clearly, the suffering and dying oaks are a tree canary of sorts. In fact, there are canaries and red flags almost everywhere if we are willing to look at the disappearance of coral, ice caps, and honeybees, as well as the rising seas. The aspen are dying, not quaking, and our oaks are leaving us. It is hard to believe. How many of life's precious functions and forms are at the edge and are frightfully close to sliding into darkness? It's hard to know. Trees are dying while weeds are thriving. Honeybees can't be found, but yellow jackets are stinging their way across America. Inner city youth see contenders, not playmates, and the slaughter is on. Living is a challenge for over two thousand American children a year who commit suicide instead of choosing life. Does anyone really feel good anymore? Or has the imbalance and decline that is so obvious in our world also begun to creep into our homes and our bodies, leaving us aching and looking for multiple forms of pharmaceutical relief? How many living earth systems can fail before it all goes over the edge?

Understanding that the living earth systems are breaking down compels us to ask, "What can be done?" The biggest challenge for us today is the decision to see or not to see. Seeing will allow us to come down on the beneficial side of life. Continuing to not see will only add to the hand of the reaper with further decay and decline. Seeing compels us to view the world from wherever we are. As an arborist I can choose to see trees as sticks in the ground from which I make a living, or I can see these woody beings as leafy friends. "Friends?" you may say, "A tree is just a tree. How can it be a friend? This term is reserved for more special and warm-blooded relationships!"

The difference in how we see the world that looks back at us can make all the difference. As sticks in the ground, we just remove the trees to build our houses. As for 'leafy friends,' we find a way to build our homes among them.

Trees, along with the woodlands and forests to which they belong, are one of the most significant carbon busters in this alarming time of global warming. They provide us with precious oxygen and wood with which to build and heat, and they provide a general cloak of comfort over the land. In return they ask only for a place to be. Do you have friends like this? Yes, they are friends indeed! And might we not also benefit by considering all significant life systems as friends and kin to the human family? If we begin to see them in this way it will be much more difficult to disregard their legitimate place in our world.

Regardless of what we do or where we are now, there is a living world that needs our participation. If we listen to the world around us the cues will be obvious: the child needing meaningful time, the finch upon an empty feeder, the dogwood tree with wilted leaves in the back yard, or the lonely senior citizen right next door. Many of the more grand expressions of life are being depressed and thus being substituted with more marginal, less beneficial and less valued, expressions. In the landscape and woods edge poison ivy is thriving and growing at accelerated rates, while cultured grapes are struggling with one pest after another. Beneficial insects like lacewings are struggling while voracious, decline-inducing insects such as Japanese beetles, bagworms, and tent caterpillars are ever increasing their populations. In the soils that support the plant kingdom the beneficial and necessary fungi of the micro-rhizae families are less and less evident, while infectious soil-born fungi like those causing verticillium wilt are ever more present. Clearly, we can't take the living world for granted. Perhaps the vigor that underlies the multitude of life forms on this earth is being suppressed.

Dynamic and healthy life is not so available now. The tipping point may have been reached. Life's fragility equals our loss.

Not seeing has allowed humankind to separate ourselves from the world to which we belong. Admittedly, we see the earth as important, but we don't feel intimately involved in it. The consequences have been huge and can be noted in different ways.

So many of our behaviors and the attitudes that support them illustrate that not seeing this intimate and interdependent connection has allowed our technologies to out-distance our conscience. The consequence has been that if we think we need something from this world we feel justified in taking it. The implications are clear to this arborist, if we continue on this way we have a very short horizon before us!

To lengthen our horizons we may need to look again at some common beliefs that may not be to our benefit regarding the challenges before us, such as the belief that science will reveal causes and set forth solutions to problems. Maybe and maybe not. Focusing on the small underlying organisms involved in this myriad of losses may keep us in catch-up mode, while the living world collapses around us. Much of the credit for MRSA is given to the misuse of anti-bacterials, particularly antibiotics. But this doesn't explain why a life supporting bacteria or organism has not consumed or fended off this bad guy. We certainly can't explain away the invading reaper of our oaks as a bacterium strengthened by overuse of antibiotics. Very few anti-bacterial agents have ever been used in the plant kingdom.

Intellectualizing and explaining away the obvious as being cyclical and normal serves to give 'normal' a very wide range. This view may cloak our eyes and subdue our concern, further delaying our response to these alarming signs. Again, we are practicing not seeing. To those who say, "Don't be overly concerned about the oaks. It's part of the cyclical ebb and flow of life." I say, "What? There has been no historic corollary or fossil evidence anywhere of a loss of this magnitude in such a short period of time. Regarding the recent rapid rise in childhood autism, there are those who credit the increasing numbers to better diagnostic tests and more accurate record keeping. Twenty or thirty years ago this breakdown of communicative and emotional structure occurred only once in every hundred thousand births. Today it appears in one out of every two hundred fifty births. To accept these numbers as being within the 'normal range' may be foolhardy. Is it possible that the quantity and quality of life is just not able to support the developmental and structural integrity of so many of our children's growth?

What is our best hope in all of this? Caring will be the verification of our willingness to see the value of protecting life's needs. Identifying with life's needs connects us to the special something, mustardo, that underlies all life forms in our world of existence. We can't be here and alive without it. All life draws from it moment to moment, and without it we are no longer involved in the living experience.

Our hope lies in the often-asleep goodness within us. If we can translate this into personal and collective acts of caring for life, then that which created us will find a way to keep us. It is within us to be caring. We are capable of being good stewards of our earth and the life upon her. Clearly we are special beings on this world. But perhaps we must foster a new attitude that suggests that we are not more special. Much of human behavior suggests that we are separating our thread from the fabric of life in the pursuit of specialness, which may be diminishing our lives while threatening the well being of the world to which we belong. Thus, we may be better served by giving standing to all of life, regardless of how we interact with it. The health and vigor of life belongs to all of life simultaneously. If certain forms or expressions of life are lost, then all of us have lost something as well. And if caring is what it will take, what could possibly stand in our way? Perhaps old habits and outworn beliefs. An example of such a belief could be that this world is only a place that we are passing through, and what really matters is that there is an eternal resting place some would call heaven. Of course, if we are just passing through on our way to heaven, we must be more special, and we can take from this world whatever we see as deserving of our special status.

Is there a better belief system for this world's needs? All theologies can find a place in life's needs. If this is not a mantra, then it is a cloak of comfort against the powerful and ruinous winds blowing about us. We have seen the human hand of taking in some of our losses, and we have noted the human hand of giving in some acts of recovery.

But what about the tipping point of resistance? Where is ours in all of this? Is there a colony collapse of our own just up the road? With the failure of so many species so evident in the world around us, can we be long immune? Are the super bugs of decline lining us up in their sights? Will MRSA soon have the company of even more aggressive super bugs? Are the AIDS virus, cancers, autoimmune diseases, and the many debilitating children's afflictions such as genetic abnormalities and autism the beginning assault on the human family? Are these losses already holding a mirror up to us that we are drawing frightfully close to? Is the future something we can assume we will enter? What are we willing to do to lengthen our horizons?

Nothing could be more assuring than if what we do and are willing to consider centers around life for life's sake. We must let life be the sun we revolve around. Any thing, thought, or action that takes away part of this sun may only continue to cloud our future.

Admittedly many of my assumptions and implications are speculative and subjective, drawn from observations in the natural environment that yield parallels and corollaries regarding the state of our world. The parallels I have attempted to draw between plant, animal, and human domains may not be documented, but I am quite certain of the reality that something is going on with our natural and living world.

At some point, and it may be sooner rather than later, society must respond to the declines and losses confronting us. So many are saying it's already too late and are questioning whether their own actions can even make a difference. Recent history suggests that the majority of humanity has not seen or appreciated our intimate connection to the living earth. Throwing our hands up is another way of practicing not seeing, not seeing the value of getting started toward caring for and celebrating life around us as inseparable from the life within us. Ultimately our efforts will need to be big. Small may not be good enough at this late hour. Then again, if enough of us truly make a small step, it may be enough to equal a big one. To know this as true, we only have to see that our American eagle and California condor still fly, and they fly over cleaner water flowing in our rivers.

Human history has often illustrated that we have wanted to reach beyond life's integrated fabric and do something more grand and more special of our own. We are driven by insatiable yearnings to become more and perhaps to prove our worth. Now the greatest challenge of our history is set before us. The taking fires are burning all around us. Will we be able to cool them down and put them out?

Identifying life as the 'pearl of great price' will, for many of us, become a new way to see. Perhaps human-kind's material extravaganza of taking and controlling would not seem so necessary if only we could believe that life, and more of it, is what we seek. We can only be as alive as the living world around us is allowed to be.

Mustardo supports the wondrous qualities of life, which occupy a narrow range and are often found in very thin places. While there is intention in the many-colored fabric of creation and a force to life, there is also a power of decline. Will we awaken to realize these distinctions and find the courage to extend the hand of caring to make the difference? Will we insist on responding under the full light of day, or will we continue to be content with the night-like reflections of a blue moon? As of now we are still gifted with time. Let's agree that it matters. Let's agree to do what we need to do. Let us keep this life and return mustardo to life's river, as it returns us to our destination. Together we must and can push back these times of subtraction.

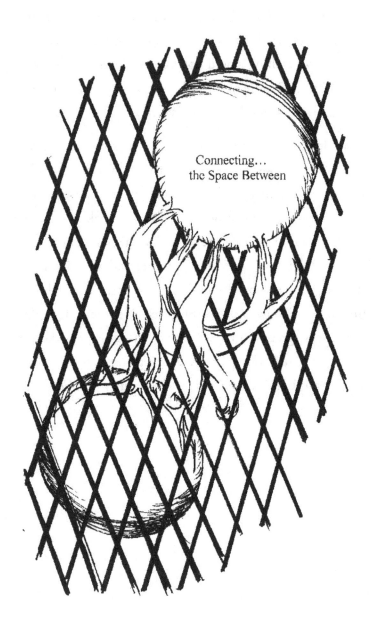

8

Connecting: The Space Between

To remember and recover the More and the wonder of our lives, we must agree that life does not stop at the end of our personal bodies. It also lives and flourishes in the fluid realm of space around us. Many of us know this, but at times the way we live our lives suggests otherwise. Our bigger and living presence may impact our world far beyond where we are, as the presence of others may impact our lives even though we may not see or directly experience them.

When the lights go out
we go on.
The lamp may have been
forgotten in the night
but it awaits our passage there.

The Skipping Stone

His son spoke tearfully of a loss. There was a pained sense of parting in him as well. Together they had come to the shallow, soothing water at the edge of a lake with their arms around one another's waist. Their intermittent tears slid easily from their cheeks into the fluid earth before them. "Father, I so miss Grandpa. I do sense that he is still here with us. I only wish I could see him and touch him," lamented the boy.

His dad reached down, lifted a well weathered, elliptical skipping stone, and in a singular motion tossed it upon the water. After a few grand leaps and a plop, the stone disappeared below the surface. Father spoke, "Son, your Grandpa disappeared from our sight, but we can be confident that he is out there someplace. Even now we can know and feel his presence."

Against a prevailing face-wind the ripples from that stone went out beyond where their eyes could see, even while they also approached, then encompassed, their feet. For a moment at least their tears fell across wide, if salty, smiles as the two stood as three in the wonder of life's embrace.

Understanding the 'space between' is an important concept in comprehending our different worlds and how we might belong to them. It may be helpful to consider the nature of space itself before grappling with the many applications of the space between. First we must acknowledge that space is far more than the mere absence of matter. In fact, space is what allows all matter to exist.

Before a place
there must be a space.

Everything that is born, thought up, or expressed needs a space to allow its manifestation. It is apparent that before there was any of creation there had to be a space in which to receive it.

Clearly, space is critical to the existence experience and our place in it. At its inception the breath of creation set us forth into a great sphere of darkness. Into this unknown, life would masterfully integrate and animate, bringing forth structure and form in which the existence experience would be born. From this intimate relationship between life's impulse and the mass of this darkened sphere, creation manifested the experience of existence as we know it. As we were conceived it was also understood that there was a large space before us that was unknowable and distinctly outlined by a deep darkness from which no light emanated and in which no life form was evident. In every instance of this unfolding and manifested existence experience, space was central to the reception of life's expressions. Much of the intention of our life journey was for us to cast illumination upon this night, to light the space so that we might better understand it, and to ask if the great sphere of darkness might become hospitable to life. Can we illuminate it? Can we know it? Might life's creations be allowed to inhabit it? It was indeed in the very critical qualities of openness and fluidity where the animation of form and structures would emerge into the space for life. Therein lie the cause and the compelling challenge of our journey. As the breath of creation came to be, different worlds and realities with unique designs emerged from life's batter and moved along together in an amoeba-like cluster. The space of life was now occupied by different worlds and realities, along with the space between these worlds, which identified and differentiated one from another.

This fluid and open space between always served as the defining and connecting component of the multi-world experience of life. While it separated the design of one world from another, it was also the fluid space between worlds that was open and available for one life form to connect with another.

Each world had its own specific design and set of laws and relationships. Early in this life's manifestation the space between worlds was so clear that life forms from one world could know or even experience their connectedness to life in the other realms. In fact most, if not all, individual beings were also represented in each and every other world, which moved along on this great journey. It may not have been possible for one of us from the vessel of earth, for example, to have exactly identified another face of ourselves in another world, but our particular essence and radiance would be available to our perception. For us to have known that we were not completely defined by our existence experience on the earth, and thus only relatively contained by the design of form and parameters of time, would have been a great comfort to us. As we have travelled toward that great space of darkness the clarity and clearness that once graced the space between worlds has been clouded or even lost. The darkness that has infiltrated the space between our different worlds has been unsettling for life. It has also unfortunately begun permeating some of our companion worlds and realities. So much of the conflict and confusion associated with man's presence on the vessel of earth had its genesis in the unknowing of this darkness. But regardless of how obscure the space between us and More may be, it does remain available to us. As we awaken to the possibility of More in our lives the space between will serve as a critical medium for us to reconnect to our greater selves and to view and meet more of life and her mysteries. It is a giving womb of nurture and protection as newness may be born into our lives and world.

The concept of the space between might at first appear to be mumbo-jumbo until we view how it applies to us and how it features a passageway of much joy and experience. If we enjoy the simple act of walking through the forest then we might say that this joyful experience is made possible by the space between. If there was no space between the trees there would also be no way for us to access the forest. There would also be no definition between trees. The space between is the fluid opening of the forest and we can move ourselves there and enjoy what a forest can offer us. From a distance the forest looks like a solid wall of trees, but as we approach the woods' edge a way inside is made ready for us. The space between the trees opens up to us so that we can enjoy the wonders of the forest. We enter and enjoy the splendors therein: the cooling breeze, the song of the warblers, the delicious smell of the organic earth, and a taste of the ground berries. So too may the space between our world and others avail itself so that we can know and discover the much More that creation has set before us. From the distancing tendencies of our present, objective mindset; belief in different worlds and realities often complicates our perceptions, and thus they are fenced off from us. If we trust that they may be there, however, they may still become unavailable to us. We can begin to know them as we trust and practice our seeing.

The Space Between

She is that which allows all
these things to be.
She brings them in and adds
life unto them.

Thus, the space between is not just a place or space between things, it is the living arena of all things possible. It is the home of the fluid aspects of life, life's most lasting and eternal expressions.

Life need not always
be firmed up.
Much of it is fluid.

The space between realities and worlds is always a fluid and open realm where visitation or crossing over from one reality to another is made possible. We can assume that the essence of visiting entities will reside in a space between worlds until such time as they step into our reality and manifest themselves here. This is particularly apparent when a lost relative, friend, or lover returns to our world as a voice or shadowy apparition. They may have previously passed away in this world, but they are not dead. Though they have moved on to another reality, their longing for our world and those to whom they were connected, allows us to greet them through the space between this world and theirs.

Those who have
left us
may not be gone
from us.

If we will,
our love
may bring
them near.

Brad Came Also

Terry, the mother of a recently departed school friend of
my son, met me at Lenape Park to place a protective wrap on
her son's memorial tree. There was a palpable longing for her
recently departed son. In her rich accounts of her love for Brad,

a space opened for his presence and I felt strongly that he was there with us.

For some brief time we sat on a park bench while I spoke gently to her about relaxing her mind fences and trusting to see, for her son was now in our presence. For the moment her mental resistance was strong, but not so strong as to completely discourage Brad's phantom presence. It was stalwart enough, however, to hold him out at a distance of a hundred feet or more from us. I could now identify his slippery form, as he looked our way while riding upon the lake breeze.

Clearly, Terry wanted to believe and was making efforts to see, but large iridescent tears kept getting in her way. I thought perhaps that she was trying too hard, as I considered the good and loving lady sitting there beside me. From time to time, I noticed her phantom son sliding alongside her, holding out his hand to tenderly catch some of her tears. Then he would leave for a moment and return with white petals of a flower that he released above her. She could see and feel the blossoms, and mother and son were clearly connecting. As the blossoms fell around her she grinned broadly, then cried even more. The broken cloudy sky above us seemed to reflect her moments of openness with moments of doubt, as the sun shone intermittently into this chilly day and then retreated once again behind the clouds.

For one last moment as we sat upon the bench, Brad moved close and looked into her green eyes, wanting his mother to see him and to receive him. Though his mother could not receive him, I could. Her love called him, and my experienced perceptions received him. Clearly she had been open to my coaching on seeing and by degree, as she loosens her mind's rein and quiets her disallowing fears, she will come to see and receive more.

Brad had crossed from the fluid, liquid space of his residence through the physical divide. I took his shadowy hand into mine. The love and comfort he wanted to convey to his mother poured through me, and her love passed back to him. His longing passed through me to her, as did hers to him. Our hands formed the arc. It was, for the moment, complete. He had returned from his fluid realm back into this existence experience, and we had received him. From his ethereal domain he did, for a moment, return to the earthly place he had so recently departed.

It was now time to remove ourselves from the park bench and follow the outlines of the lake. As Terry and I walked along together, the cold breeze slid over the lake waters surrounding our bodies with its chill. Throughout the walk Brad looked out of the ethers, wanting to touch his mother's lovingness. As a curly-whirly his outline remained remarkably consistent. Comfortably present at our eye level, he again caught Terry's tears and blew them about as spring blossoms.

From time to time we stopped and she spoke fondly of him, while the phantom son swayed to and fro. She spoke of his beauty. She spoke of his gifts. The phantom son clung as close as the lake breeze that embraced us. He was so close that on one occasion warm air encircled us. Numerous petals of white flowers continued to settle around us. The last one stuck on her cheek, affixed to a stationary tear. Her mind reins were beginning to be loosened, and Terry's green eyes opened in an emerald willingness to see.

Our hands together touched.
My hands were our hands.
From cold to warm in a
moment's touch.

I spoke about his presence here with us, and about the fluid realm of his current residence. I told her how I thought it was for him. "When you call to him he is here, very close, just beyond a porous veil. How else could he make those tears into a cascade of flowers?"

Terry spoke to me of one lucid moment in his last days. He sat up, and in a very clear voice he asked, "Mom, where is that man who was carrying me? Why would he do that, and what was he saying to me?"

I responded that Brad left this world before his time, but he was not alone, nor forgotten. This was a young man who warmed the world while he was here. Those phantoms, Benginers, or maybe angels had come to meet him at the door. His painful battle with cancer was over. The letting go of this world was complete, and he would never have to revisit this pain. Why had they put him down? He had resisted a little. The Benginers carrying him to the door recognized his hesitation. He resisted for his mother, so that they might have one last goodbye, and they got it.

The three of us held hands. What a lovely walk it was. We spoke of seeing and of remembering how it is and how life was. We spoke about the world from which Brad was transitioning, including where else we are and how to know it.

Someone's kin was loved today
in a very real and
lasting way.
Mom became open to Something More
seeing and joining in
how it is for her son now.
My privilege and my pleasure
was to be a lamplighter on the way.

If friends or relatives were present in the space between their current world and ours, how might we notice them? Their fluid presence allows no end to how they might first knock at our window or attempt to get our attention. As with any other being or presence out there that may want to enter our world of earthly realities, preparation is the key. This is true for both the visited and the visitor. It must begin by us being open to the unusual. We need to have a quiet understanding within ourselves and be open to signals and signs that may come to us from beyond the veil. I look for faces in the open or cloudy sky. I see them in the smoke of woodstoves as it settles over wooded hollows. There may be a sign in the ice I am skating on, or I may connect with a meaningful image in the canopy of a tree. In these very sketchy introductions our attention and our trust will be measured. This is not a simple thing. Early in our receptions something stupid often gets in our way. If we are not successful in a more clarified visitation we should not worry. We may still be in the preparation stage of this incredible experience of transfer. If we return to whatever it is that we do, opportunities will arise again. It is important to remember that early on in our discoveries the opportunity to part the veil may be a momentary thing. We cannot force anything. The opportunities are countless, and the possibilities are endless.

Before leaving this touching visitation between Terry and her departed son Brad, I would like to mention one other occasion when Brad stepped out of the fluid into our perceptual world. It was midsummer of this same year at a school picnic, which my daughter Meurcie organized.

"Daddy, would you cook for us?"

"Of course I will."

There at a blazing cooking fire on a hot July day, I was amazed to see three wood ducks. The most secretive waterfowl of our eastern habitat walked confidently up to me while I was preparing the picnickers' food.

Within minutes these wild and impossible to approach wood ducks were walking among Meurcie and her classmates. After a moment, but not more, these chattering ducks were being called Brad, Kyle, and Bill after the three students who were lost from their class through accident and illness.

It was truly a sight to behold; these high school teens welcoming back their one-time classmates with joy and ease. Who or what else could better explain this juxtaposed order of things; wood ducks and those teens were comfortable together, receiving treats, and touching one another.

As the afternoon grew into evening, the unlikely visitations ended as these beautiful waterfowl took their leave. It was clear that this magical rendezvous of old friends had been important for both sides as the duck phantoms set off to return to their world. Tears moistened lovely young faces, six colored wings were spread, and the crossing over was complete as the spirits embodied in the ducks were given back to their current habitat in the space between.

I have often identified my mother's visitations as simply curly-whirlys in the open sky. I lightly gaze upon her, and with a deeply drawn breath, I smile. She seems fine and comfortable in her present reality, drifting by for a moment or two, and then she is gone. As a curly-whirly she resides in the space between her new abode and ours; looking in, then moving on.

At our large family events, however, she often makes the effort to

278

manifest in form. How do we see her? How do we greet her? When she greets us at our annual gathering in late August she usually comes as an impressive snowy egret. She often comes a day or two before the multitude of Reddings arrive, and she comfortably shares the large pond called Macanudo with us. Sometimes she even walks among us. Even the most cautious of Reddings agree that it must be her. With the exception of this occasion, there is never a snowy egret at our property, nor is there likely one anywhere in the surrounding countryside. It feels so nice to see and greet her as she expresses her presence in her snowy, white plumage. When the gathering is over she too is gone. The egret must melt away in our world as Mom's essence slides back into the space between for her return to her sphere.

The space between is also beautifully illustrated in my favorite nighttime habit of walking beneath the stars. The quieting peace and bounty gained from the glimmering cathedral above me is an enriching, subjective experience. I sometimes wonder why I don't bump into more humans doing the same thing. I do, however, sometimes traverse the paths of otherworldly beings experiencing life's wonder beneath the firmament. As I turn my eyes skyward and drink in the vision of the glittering stars, I am set to wonder. The experience for me is absolutely sacred. All is made possible by the space between the distant stars and me. The twinkle and the wonder come to me through the space between. Were I there upon the star it would not be tolerable. It would be too hot, too cold, too volatile, or too something. The inspiring shimmer from the star lives not on its surface, but in the space between. Between the origin of the star and this tiny, earthly ant is where the magic, joy, and inspiration come to be.

My eye is open
but my mind is closed.
My eye does not try
to reach the star
but it does want to receive
its glimmering light.
In the night it comes to me
excitedly crossing the dark sea.

The space between is so often overlooked but is very important to us. When touching or contacting the More of ourselves we need to allow a space for this to occur. Remember that:

The light coming from us
is the same light that is coming to us.

How is the space between experienced in a subjective context? From a subjective point of view, when growth or change is going to occur in our lives it will happen in the space between where we are and where we want to be. In a truly interpersonal relationship the space between self and others will be experienced as a condition of we-ness. Only in the special space of we-ness can one or another add to the experiences of love and friendship where both are involved without either feeling threat or demands to our personal constitutions. The critical mixing bowl of we-ness is where self and others can integrate their personal vibrations and visions with the Something More of life, while opening new doors which allow new understanding.

The experience of love and friendship and the expression of hope and joy are perhaps life's most giving and sustaining conditions. When we infuse care and compassion into the world, a trickle or ripple of goodness goes out into the space around us and seeks to be received. When it encounters another, a space of we-ness is manifested. This can lead to potent acts of co-creation in an otherwise singular, if not lonely, disposition.

Many of the challenges facing us and our world will best be resolved by our understanding that we must perceive and value the space around us as well as honor the space between us. So much of our lives are lived beyond our skin as vibrations and ripples, which may influence and sustain much that is possible for us. As we begin to understand this we will be encouraged to move beyond self-centeredness to a more inclusive connectedness to our world. We will understand that much which is good and giving results from these relationships of we-ness. As we come to know this we will then need to consider: how do we communicate to others that they are beginning a birth into we-ness that is necessary for gladness in their tomorrows? How do we tell them that the time of I-only is coming to an end and the era of we-ness has begun? How do we let them know that I matters but that we-ness is a necessary focus and the space of life's concern. Our personal childhood has reached its end, and the collective journey of the we must continue. Thinking and acting as we begins to establish necessary connections that are vital to what we seek to become. This is something life needs to do collectively.

Coming together will be the best way to get done that which needs doing. The task will benefit from the blanket of protection, warmth, and support that is afforded when like individuals become an intertwined tapestry. Woven together, we will all be so much stronger than we would be as individual threads. Individual ripples of good intention are a good place to begin, but together we can engender a wave capable of pushing back the obscuring night, allowing us to know the freeing passage from here to there.

In we-ness the qualities of love and support become integrated into a common space of openness, with the world around us allowing others in, not shutting doors to keep them out. Together our collective vision of goodness and caring will create a space that is supportive and strong, so that if one becomes weak, or ill and falls down, others will lift them up.

The sense of I is a difficult thing to give up. While it is the design of our presence here in the existence experience of earth, it cannot be lasting. Safe and meaningful passage through the night must be a collective journey. No one takes a singular journey across the great sea. Though we may think of ourselves as apart and alone, we really belong to More, and that's the way it needs to be as we make our way from here to there.

Seeing into other realms and receiving from them begins by establishing a space of we-ness not unlike that which occurs between ourselves and others in true friendship and love. It all begins with inner preparation and openness, to be sure, but the earliest cues are happenstance and touch us with something more than an ordinary impression. Something impresses us as being different and valued. We may not be able to put our finger on it, but something definitely clicks. Do we feel a warming sensation within us? Did we hear something? Did we see something? Where did that beautiful sound or song come from?

If this was an earthly experience we might ask, "What is it about that person that touches me in such a special way?" In this world or between worlds the space of we-ness can only be orchestrated by a common denominator of interest. From either here or there we begin by paying keen attention to one another. Though we may be expectant, we know not to apply pressure. We can't force we-ness! If something is touching us from beyond, applying force will only push it away. Attempting to force relationships in this world may similarly result in creating distance, rather than fostering the love or friendship we desire. Confidence and trust in what is coming to us is very important. A lack of basic trust can only weaken the quality of we-ness and thus reduce the overall amount available to us. A perceptible give-and-take identifies we-ness as a special space where newness is being born and where we accept things on the other's terms as well as our own. We don't judge or overly discern. We don't sweat the small things. Something special is born in the moment-to-moment give and take. As something is given, something is received. We all know how quickly the fabric of friendship and love can disintegrate when the space between one and another is abused or misused. This is also true in connections with other realms and the beings thereof. As noted, these relationships are not for show or for entertainment. Living beings are reaching across the divides, and these connections have real and special value, both here and there.

As a connection is developed and refined, old friends and kin will greet us in more and more ordinary ways, expressing as something that occurs naturally in our way of life. In this way the greetings will become more lasting, and interruptions to others' expectations will be less threatening. We may even learn some of their voices. These powerful inter-worldly communions are precious. Nothing good can come from blowing their cover. When and if this mistake is made we can expect a long, dry spell.

The space that separates one world from another is also the space between the realities that offers possibilities of expression and we-ness. It is where so many of our discoveries will originate. Each reality represents its own unique design, and the space between is where these worlds may meet and greet one another. In this space different forms of life may meld and become integrated for a period of time or expression. Thus, meaningful contact may be initiated or received between worlds. It is my thought that interworldly travel is never permitted with beings as is, but rather can only take place after certain filters are employed that keep what belongs to earth on earth (and what belongs to Javunda on Javunda). Fluid essence and radiance can pass through the filters and when received, can manifest in one way or another in the space between worlds. Form can be co-created once this essence is received in a space of we-ness. It is then manifested, for however long, as a presence belonging to the here and now.

The form or structure of these otherworld beings is tenuous at best, and in most cases we might pass our hands through them as if they were phantoms. This does not diminish their legitimacy or lessen their authenticity. Their essence is giving and powerful, and sometimes it is manifested in legitimate forms of this world. There will always be some telltale sign that these beings originated in another realm. The long and sideways leap of Croaker Joe is a great example. I buried his body once, but he did not leave this realm, and thus he did not die. Following is the saga of this remarkable creature.

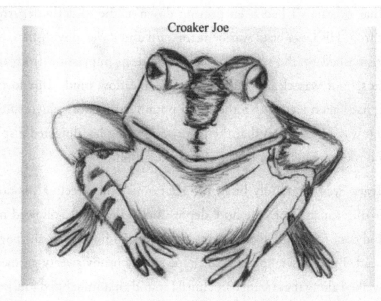

Croaker Joe

We buried his body once,
but he did not die.
These many years have passed,
Croaker found again a door.
In his sideways leap he said "Hello!"
as he landed upon my pinewood floor.

The Life and Times of Croaker Joe

The giant frog was here again. He had the same greenish-yellowish face and deep-set, large eyes with ribbons of white radiating around them that I remembered. If the sheer size and expression of this childhood,

285

leaping friend did not validate his identity, then his fairly uncoordinated jump, more sideways than forward, was sure confirmation.

Fifty-two years had passed since I last looked upon Croaker Joe. On that occasion I had been peering down at the recently departed giant frog. His large head was bent forward and covered with flies, his body smashed by the tread of a cow. The deep impression from the bovine's hoof was clearly outlined in the meadow mud. This lovely being had fallen victim to a thousand pound ruminator, which surely had no way of knowing that the giant, noisy frog had lingered a split second too long between her hoof and the ground.

Teary eyed I carefully lifted his gelatinous body, peeling his now paper-thin carcass from the hoof depression in the mud. I allowed my dog Judy one final sniff of our intriguing friend. Sliding my tee shirt over my head, I gently wrapped Croaker Joe snugly in my sweaty garment and walked along the stream bank until I found an uninhabited muskrat hole. Gently folding my shirt back from the unusual amphibian's head, I took one final look before I slid his wrapped body into the earthen tunnel. Securing a couple handfuls of dried grass and mud, I stomped the opening shut with my foot and placed a large stone on top to mark Croaker Joe's last and final resting place.

A deep sense of loss passed over me. At that time, in my sixth year of life, I had not yet separated the truly phenomenal acquaintances from the normal and predictable life forms of our farm environment. Croaker Joe came into my life at the same time as Cheezer Wheezer (see *Something More*), and while both of these beings captured my attention, both were greeted and affirmed as matters of fact. As a young child, these two critter-beings didn't register as unusual phenomena, which I now know them to be.

Croaker Joe first greeted me in the lower meadow along a meandering stream in the summer following my tractor accident. It was not unusual to hear a volley of assorted frog talk in the late afternoon and early evening hours of summer. One afternoon as I followed the stream out of the woods' edge, I heard a frog croaking like I'd never heard before. "Barraaat. Barraaat," resonated off the woods and echoed through the meadow. I hurried to the meadow fence and slithered under it. A short distance before me, I noticed a handful of cows and a couple of calves gathered around in a semi-circle. "Barraaat. Barraaat." They all lurched back and there he was. Croaker Joe was immediately and appropriately titled. A full fourteen to sixteen inches long, this frog was almost as big as a full grown chicken.

For over a year Croaker Joe would meet me at stream's edge and leap his silly self along with me. On some occasions he would spring among the cattle while I herded them toward the barn. Unlike Cheezer Wheezer, Croaker Joe was not bashful nor did he seem to have any fear. I feared for him though. I was afraid that it was only a matter of time until one of the hundreds of hooves of the cattle herd would come down upon him like a sledgehammer. For the longest time he seemed protected. He would enter one side of the grazing or running herd and traverse the group, leaping higher than the cows' backs. I would watch and worry until he emerged from among them. No man, dog, woman, or child would allow himself to be caught up among the beef cattle herd, but Croaker Joe seemed to have no fear.

One of the many attributes of Croaker Joe that endeared him to me was his willingness to greet me halfway up the hill from the stream. I would leave the house or barn up on the hill and start the quarter mile walk down to the stream bank. Somewhere midway down, out of the grass would flop this long-legged, glutinous mass. With his awkward looking yet surprisingly efficient sideways, leaping, lunging, flying gait he continued to move with me as I proceeded with my day. If I was moving the cattle, he seemed to want to help, fearlessly and effectively negotiating their many dangerous hooves.

To my surprise and delight some five decades later, Croaker Joe returned to visit me. Our renewed acquaintance played out through the hands of my sixteen-year-old son, Orrian. I was in an especially appreciative and grateful mood as a slow rain was rhythmically falling on the house roof. It wasn't much, but in the midst of a long and painful drought, it held out hope that moisture would finally find its way to eastern Pennsylvania.

A celebratory mood was already at hand when Orrian approached me with both hands behind his back. "You'll never believe it, Dad. You will never believe it," he teased. From day one Orrian had been a toad and frog enthusiast, and he had become very adept at knowing where they resided. This keen sense of where they might be allowed him to keep company with them almost constantly.

Imagine my surprise and delight when he whipped this striking likeness of my childhood friend from behind his back. With a squirm, the giant frog was soon dangling by one leg from Orrian's firm grasp above the floor. Orrian quickly regained a two handed grip around the grand amphibian as I regained my composure. The thought that Croaker Joe had returned from the ethers and was once again paying a visit to me here upon terra firma had left me breathless.

In the next instant Orrian lifted this behemoth of a frog up to his face and deposited a kiss upon Croaker Joe's nose. The frog responded by overpowering his two-handed hold, leaping into the air and landing with a loud splat upon the yellow pine flooring. Another leap, this one more sideways than forward, quickly followed. This confirmed his true identity, of which there had been little doubt. Croaker Joe was back. Incredible.

"Orrian," I said," where did you find him?"

"Pop," he replied, "he found me. When I heard the rain I stepped outside and splat, he jumped out of the night and landed across my boot."

Totally amazed, I listened to Orrian tell his account. It was strikingly similar to the story I shared with my young children about my childhood friend, Croaker Joe.

As Orrian recounted his surprise at the way he was greeted by this phenomenon as he stepped outside, I recalled the way in which Croaker Joe would continually surprise and delight me with his sudden appearances. He would materialize at almost any time of the day and almost any place within a half-mile radius of what might be expected to be a frog's habitat.

Croaker Joe launched himself off the pine floor with an awesome leap. It reminded me of the way he could cross the stream or any other obstacle that he needed to clear. His heroic sideways flight ended with a telling thud that set a smile across my face and a deep inner marveling at how the expressions of life can be so staying. Life may depart from our perceptions, but it does not necessarily quit.

I suspect that the magnificent leaps he took across the pine flooring and traversing the meadow are akin to the way he entered this realm of existence, the way he left it, and now the way he returned once again. In what nether realm had he been sustained? Did he belong to Javunda or yet another reality? As a frog, his earth form, he was quite magnificent, a substantial being!

So many years ago his earth form had been stepped upon and, by the design and laws of this world, he died here. But he did not end. He lived on in another realm, recovered, and once again returned to a place I suspect he greatly loved. In the hands of my son, he greeted his old friend once again. Although fifty years had passed, Croaker Joe seemed not to have aged at all. In the attributes of earth time, becoming antiquated is part of the design. I couldn't help but wonder, "Croaker Joe, where were you all that time?" Since that fateful day in the meadow not a single night had seemed to pass for Croaker Joe. Was he held in suspended space, or did he pass into another world, a place like Javunda? For Croaker Joe time may have been suspended. He still looked the same, but for me fifty-two years of struggle and toil had changed my face considerably. At some point my time here will be done. But will I be coming back again? Will there be a place to come back to?

Croaker Joe was released late that rainy evening into the arms of Happy Tree's forests and ponds. More than a hundred days have passed without sound or sight of his presence. For now at least, this is the life and story of Croaker Joe. I remain certain that at some future time, in this world or another, a familiar friend will cross my way, and I will know this life in its leap and its laugh. "Barraaat. Barraaat!"

Once we understand how places meet in the space between we may be more open to receive. We will be more tolerant of fuzzy inscription and appearance early on in our awakening. A great effort may be involved in life coming from the beyond to meet our lives here. Travelers may have the most to do in their preparation and transfer to fluid essence, but receivers will have work to do as well. They must put their minds on the couch, create a space of communion, and be open to receive.

Getting started in seeing can be facilitated in different ways. Finding a time and a place absent of interruption can be helpful. For lack of a better term I refer to this as a place of communion. This is a place and time where and when conditions will be most favorable for quieting the mind and letting impulses and impressions of other worlds or realities come in. For me the wooded hollow of Fairyland is one such giving place.

It is my belief that in our early days of seeing, the transfer of beings from other worlds will be received as essence or radiance, as in tap screws and curly-whirlys. In this way the transfer is given more gently and is less likely to be shocking than other manifestations, such as an alien form might be. Even after all these years the radiating light of a tap screw never fails to take my breath away. Curly-whirlys satisfy my inner yearning for mystery and more, and they always put a smile on my face. When I catch a glimpse of their fuzzy, sketchy outline I know that someone or something is looking into our world and may even emerge in form at one time or another. In almost every one of my personal experiences of visitation from there to here the form that was manifested was a singular being: Cheezer-Wheezer, Croaker Joe, Cyclops, and Melix (See *Something More*). An exception was the lovely mother and daughter that emerged from the hickory tree. This leads me to believe that otherworldly being-ness passes through filters as points of radiance and, when manifested, all of this radiant essence coalesces into a singular being. On a few instances of visitation I clearly perceived a collective of tap screws before a being congealed and could be recognized. The Orange-Haired Lady of Fairyland comes to mind here.

The Orange Haired Lady

In her beauty and her dance
This phantom lady held me in her trance.

From what reality or distant world had she come
To twirl upon the waters of a country pond?

The Orange-Haired Lady

It was a midsummer night in the wooded hollow that nestles the two-acre pond of Fairyland. As I climbed up the footbridge crossing Ridge Valley Stream, the night songs and nature's reverie were deafening.

Ridge Valley stream separated our cabin from the wonder of Fairyland, and at times it almost felt as though the footbridge was a doorway to another world of wonder and mystery right here on planet earth. The brilliant half moon adequately illuminated the bridge for safe crossing. Upon stepping down on the far side of the stream the vapors from Fairyland met and obscured my way. They were unusually dense. What wonders might I meet tonight? The mystery and the magic were almost touchable in the dimly lit, dense mist that was swirling about. Soon I was sitting at my usual spot, on a stump by a small dock at the side of the pond nearest to the cabin. With breath drawn and my mind just a little uneasy, I spoke my normal nighttime greeting when preparing to receive any spirit being, tap screw, spacer, phantom, gnome or the like. "Hello my friends, so good to be with you again."

No sooner had I spoken my greeting, than I noted a cluster of fifteen to twenty tap screws quietly twinkling and descending in the vapors over the surface of Fairyland. Although tap screws were almost predictable companions in my nighttime discoveries, this was a bit unusual. I had never seen them descend into water. Wouldn't the wetness dampen their glow?

They often lined the stream and circled pools of water, but I had never seen them in the water. This night I did. They seemed to congeal at a spot under water and they emitted a soft, visible glow. Soon, I was seeing a cone of cooling water vapors swirling above the glow. At the same time, the surface of Fairyland came alive with ten to twelve more of these vapor-fairies, from whom the pond has gotten its name. In an evenly spaced, almost organized fashion, the vapor-fairies moved slowly about to the sounds of the night, which seemed to be orchestrated music. Clearly, the nighttime Fairyland waters were being prepared for something special. Above the noisy nighttime sounds I started to discern a melodious noise with chime-like resonance. I looked back at the congealed glow beneath the surface of the water and noticed that a particular cone of cooling vapors was aglow with a striking, orange radiance.

Soon a milky-opaque fluid stream was entering the orange vapors, and slowly they coalesced into a body form. As the underwater glow lifted completely into the vapors rising above the pond a six to eight foot fluid lady took shape upon the water's surface. The vapor cones gathered around this glowing apparition and seemed to become part of her dance. Who was she? It didn't matter, her presence was magnificent. I noted her deep orange hair falling over a lacy gown, which clung to her ethereal body as she moved gently to and fro. On two or three occasions she seemed to gaze at me directly with emerald green eyes. With each brief glance, my heart seemed to stop and a twinge of fear crept into my mind. She loosened her gaze and again I was fine.

A deep emerald gaze
powered from her eyes into mine.
My heart stopped.
Some fear crept into my mind.
Only when she loosened her gaze
did I again feel fine.

What a visitation! Her slow, spinning dance was accompanied by the sound of chimes as her arms opened and her hands were splayed into the vapors. The entire pond seemed to be illuminated by the magical, orange glow of her presence. As she moved slowly about I noted how her legs, gathered together under her gown, did not step or move. Instead she seemed to be moved by the gathered vortices of the other cooling, swirling, synchronic vapors also present on the pond. The space between her manifested presence and these other vapor vortices seemed charged so that one supported the other and maintained a constant distance from each other. From time to time she would extend her hands into the vapors about her and they would glisten like jewels. Although she displayed clear form and striking color, her gentle movements meshed with the other, more typical, vapor fairies. The entire surface of the pond was alive in this moving dance.

I couldn't help but notice that the normal, nighttime noise had reached an even higher crescendo during the lady phantom's visit. This was unusual at Fairyland, where startling nighttime visitors would typically quiet the woods completely. Cyclops visiting from the beyond would instantly suppress the frogs, peepers, and owls. The bobcat of this world would completely still everything with its stalking presence or its loud screams.

There she was, stunning in her glow and presence. Again and again she would briefly seem to gaze at me with her emerald eyes, and I would lightly tremble until she lifted her gaze. After a period of approximately two hours, a relatively long visitation, she was gone. Ascended or descended, I couldn't be sure, she had seemingly melted into the background. Her glow was gone, and so too was the Orange-Haired Lady of the Night. The sound of chimes continued for approximately five minutes after her departure, which encouraged me to believe she would make another appearance. She did not. Soon the chimes were gone, and a band of mosquitoes began to feast on my body in earnest. This was my signal to return to my cabin and take my wonder with me. I wondered and waited, for days that stretched into months, hoping to see her again. Had she come to see me? Or, was it just by happenstance that I was there when she visited the magical waters of Fairyland? Had she come before? Would she come again? The nighttime creatures seemed so comfortable with her presence, calling out and singing in deeper pitch and joined in her rhythms when she was near.

Once again I felt blessed to have been available when another reality allowed me to look in. A space between worlds had opened up to one of the most giving experiences of we-ness that would ever come my way. The Something More of life had made itself available. What a beautiful and giving interlude it was. And those angelic chimes may have signaled and defined the way in and out of this world for her passage through.

The space between is always involved in the passing of essence or beings from one world to another. As we enter spaces or receive something or someone from them, the clear, opaque, or dark light will help identify what or who is coming through. It is often reported in the accounting of near death, or edge, experiences that a guide appears and aids in traversing that space between. In some cases it is said that a light is seen and followed, while in others a voice beckons the traveler onward. Though these have not been my experiences when crossing over, I have no doubt in their validity. I am left envisioning a passageway between two worlds or realities, such as a great and impenetrable mountain range seemingly blocking or obscuring one realm from another, but with hidden access through the peaks. Once again I am reminded of the distant look of a forest. From afar it appears as a wall of wood, and there seems to be no way in. It is only as we come close to the woods' edge that a space between the trees is discernable. Might it be that death or near death allows us to come close enough to the mountains to perceive a way to pass through them?

As one is prepared a key is turned, a door is opened, and the blocking mountain lends availability to the other side. Cheezer Wheezer, Croaker

Joe, and Cyclops may have had such a passage enabling them to show up on short notice and respond to signals with little delay. It is also possible that these characters have existed for a long time on the earth and are very skilled at slipping in and out of form. The lady gnomes from the hickory tree seemed so comfortable that I am certain they lived in a sustained and abiding way. Judging from their Elizabethan dress I think it is safe to assume that they were mother and daughter for hundreds of years.

Coming from the tree
and being received into the tree,
time no longer moved for them.
They were so happy to have a home.
This day was the same day
as yesterday.
Tomorrow would not matter
for today would never go away.

It is difficult to know the exact home or point of origin of these otherworldly travelers. As we see more and trust more we will better understand their comings and goings. At the same time we may come to appreciate the wonder of so much more as we are open to give and receive from the space between realities.

The expressions of character of these inter-realm travelers give us cause for reflection. Once these beings arrive on earth their personalities and expressions seem to be locked in. Cheezer Wheezer was a grumpy guy. Did he come from a grumpy world? Witchie Willie was hard, never smiling, alone, and powerful. Fixed in her stare and in her countenance, she never flashed a grin or expressed a sense of joy. Croaker Joe was always a source of loud, echoing chatter and always had a sideways leap. He never could straighten that out!

When I think of Margie's pained spirit, the night phantoms, and even Witchie Willie, I suspect their long-term residences were clearly in the deeply cloudy or even darkened spaces. The Benginers, on the other hand, seem to reside in clear and clarifying spaces either here upon the earth or in the spaces immediately adjacent to it. They are friendly and helpful, but always stern and quietly serious. They seem to enjoy stepping in and lending assistance, but they don't seem capable of feeling or expressing joy. Simple joy seems to be a quality that is nonexistent among the beings that have greeted me here on this planet. Is the expression of joy one of the unique splendors of this existence experience? Is that why we pain so much when it is taken away from us?

Did I transport my joy to Javunda following the tractor experience? I know I felt and experienced a great deal of joy in that special place, but did I express joy? My psychic memory recalls a severe sense of compression leaving here and going there. Was this a consequence of passing through those filters between worlds or squeezing through those passages? The sense of general and specific chest compression is a consistent, subjective recollection when I reflect on my edge experiences. When someone shares their physical sensation during a heart attack with me it resonates to me in a similar way. All of this makes me ponder, when passing between realms, whether there isn't a limited range of expression and behavior that is stamped upon us for the duration of our visit. It is impossible to know as we are looking out into newness while the other is looking in at us. As for the filter passages, it appears that coming and going by way of them is a more difficult and painful process, because the visitor coming through to us, by us, and for us must feel our presence to be clear as a crystal. The visitor is almost completely dependent upon the receiver as he takes his cues and presence here. It is only through us that his presence here will be protected and manifested. If the contact is broken he is quickly and completely gone, maybe never to return again. Melix (see *Something More*) comes to mind as an example. Filter travel makes for long, expectant pregnancies. A dream or intuition signals something is coming, but the delivery is seldom quick. When Melix came through I failed to completely receive him. In an instant he was gone. Cyclops followed Melix by approximately eighteen months. He too likely came by way of filters and probably originated from the same realm as Melix. Both showed a singular and powerful eye, both were beings of apparent strength, and both seemed out of place here. While Melix's power overwhelmed me, it probably also prepared me for the coming visitation with Cyclops.

As we move on toward the discovery of our long and lasting lives, newness will tempt us as we are ready. It will greet us as we allow it. The old and existing picture of who we are will need to allow a space between the frames from which we will exercise our seeing. If we will allow this, then so much wonder will be revealed to us. We will come to know our lasting value as we enjoy opening a door to so much More.

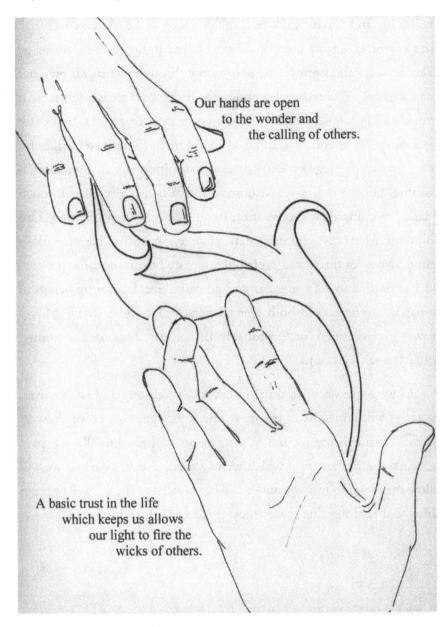

Our hands are open
to the wonder and
the calling of others.

A basic trust in the life
which keeps us allows
our light to fire the
wicks of others.

9

Who Are We?

Sailors of Fortune

Awakening to the More of life implies that we are also aware and protective of the quality and value of life all around us. As we step free of the limiting conditions of our present world, compassion for the many others will encourage us to extend our hands to them. In that we all voyage together in this time and place of More or Less, we might be likened to Sailors of Fortune as we extend our hope and vision of more.

As Sailors of Fortune we understand that we are all human. The difference between ourselves and those we want to help, illuminate, comfort, and befriend is a matter of degrees. The Something More of life burns deeply for us. Our yearning for it is an imperative. Our focus in all things is life, as we work to separate ourselves from the darkness of this world. Simultaneously, we want to bring others to join us in this new-found More. Perhaps the most that we can do, and the thing we do most naturally, is to extend caring, along with warmth and illumination, to those around us. This is always a good and right thing to do, and if we feel an attunement with the perspectives of this unfolding world view then it becomes the obvious way of our now lives. We have accepted and know that we are on a voyage over time upon a great sea. Intrinsic to our sailor's identity is knowing that, while we belong to our vessel earth, we must navigate and make passage upon the large and unpredictable sea of time and space. The successful completion of our voyage is assured only when we reach our destination. The protected harbor is before us. The destination is that one day with a beginning but not an end.

To accept these perspectives we must also understand that the ups and downs of our voyage can never really be foretold. We have no way of knowing what storms might challenge our sea craft, what conditions might arise within our vessel, or whether our ship will remain seaworthy throughout our long and sometimes hazardous journey. Regardless of all of the unknowns inherent in such a voyage, competent sailors know that they must remain committed to the vessel until a safe harbor receives them.

Obvious signs are telling us that time is of the essence here. Our journey is handicapped, indeed almost stuck, and an intuitive sense tells us that these may be our final days. To navigate our vessel out of the darkness and away from stormy seas we must put forth great and genuine effort within and around our vessel. We must begin by clearing and clarifying the hold of our ship. What is good for the earth is also what will be best for us. Much of our cargo is no longer necessary, and it needs to be cast off so that our vessel may become more buoyant and move more freely upon the sea. Some of the cargo that might be jettisoned for our ultimate benefit may include distracting ideas, outworn beliefs, manipulative minds, and excessive technology; all of which have demeaned individuals at times while creating tensions about us and beyond us. We also need to identify and support competent sailors with abiding trust, stalwart character, and deep courage who can effectively perform on the deck. We must find those who are not drunken by the darkness, but rather who possess belief in the promise of the journey, while responding to the needs of our vessel.

Much of what needs our attention is found in the obvious living arena of our immediate world and the spiritual and etheric spaces which surround us. These intimate and open spaces around us remind us of the value of right thought and caring vibrations which will differentiate the light or darkness that adheres to us and the space between us. The fortune within us and the work we do around us will vary from situation to situation. Being a Sailor of Fortune is where we will begin, or where we have already begun, and where we will continue to be until the time of lostness and darkness is passed through.

The perspective of More and the onward journey are important for our confidence and commitment to break free of old habits and limited thinking. We are not a static fixture. Instead we are a dynamic unfolding creation in the hand and service of life. Our moment-to-moment and day-to-day presence must imply the intention of life. We are not just happenstance. We belong to a purposeful journey. What might we want our presence of caring to signal to those who are lukewarm, distant, or cold to our intentions? We must remember the all-ness from which we have come, and we must stop living in ways which are pushing our tomorrows away from ourselves. We must never disregard the value of our world and the creation to which she belongs.

While we remain committed to the world around us, we will no longer allow ourselves to be bogged down by others' negations, weighty needs, or silly games. We stand serene and without judgment. Yes, we are anxious to be on our way and want others to feel and share in our awakenings, but we will not push, nor can we carry. Rather, we will tempt with our warming goodness and understanding.

-

Our Pledge of Purpose

We will not do hand or mind battle with the darkness, neither as a space nor with its emissaries. We are aware, however, that extensive efforts to free others from it and move them through it may allow us to become vulnerable to it.

Light shall not enter darkness
to destroy it
or even to replace it,
but rather to illume!

Our disposition in this struggle will be the expressions of our love and compassion. Our love will not venture forth to conquer hate but rather to offer understanding. Our lives will not willingly enter the cold and darkness of the night, even when it is bound up in another human being, but rather they will share its warmth with likeness. Our caring shall always be available to ease the afflictions of those around us.

Though we may have our opinions, we will not aggressively break down others' beliefs, behaviors, and habits of any kind. The most we can do is to allow our lives to offer options or alternatives to the dark and even the dangerous, which may whirl around us.

It is not about pursuing the darkness,
it is about extricating ourselves from it.
We cannot win with a drawn sword.

Caring shall be what we hold
in our open hands.

If there is to be one quality of life that distinguishes us from most of the world around us, let it be caring. A caring person expresses a confident and strong presence that proceeds gently in the world, connecting with that which is of life, while avoiding that which isn't.

In all that we do
shall be expressed
the affections of good intentions.

Caring is difficult in a cold world. Regardless of our intention, bringing light into darkness can be a painful thing. If the unknowing darkness feels as if it is being destroyed or even neglected, we may be denied. The illuminating warmth of our being may be pushed away. We are challenged to move about with the soft light of morning as we represent the creation, which fuels and guides our way.

We must move about the world
in the soft light of morning,
while our work needs to be done
in the evening light of day.

We will be aware that it is not always easy to distinguish between those who may respond to life's leanings and those who are living out a physical existence but whose future is boarded up and closed.

Are You Coming?

How can we recognize someone who is outside but not completely lost to the More of life and who may be willing to respond to our beckoning? In this case we are reaching into the obscuring shadows and will need to determine if we are being received. There may be some appropriate questions we want to ask, and the answer to these questions will help give to us the guidance we may need. "Are we getting back some of what we are giving?" "Does what we are seeing on the outside feel right on the inside?" It might be helpful here to reference the work of Piaget, the highly respected Swiss psychologist, who introduces us to a process of accommodation and assimilation, which may serve as a key for us, so we might have these answers.

It was my good fortune to have met this man. He was so beautiful in his age and presence, and he captured my attention with one of the most revealing seminars of my university stay. He spoke of how cognitive structures, the highways of knowing that can process and organize information, develop in our minds at different ages and times which allow us a way of viewing the world around us. These un-seeable but obvious biochemical mechanisms of the mind are connected to how we function in our lives. He taught that thought and behavior is always an interplay between these internal structures and our interaction with the world. As we perceive the world and act in it, there is a constant exchange of assimilation and accommodation between our mental constructs and the world around us. Assimilation refers to our ability to bring something from beyond us to within us. As it would pertain to the awakening to and discovery of More in our lives, it would imply a new way of seeing and believing. Accommodation refers to the balancing aspect of this process, which almost simultaneously requires us to make internal mind or perceptual changes that allow these thoughts, possibilities, or perceptions to become part of our presence, or being. A simple illustration might be that of a piece of fruit. If we see an orange and desire to have it, the process of assimilation has begun. Assimilation can only be completed as we make the effort to accommodate to what we see and desire, in this case the orange. Thus we must literally involve behavior of accommodation such as reaching and grasping the orange, then chewing and digesting, and finally our body has assimilated this tasty morsel.

~ As we change the way we see things
the things we see are changed. ~

Another illustration involves friendship. When we meet someone who we perceive as being nice or comfortable and fun, thus having value to us, we begin to trust and invite them into our personal space (assimilation). Simultaneously, we must provide time for them and allow a give and take relationship. We must be open to their thoughts and values (accommodation).

If we refer to this process of assimilation and accommodation as it pertains to our hopeful efforts in the world around us we will benefit greatly. Not only will this process clue us in to those who are willing to awaken from their sleep, but it will also guide us in how much illumination is appropriate. If we are to administer to them, we must be aware of how much they are ready for. The process of assimilation and accommodation of something new is best achieved through a balanced and orderly process of change. It is important that we don't expect someone to come too far too fast. Existing belief systems, degree of mental-ism, and willingness to see are all critical factors. Once again:

We must not shine a light
too brightly
in sleeping children's eyes.

The process of assimilation and accommodation may be very revealing and helpful to us. If others are seemingly open to our expressions regarding the wonders of life (assimilation), we might expect some changes (accommodation) in their relationships to our world. They may become more reverent and more appreciative, and may express more positive attitudes, along with care and compassion.

For me, Piaget's work is a refreshing understanding of the unseen pathways of our mind. It encourages us to believe that we can, indeed, change our once cold or limiting thoughts to new mental structures that might correspond with new behavior or function. If a light or memory is turned on, from within or from without, and we indeed see or receive it, we may witness the beginning to a new and growing view. Assimilation almost always precedes accommodation, or change in us, but together new function may be born.

If we can again turn another around,
we have lifted them above the ground.
Some of their light once lost or taken
may again be returned as they awaken.

It can be very rewarding to see someone moving from old destructive habits toward something new and giving. As we infuse the old with Something More we initiate changes in our lives that amount to life-sustaining thoughts and feelings. If, in fact, there is a true interest in the assimilation of something more, then we should see real changes and accommodation in our lives.

If they begin the effort
to get unstuck,
they probably will.

Sadly, there is so much that needs to be done in these times that we cannot linger. We cannot carry anyone out of the darkness! If right thought is evidenced with right action, our compassion, our guidance, and our illumination are justified and rewarded.

How Will We Know?

Until we afford the canopy of goodness and make it available to others around us, we probably can't know for sure. This is where it gets difficult. We have so much mustardo to protect, yet if we are truly Sailors of Fortune, we must allow an opportunity for one and all. How does it work in the gardens of good and plenty of the rain forests?

The following impressions, left with me following a sojourn into the Amazon River Basin, provide illustration.

Although it is built upon relatively poor soil, the rain forest is abundant in life of many forms and expressions. The first and most obvious observation is that where the colors, songs, and presence of life are richest are where the cathedral canopies of large trees cover the vegetation and water beneath them. When canoeing past areas that are timbered selectively or completely, the loss of life's richness and abundance can be clearly observed. If only one or two species are selectively removed, such as ebony and cotton trees, an established, if limited, ecosystem remains. In time, small trees might become large protective canopies and these forest niches might become healed and grand again. On the other hand, where indiscriminate clearing is practiced, life seems all but completely lost. Yes, some vine-like plants snake along the now naked soils and over the remaining stumps, but the thought that a thriving community of life could ever return there seems most remote. Where the grand trees end, or are timbered, savannahs begin, featuring tall grasses representing a monoculture with few life forms. Not only are these areas devoid of the elements that add richness to life such as flowers, reptilian sounds, fruits, and cool breezes, they are also vulnerable to frequent fires, which can consume these grasses and any life among them. While the underlying mantle of earth in the rain forest is slowly enriched and protected from erosion, the treeless savannahs are not. At best, the soils are lacking the necessities of simple life support.

Thus the space of the savannahs seems to be essentially barren or even dying, while next to these tall grasses the rain forest exists with countless thriving life forms. Life is layered from the forest floor to the upper canopies of the large mangoes, ebonies, figs, mahoganies, and others. Animal and plant life in many forms springs forth in every conceivable space beneath these spreading canopies. Along with affording protection from the relentless heat of the tropics and providing life-sustaining oxygen and transpired moisture, these large trees allow these many countless life forms to thrive and propagate in their understory.

In further illustration, the majority of these trees and plants are not invasive. They do not force propagation of their population upon this rich fabric of life. However, they achieve their necessary stature because what they offer their ecosystem is so compelling. Sweet odors, vivid colors, and nurturing fruits entice other critters and creatures to come and enjoy what they freely offer. In so doing, winged and legged life forms move their genetics around, cross pollinating and nurturing, and thereby further strengthening and coloring their environment while supporting their survival.

I see a valued metaphor in this illustration for humankind's awakening and recovery. The interconnectedness of life is so necessary. There is a certain richness in the fabric of integrated and multiple life forms that may satisfy much of the need and warmth that's wanting among us. A monoculture of bottom-line type thinking and living diminishes our value and lacks the richness necessary to sustain this creation. The rain forest thrives upon relatively poor soil, which symbolizes the cultural limitations and materialism so evident today. But if we collectively agree to express the goodness of life, what a world it could be! Let us gather under the canopies of goodness and caring. Those who demonstrate such qualities, along with a positive vision, will be so compelling that others won't be able to help but be open to the sustaining gifts of their lives.

The more we can lessen our dependence upon an aggressive and competitive mind field and initiate an awakening to the More of life, the more easily a carpet of comfort may spread out before us, flowering and colored by hope and joy. As we come to see, the 'buds of belief' will begin to swell and the 'fruits of satisfaction' will follow. Together we will celebrate life with a renewed sense of trust, and in many ways we will add more life to it. From in us and around us we shall know life's secret of the bloom.

Thus we will know that
we are the ones
we are looking for.

As we begin to sense the wonder of it, we should not hesitate or wait any longer. Instead, we must be about creating the conditions necessary for our recovery and the illumination of others around us. Let it begin within ourselves with a quiet imperative. We must be prepared to nurture and guide the awakening interest in others. We must allow this nurturing guidance to indicate the basic trust that we have the means and the support to do these things, to awaken and answer the call of life, and then, in return, to add more life to it.

All hands on deck!
Any effort given will not go unnoticed
but rather will be returned in kind.
We are attentive and we are present
as we begin our way into
everlastingness.

Reflecting back to the rain forest, whatever comes within the spreading canopies of the large trees seems to have a place and serve a function. While there is decline of one sort or another, there is always a greater abundance of collective life than the total of accumulated decline. The process of subtraction is held at bay.

Yes, trees are dying, and life forms prey on one another. Dominant animal forms diminish others, and strong winds sometimes wreak havoc among the community of life. At the same time, all of the plants are growing, and all of the animal forms are busy expressing song and color. In other words, the preponderance of what is happening comes down clearly on the side of the living. The atmosphere is made ready for life, and life responds.

This can be our model. The way of our lives will cast its canopy of goodness, trust, and support over the part of the world that we occupy. As others are touched by this, they will also express life's giving qualities. We cannot be preoccupied with every thought and action, because the balance of what's good shall replace what's detrimental. There will be disappointments resulting from negative thoughts and actions, but we will not be alone. We have gathered much pleasing and giving support around us. We must venture onward, knowing that we are nurtured and stayed in life's embrace.

That to Which Our Lives Must Call

The human condition today, as reflected in individual lives, defines most of us as hybrids. In part we are alive, belonging to eternal life, and in part we are dead or dying, expressing the antithesis of life. Few, if any, are completely alive; and few, if any, are completely lost or dead. We as hybrids are not of the dark, but somehow the dark has entered us in varying degrees. At times we find ourselves in the gray or shadowy areas surrounding the night, and this puts us in a position to be both giving and taking. The taking acts are cold and manipulative, while the giving acts are warm and helpful. To one degree or another we are living in and out of life at different times. Our lives are filled with elastic moments; sometimes being pulled toward life, and at other times being pulled into the shadows. Manipulative thoughts and behaviors represent our biggest obstacles as they always separate and divide us from the world around us. This fragmentation causes the staying power of connection to be lost, leaving an opening for the intrusion of Less.

We are not Coins

Who we are
must be the same
on both sides
of our selves.
Not then good
but now bad.
Our sides are only in the middle
at the centers of our being.

As Sailors of Fortune, at any one time manipulative shadowing thought and behavior has been sequestered by our allegiance to life for life's sake. We have answered many of the challenges set before us upon the darkened and troubling sea. We understand there is More before us. The extension of our presence into this world suggests a deep satisfaction that we are coming free of Less and moving toward a lasting destination. We are now in a position to lend a hand toward those less fortunate still held in the tentacles of the darkness of manipulation and taking. We understand that the very thing that withholds the more side of life from the ones leaning toward less need to control and have delivered to them what they feel is absolutely necessary. Manipulation has become an integral part of their lives. Bringing those in the dark to understanding that life will keep and support them to the degree that they are open to it can be very frustrating. As they work to trust and then relinquish their manipulative control, we will need to provide them with support and large helpings of patience. Slipping and sliding will be evident as they work to walk away from the darkness. Returning to old habits that had seemingly worked for them will be very enticing. On some level they will know that the things they have, while not lasting, became theirs by way of the art and skill of manipulation. They were good at taking what they thought they wanted because so much of their lives was spent practicing how to get it.

The frustration for us and the struggle for them can be very intense. In times of slipping we can sense that behind their eyes they are saying, "No! I won't give it up!" What they are also saying in these periods of doubt is that they will continue to allow darkness to pour into their lives. Good people can be conflicted and confused. The shadows have crept into their lives leaving their mustardo very low in times of pain and sorrow, but when joy and happiness returns to them they are very loving and productive people.

The greatest challenge with the hybrid condition is to bring people back to a meaningful connection to the consistent expressions of caring. This reconnection can only occur in degrees as they simultaneously relinquish their manipulative skills. As they give up their need of taking, they will loosen the grip of the night. During these efforts they should begin to feel more intimate with the living world around them. Instead of feeling separated and divided they will begin to feel connected to the More of life.

Expressed attitudes and mindsets will reflect their leanings and the degree of recovery regarding their places in life. They cannot truly be with life if, in one instance, they are taking from it and at another time they are giving to it. When their minds and thoughts show allegiance with the night they are rigid, manipulative, and controlling. The transfer of information from their lives is specific; expressed in words, numbers, and formulas. When they meet with ignorance and doubt, their minds will attempt to replace what they see as wrong; even if, in fact, it is right. To support their positions they will offer up subduing, or absolute, pieces of information. However, when their minds are operating from caring, life-supporting perspectives they share information and knowledge with sensitivity. Ignorance and doubt of others are met with warmth and support.

> Right thought fuels our lives.
> Wrong thought fuels the night.

To truly clarify the darkness, their efforts must be employed in the service of life. The simple measures of caring and warmth will be indicative of how they are doing. When in the service of life they will know to support it, add to it, and not take from it. Acts of manipulation serve only the night whose shadows they are attempting to evade.

From the emotional center of hybrid people the level and expression of their passion is very indicative of where they are in the pull between life and darkness. Passion, not to be confused with anger, is one quality of life that disappears by degree from those who are slipping into the night. Passion underlies our characteristic of caring, and as caring improves passion can be assumed to be present. It is so important in our recovery from Less to know that, from an action and behavioral viewpoint, caring is the single most defining characteristic of those committed to life.

As awakening occurs people are held to a higher standard. The measures and consequences of their presence become more important. More is given to them, and more is expected from them. As long as they vacillate they are not moving toward life's call and may, in fact, be without its protection. A life must have just one unifying expression. We can't have goodness in our hearts with taking and deception in our heads. The struggle can be intense. When life-giving and sustaining behavior is defining the present, we are protected from the habits of the past which allowed the darkness in.

Freeing ourselves from the night and coming back completely to a caring life can be very difficult and even fraught with danger. The energy that is expended in this struggle to clarify our lives can lead to exhaustion, which leaves us open to subtracting motives. Neither the tentacle nor its night serving extensions will willingly release someone it has been wrapping up for the night. There will be a critical and defining point in our life. We must respond to the weight of the night, even while we are extending joy into creation. We don't accidentally become the darkness. We must avoid the thoughts and actions that can allow us to be seduced by the night serving behavior. We must clarify and declare ourselves!

Post-partum depression is a good illustration of how some, due to their hybrid identity, must fight and struggle to maintain a joyful existence. A woman brings forth a beautiful child, one of life's ultimate expressions of co-creation and life-giving celebration. Soon, however, the tentacle reaches out and troubles her to the very core of her being. Habits of her past have let the darkness in. Now she falls deep into a dark depression. Her mustardo is drawn off, and the night holds her under its spell. It has come for her and the life she's borne as well. It helps itself to a double helping of mustardo. As the situation escalates, the mom hears a voice she can't shake, and misery is her shadowy companion. In the worst-case scenario her child is harmed. A dark voice has guided her toward the wrong, and her other children may be harmed as well. In this instance, we see the tracks of the tentacle. The timing is uncanny. In the face of life's celebration is life's taking. A shadowy tentacle reached in for all the mustardo it could take. Living between the night and day was the opening that allowed the darkness in.

If life-giving and caring friends or professionals get involved in this mom's depression the outcome can be very different. Still, the struggle can be difficult and painful. Society in general is unaware of what's going on. If this mom hurts her children, severe punishment and incarceration may be her discipline. Separated from family, alone and confused, the tentacle will have easy pickings. As she hurts, others will try to lift her up, bringing her fresh allotments of their mustardo. In pain and separated from life, the night will feed upon her, consuming time and again the precious fluid from life's river.

A parting word for all of us hybrids, whether we have essentially lived in life or have lived in the tentacles of darkness believing that our presence on earth didn't matter. We all must remain in charge of our own deaths! The fact that much of our time was spent in life extends some opportunity for us. If we are aware that we have closed a door on this world we may be able to open one into another. It will all be in the blink of an eye, as the shadow world will be dancing about. We must not look their way. Instead, we should ask for Something More. If a door should open, we can enter in and the shadows will be gone forevermore.

When you die
the shadows will dance about.
Look not in this blink of your eye.
A door will open, just enter in.

As people seeking to extend the horizons before them, some will sense that they have already begun and have even essentially completed the preparations by opening a door to More and sweeping the darkness out. They will also serve to help open the door for others, which will further extend their value and fortune to life. As they continue to do this, so much more of life's splendor will be received.

Those of us who have heard the call and are responding to the relative urgency of these times of subtraction can benefit by what we might expect from different people with alternative behavior and values. We need to distinguish where our time might be well utilized, as opposed to where we may be wasting our time. We must clarify what interactions will nurture and protect our mustardo, and which would distinguish us from those who seem bent on throwing theirs away.

Life-Leaning Hybrids

It may be helpful to delineate some of the characterizing qualities that can distinguish one type of Life-Leaning hybrid from another. We could begin with those whom we might say are Happy at Home. The More of their lives is presently hidden from them by their singular focus on the immediate world around them. Reflection and meditation are not a big part of their lives. Going along to get along is their modus operandi. They are not easily opened to more because they are totally involved in what is right in front of them. It could be said that these are good people who are so focused on the little picture of their lives that they don't know that a bigger picture exists. The unseen aspects of their lives are kept from them by their complete focus on their present reality. They are limited by the objective processes of the mind, along with perceptions limited to earthly senses. Their 'reality' based thoughts and judgments are supported by culturally conditioned mental fences.

These people are many in number and at times they can be reached. In a broader sense we might think of them as being home reigned. Life for them is limited to their personal space, which may be beautiful, and which may have many life-giving qualities. They are so busy at keeping their houses in order, caring, working, and playing in the earthly world, that they do not fully realize that there is Something More just beyond their door and windows. Once introduced to the windows, they may begin to show interest and begin to reach for the More of their lives.

There are others who seem to operate almost exclusively upon logic and are essentially clueless. Emotion and passion are infrequent qualities of their expressions. When exposed to a scene of life's joy or natural beauty they offer little or no response, unlike how it might excite those who have awakened to More. For instance, if we were to ask them to spare the early spring blue bonnets that decorate their lawns for a few days, they would continue to mow their grass without thought. Ask them to recognize that there is something special about these early season flowers, and they are clueless.

They will pay to have flowers planted, but they will not give value to similar color or texture in the natural world. The flowers under their control, located where they want them, are the only color with value to them. Even so, they may not seem to notice the beauty of either. The beauty of life in general seems to go unnoticed, thus Clueless seems to be a good designation for them. Unfortunately, life does not constantly resonate within them. From raising their children to celebrating their religion, almost everything in their lives is done by form, recipe, and thought design. Their mustardo is often limited or is sometimes spent, leaving them with bouts of depression in a pervasive state of emptiness. Without someone lifting them up they will continue to function in this world upon the highs and lows of ambient emotion and limiting thought, until time runs out for them. Regrettably, the dance of life may not come their way again. Clueless people are not highly practiced in manipulation and consequent taking from our world, therefore life loses very little from them. Unto themselves, however, life is often lost. They are very difficult to reach and are just not open to newness or to Something More.

These people are harmless, although disconcerting to be sure. We need to limit our contact with them because they often seem to be surrounded by a percolating sea of sadness. We don't need it to splash upon us.

Clueless

When my life ends, that's it.
There is nothing more.
I'll live out
this life as I must.
There isn't going to be anything else.
Quite sadly, for them there may not.

It must be our hope that if the life of someone who is near or dear to us epitomizes the aforementioned limitations, our hopeful vision of the Something More of life may be able to entice them so that they may be open to processing the idea or vision. If they do we will soon see changes in their values and behavior that will indicate that this newness matters. They will also show by intrigue and questioning that they are open to beginning the process of assimilation, bringing the newness in and embracing it. Soon we can expect mental constructs to have accommodated toward beliefs and behaviors, which allow the expression of their lives to reflect an interest in belonging to the More of life.

The Light that Meets Them

The powers of darkness with which they play_
have bitten into our tomorrows
and are already chewing on our today.
To throw open a window
may not be enough.
They must also open their doors.
Knowing shall greet them, if they are willing to climb.
If the light that meets them should also blind,
we cannot wait and fall farther behind.

Outsiders, another group of hybrids, defines those people who are essentially empty on the inside but want to imply that they are satisfied and successful. There is always something on the outside that will cure, entertain, or excite them. Their inner selves are seldom rung up. Enjoying themselves by themselves is impossible. To meditate or reflect for even an hour would be torture. Outsiders are very uncomfortable being alone. All sorts of pharmaceuticals are employed to wake them up, make them rest, and respond to nervous tension. Their inner beings are buried so deeply they just can't reach them. It's been so long since they've called home, they've forgotten the number!

These people have lost touch with life's meaning and vigor, and they have difficulty retrieving mustardo from life's river. Their vigor is limited, and they seek to borrow it from others. Outsiders are almost completely dependent upon the external world for any zest for life that they may experience. Expressions of happiness and joy tend to be episodic. They are, however, intermittently capable of expressing half-hearted interest, with periods of celebration punctuated with bursts of laughter. Plans are made and times prearranged for their celebrations.

Now they know that it is time to eat, drink, and to be merry. A party, a birthday, a sporting event, or a reunion may be a good, safe opportunity for their celebrations and expressions of seeming happiness. If time, circumstance, and opportunity are prearranged, then happy they will be!

Outsiders

See all the fun I am having,
listen to the music turned up high.
Gosh, I must be something with my new dance steps.
How about my 'do,' and my new threads?

Is there a way to revive the Outsider to the spontaneity of joy and happiness, so that the celebration of life becomes a moment-to-moment thing? If someone were to throw these people a lifeline, they might be able to hold on to it. Can they grasp it tightly enough to be pulled back from the edge of lostness so they might be disentangled from the night? Will they extend the effort? They often advocate the theology of a distant God, which puts them at a safe distance from the 'all' of life. When all is said and done, they have faith that the heaven factor is going to work for them. Recovery is a slim but real possibility for them.

-

Life's Keepers

Awakening to and seeing the value of life and the promise of more presents us with the challenge to do what we can in these times. Many have already done this naturally, but the difference now may be that we have a deeper appreciation of the longer view of life and our place

323

in it. We may also have gained some appreciation for the fragility of life and creation in general. The challenges set before us ask that we extend these fortunes of life in many ways as different contexts and needs provide us with opportunities. As we stand in for life with our hands extended, conditions around us, as well as the timing of our personal awakenings, may identify us in different ways. Together we must extend the effort to keep life as life has always kept us.

As keepers and purveyors of life's promise, how might we appear to another? And how might another keeper appear to us? Our focus is in the near future, our attitudes are open and connecting, and our demeanor is clear and comforting. There is a serene, quiet, translucent quality about us. We are often alone but not lonely, while extending a warmth that can touch the soul of another.

> We draw from life's river,
> but we fish from the sea.
> We are all fishermen,
> we fish for one another.

Should there be reason to be afraid while we work to retrieve that of life (mustardo) from the world around us? The perceptible presence of our efforts may be of some concern to the powers that be, which always work to sustain things as they are. It is so important to remember that our efforts are of soft illumination and not confrontation. Even so we may be seen as a threat to those with limited seeing and hardened belief systems that have effectively withheld life's promise and wonder. From their perspective our threat may be implied as, "What's wrong with you? Such nice worker bees you used to be!" Still, however, we should not be afraid or hesitant in reaching out into the obscuring darkness to retrieve something or someone of value. Life's staying vibrations will comfort us. These currents may be invisible, but they reach deep within and around us, and their light will guide us as we joyfully attempt to trumpet life's yearning and awaken it. Where it sleeps, we will accomplish what we can without becoming attached to the results.

To what extent should we go while trying to retrieve someone from the shadows? As we call out to life our vibration will precede us. Beyond this, the most that can be done is communication with a simple smile, a few words, or a brief hug. A brief or willing exchange might proceed something like this:

"No I cannot carry you, you must find the strength from within you."

"But I just don't have the strength."

"You will gather strength from a now elusive fountain that you have not yet utilized."

"Where shall I find this elusive fountain?"

"It is found both within and about you. With a thirst for life's wonder, along with small efforts, this water can be lifted from its depth. As your thirst is satisfied this fountain will no longer be elusive, but instead it will be quite artesian. The more often you return to this fountain, the more easily its life sustaining water will evermore gush out. You will soon be able to confirm for yourself that without coming to this sustaining fountain, something precious is and was missing. The secret of this once elusive fountain is that both a thirst for it and the quenching waters from it are necessary. With this you will now have all that is necessary to lift the obscuring curtain and return to life's embrace."

When with it, all is right.
When away from it, all is wrong.

This is all that is being asked. Anything less is not enough, anything more is not necessary. Only now will we truly know if we will choose the onward journey or rather slipping and sliding into the deeper night.

The way to More
is to begin
to take less.

A long discourse of exhaustive reasoning will likely be ineffective and may instead leave us tired and exhausted. Should we bend for them or go halfway, so to speak? No! Never! We must not risk throwing away or contaminating the ample amount of mustardo that surrounds us. We must not overlook the many, maybe countless, unseen in our wakes that are supporting and depending upon us. Each of us must stay where our life is true and not bend to accommodate uncertain calls from the shadows. In all of this that we will do, remember that we do it for ourselves. We are the ones we have been looking for! Only then can we adequately stand in for the many wedged beings behind us. We must lead them and honor them, and we must do the things that remind us to stay where we belong. Our place in this time of recovery is to extend our presence if someone is returning from the night. We will receive them, but we cannot carry them. It is not always easily done; but, once again, we are not alone in this.

With so much to do
it's so nice to know
that we are not alone
in seeking life's glow.

There are already many among us who stand in for life like the grand trees of the forest. Similar to those grand arboreal beings we stand beautiful and strong, providing a space and place where many layers of life coexist simultaneously. We have quietly been touched by the Something More of life, and we encourage and facilitate it. In and around us the conditions of discovery and recovery are fostered and protected. Different challenges and opportunities to express our fortunes may further define and identify us. It will matter not how we identify ourselves. At times we are functioning as Sailors of Fortune. Sometimes we are serving best as lamplighters, radiating understanding and warmth from ourselves. Other times we are simply working toward keeping the cloak of green alive in our world, and thus we may be known as Edenites. Keepers refers to all of us who stand in for this world, regardless of how we answer the call of life. We are the Keepers of life's hope and promise, without whose trust and caring life may have already vacated these premises. At times the service asked of us will imply different things.

Throughout the trying and giving time ahead of us we will be protected from the cloaking shadows because we know who we are, and we know who and what we are looking for. The unrelenting strength and conviction of Life's Keepers are the fortunes in the gifts of life they carry with them. The implements of difference for these Keepers are kindness and compassion. They are committed to constantly carrying this goodness in a sometimes cold and uncaring world. Keepers are found the world over. Like the stars that adorn the night sky, they appear sometimes clustered in groups, but they are more typically scattered one here and one there, almost like dispersed brothers and sisters.

Some of these pillars and providers of life may not even know they are Keepers. This was true of my mother who somehow cooked for, bathed, and clothed fifteen children and cared for ten thousand chickens, a herd of cattle, and a large garden. What made these huge efforts so special was how caring was directed to where it was most necessary at the moment. She experienced joy in doing all of this, and she was nurtured by the relative health and gladness of all that she touched. Keepers like her are busy living their lives, and they are too humble to think of themselves as very involved and very important to life's journey. What these people have in common is that they are deserving, and they are prepared for the Something More that they have witnessed and stirred. While many of us need to be awakened, the Keepers are already seeing. They already sense, if not understand, the struggle looming before us, and they take the lead in the much that needs to be done. They are practicing with and freely utilizing life's most powerful energies. These are strengths about which the forces of darkness have no comprehension. They are pushing back the shadows by illuminating the night as they loosen the grip of the tentacle with their skills of caring and compassion. They are life's decisive advantage!

When a person's sense of value is lost or obscured she has little real sense of connection to the qualities of life. But if another can extend a sense of value to her, she may be able to be brought back to where we all belong. An arc of light may symbolize her recovery.

Keepers understand those who are lost under the weight and doubt of these times. They know that their burden of unknowing and inertia has much to do with the night, as the condition of darkness has taken or obscured their value and mustardo. Their light is so greatly diminished that they struggle to find their way out. Keepers skillfully find ways to extend a hand to them.

The Arc

We must somehow excite
holding for them a mirror.
Once they begin to see a little
they will be able to see a lot.
Light coming to them will join
with light coming from them.
Together, this light will warm and illuminate
and help them find their own way out.
In us and through us they will feel
creation's promise is still about.

The Lamplighters

As Lamplighters we attempt to awaken critical amounts of life within others. We encourage them to reclaim their mustardo and find their way out of the habits of darkness and confusion. By lighting an internal wick, which fires the promise of life in each individual, we are lifting the wounded up and avoiding the quandary of trying to carry them. The light given from their newly lit wicks will support and guide them as they couple again with the breath of life and separate from the nighttime shadows.

Love's Last Supper

Lift them up
Wrap your arms around them
Let them see
So they too will believe
None may be left behind
Before life's last meadow gate
Is closed upon them

The fact is we can't carry anyone. Each must come back to life in his own time. But what a gratifying cause this will be, extending our fortunes and seeing so many being found who once were lost. There may be no greater good than this, to coax a sleeping comrade out of his slumber and witness this fellow sailor coming back to where he belongs.

As time and light continue to diminish there will be a sense of urgency. The days of prodding, coaxing, and explaining are over. If there are still some who may be recovered, it must occur spontaneously. Our fortunes will burn as a bright torch in the late evening light, and the hope is that some will yet be awakened. Our torch offers both protection and illumination as we move quickly away from the never-ending night closing in about us. As Lamplighters we may assist others in finding their way, but they must follow without fuss or hesitation. Our beckoning light will allow them to differentiate their newfound hope from the dangerous places they have been.

Edenites

As depicted in one view of creation, the Garden of Eden is described as a vision of what the world could and should have been like. Edenites continue to support and nurture that vision. They understand how humankind's excessive eating from the Tree of Knowledge has led to the troubling world of today.

From within the peaceable circle of life, the Edenites sustain a quiet accord with this world, and they may add a larger view of understanding for all of us. The Edenites' simple and reverent relationship with the earth reminds us that we may have eaten the fruit of the Tree of Knowledge, but now we are threatening to consume the tree and the entire garden in which it resides!

If, in fact, our excessive appetite for knowledge has yielded us countless facts and formulas that we point to as our intelligence, then how did we become so oblivious with regard to a healthy and sustaining relationship with our world? Is there something about the excessive consumption of the 'fruit' of this tree that we have misunderstood? Perhaps without the shadows cast from a tempting serpent there would not be a person among us who would kill the goose that lays the golden egg. The knowledge and technology that has evolved from the 'forbidden fruit' may be something we did not need or want.

So, Edenites, we know who we are. We need to come out from our protective gardens and join in the work that needs to be done! The quiet way of our lives has provided us with bunkers of protection against the darkness, and we can help others navigate its uncertain waters. Our dream for life is not yet dead, nor does it need to die. We are needed to assist in igniting the glow in others, so that they might see what we already know. We must encourage them to awaken from their slumber and place their hands upon the oars. Together we will share a reverence for life while keeping our dream alive.

Keepers of life's lasting promise, this is our birthright and it is also our duty. We must continue to hold our love high for it is this world's brightest star. As we are alive with it, others shall follow its beckoning in the middle of their nights. Following the compelling glow of our presence, they may lose their doubts and never again feel small. As they awaken from a cold and deep sleep, our way shall hold out a life for them that will never again be taken away.

Your love is your brightest star.

It must not be bound up by selection or definition.

As you travel it must belong

to one and all.

As we reach into the darkness to retrieve others we must remember to protect who we are. When we feel exhausted, tired, or even confused, we must know to step back from our work in the darkness. One who is weak in the light of day may more easily fall in the cold of the night. Recuperation, among other things, will be a type of fasting from this world. While working at awakening those around us we will need to remove ourselves from this world's demands. We must reassert our navigation to avoid drifting. We must move away from shapeless thought and the entertainment of ill play or idle values. Morsels of this world's foolishness have already cost the lives of so many, and through association they may now be obscuring the way of others toward the eternal day.

There is much at stake. My concern is that, while some may be freed of the tentacle's grip, others who are reluctant but not completely lost to life have been deeply wounded by the night and may experience its compressing hold upon them, even while they hunger to be free of it. It will be with those held by restraining forces that our struggle will become most intense. Through these deeply conflicted people the tentacle will remain an active threat to us and to our onward journey. If we are successful here, the forces of darkness will slip back into the deeper night, and we can separate from it. If we are not successful, we may need to leave those who won't awaken from their nighttime sleep alone with the darkness. A last and most difficult act would be to separate and divide. This late twilight hour would become life's last dance of resolution and clarification. The time would come to be known as the night of the watchtower.

Keepers, all hands on deck! Even if some must be left behind, this vessel must remain seaworthy. If this face of ourselves and our existence here on earth is lost prematurely, the rest of our being will remain. We will remain alive, secure, and protected in the other spaces to which we belong. Our mystical and fluid self will remain suspended in and about the space of earth within her sister ships.

There is so much before us, so much made eternally available to us, that clearly we are honored to stand for life in these times. If we keep this Something More in focus, we will go happily about the difficult work of clarifying the deck of our vessel. The very existence experience itself will be firmed up or relinquished in the process. This is not idle play that we are about.

It must be life and more of it,
nothing less will do!

Life's last calling signals the time to push the darkness out. The cleansing that needs to be done will reveal those who still might come. Human minds have given the night something to cling to and have afforded the darkness a comfortable home. Attempting to discern what has been completely lost from what is merely obscured by darkness may be our greatest challenge in the coming of this last day. We must skillfully enter the space of we-ness between ourselves and others to reclaim what belongs to life before it succumbs to the night.

We will move along together now as the recently recovered travel with us. It is only the light of our collective mustardo that will keep the edge of night from surrounding us. As we traverse the harbor straights, our final passage will be the great divide. We will finally be separated from the threat of never ending night as we break into the awesome, lasting light of eternal day.

As we approach this final passage care and compassion will be our fortunes. We will be as brothers and sisters to those who have recently been recovered. As siblings of fortune, one gets up when another gets tired. When one becomes exhausted another carries on. One remains certain in the face of another's doubts. All together now we are clearly friends of fortune, brothers and sisters in life's family.

Life is Calling

Brothers and sisters
all together now.
If they cry, we shall comfort them.
Should they laugh, we shall laugh with them.
If they extend their hands
our goodness shall be given to them.

If they have doubts
we shall reassure them.
If they should stumble or cringe,
in old habits of darkness,
we shall ask them up.
Our light will illume for them.

We must respond to life's last call knowing that we will follow the evening light before the cold and lasting night settles upon this age. We know who we are, and we know who we are looking for. We must hold a light gently for the many that will be found deep in the shadows of the night. It is not a shadow of their making, but it nonetheless cloaks them in a cold night's stupor. We must look for an arc of light and listen in the chilling night air for anyone calling.

As we attempt to reach them we may need to reassure them by explaining. From life's light their rightful domain, their journey, has brought them adjacent to the deep darkness of space. They have somehow slipped into the shadows, and night is settling upon them. In trying to negotiate these shadows they may have jettisoned their feeling faculties along with a genuine enthusiasm for the life to which they do belong. Habits of their minds have left them confused, vulnerable, and separated from us. Even now the nighttime web is spun tighter about them. We must remember to not allow those whom we have helped to cloak our conscience with their shadows. They cannot be held fast by our hands alone, they must also be extending theirs.

As your hand reaches
into the darkness,
their hands must extend willingly
into the light.

As those close to Life's Keepers are protected and freed of the night, they begin to join in life's call. A safety zone begins to form, and those within are protected and free.

So Keepers, be willing to be willing. Go forth into the night, knowing the extreme difficulty and challenges that await us. Always go forward enthusiastically. Protect your mustardo at all times! If things go badly, return to where we once belonged, where we are warmed and life is long.

So much shall depend upon our perspective.
With an outlook to the rest,
we shall achieve the best.

Be vigilant that the satisfaction of the newly awakened is emerging from their being and is not distilled from another's offerings or, even worse, feigned from the night itself. A basic trust should be evident about them and integral to their return. Their path back must be their own; they must not seek to borrow another's. Their minds may navigate but must not dominate. Thoughts and fears, questions with demands, may not belong to them at all.

When working at the edge of darkness,
guard your happiness like it is your home.
It may be shared as it is received,
then it must be guarded
and grown as it is freed.

If they are coming back,
happiness they will not lack.

-

In our very last moments we shall all belong to the Watchtower. Our eyes will strain looking for late lambs, so that they will not be left behind when the last gate closes on life's meadow. Are there any others coming?

The Watchtower

The Watchtower is all but over
Only moments remain
A large golden orb settles into the sky above us
Time is all but gone
The great divide is complete and locked up
Our mustardo has slipped from the tentacle's grasp
Is it content to see us go?
We never know how to ask
Without our light and borrowed warmth
The long galactic night froze up tight
How good it is
We now reside happily in this world
Of the double sun
Time is naught but in the past
In ages long gone by
We do not see it, nor do we need it
So many lives
It's done
The night is lost and far
Be gone
It shall never be our home

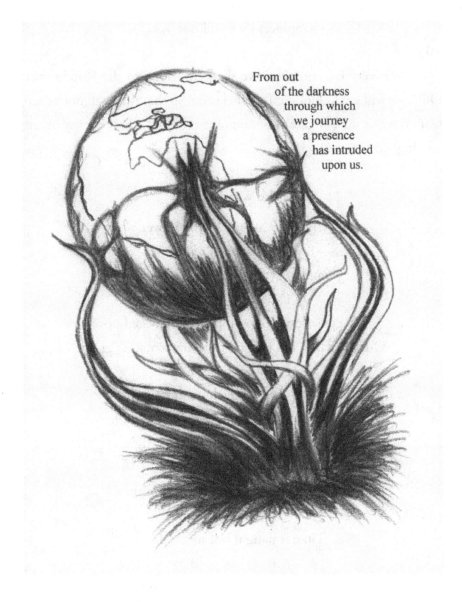

From out
of the darkness
through which
we journey
a presence
has intruded
upon us.

10

The Tentacle

Entering into Darkness

Accepting the proposition that a low flow in life's river is evidenced in this time of subtraction, and considering the assumption that some force or entity may be drawing off its precious fluid, we have come to a point where we must reflect upon the conditions that precipitate such circumstances: the force, the tentacle, and its domain, the darkness of the night.

For those living on the earth today things have become quite sticky. In fact stuck may be a better term. Appreciating that we may be stuck is evidenced in the power of Less and reflected in the process of subtraction. Remembering how it was and who we were and now are can add a great amount of understanding of this nighttime force as well. In place of the illuminating conditions of our beginning, unknowing is obscuring our place in life and deeper darkness is looming. As we struggle to sustain the More and avoid the Less, being alive may be less than fun.

Dancing with the Darkness

From the all of life
and upon a
realm of always day,
we have journeyed into the night.
Now deep into perplexing darkness
we are found in fright.
The mind, body, psyche, and soul
are really trying to see
how all this darkness
is different from me.
They say there is more night
behind us
than obscuring darkness
before us.

In the early times, the entire fleet of worlds and the realities that defined them were very knowable. While each realm expressed unique structures and relationships, all fit nicely together. The cohesion in this amoebic-type fleet of life was afforded by life's connectedness, the force of belonging. Before the darkness set up about us we knew ourselves to be integrated beings of different worlds.

Into each place
we had a face.

This possibility leads to one of the most exhilarating, though admittedly most potentially difficult to believe, propositions of the

Something More of our lives. Individuals expressed one face in this world but also belonged to other places in other worlds.

So, though we journeyed as a single burst of creation, we simultaneously belonged to different realities and different worlds and were passengers on different vessels. A space between separated and defined one vessel from another. As we entered the darkness a very long age ago, the space between us was easily impregnated with the night, obscuring our connectedness and much more.

As we approached the
place of night
looking back at our
space of light,
we sensed indeed
there was much to do.
As we noted how deep
the darkness grew
long shadows were cast
such that we
lost much, forgot even more,
and were left helpless to hold
the nighttime out.
Much darkness entered in.

As we were born from sacred life, the realms to which we belonged and the space between these realms was also sacred. Now, as we note just how much of the darkness has infiltrated our vessel of earth and the minds of its inhabitants, it's abundantly clear how the space around us was first compromised. To enter our world the night had to first infiltrate the space that enveloped us, the space in which our earth is suspended. It did this quite easily as we entered the sea of darkness in the manner of our intention. Not knowing the nature of this obscuring darkness we weren't able to repel it. In a very short time our early perceptions of who we are and the conditions of our journey were obscured.

Here are some of the conditions meant to steady our bearing during our long journey. From the beginning of our parting it was understood that the great mass of darkness before us was uncertain and maybe even unknowable. The staying intention of our journey was to carry our presence in the way of life into this darkness. It was understood that if our presence was not great enough to warm and illuminate this darkness, then we were to go onward. We would not be forgotten. "There is a place made before you of protected harbors."

And of those conditions in our parting;
If we cannot warm the cold
If we cannot illuminate the dark
Then, carry on our wayward ones
Lift your sails and go on
Toward the world of the double suns.

I truly believe that the testimony of my life is given in part so that we might be assured that the multiple worlds and realities that have protected me at the edge of life will now offer their considerable care to bring us back to where we once belonged. As I have been protected, we together may be protected as well. Is not the Something More both a message of recovery and a sign along our way?

From those early days of our parting, "From time to time, a sign will be given you and you shall know the way through this darkness.

Together we will guide you throughout your unknown journey and if necessary we will find a way to help navigate your safe return." As regards our safe passage through the unknown of this great sphere of darkness remember this, "Above all else always travel forward, do not turn around. Most importantly, do not become like the darkness!"

> I really can't say for sure
> it's really hard to know
> lost maybe, forsaken no
> a meteoric light must show
> just before this time of last
> into the day our creation pass.

Maybe we can better know the nature of the night by considering some possibilities. Groping for understanding may be the best that we can do, since its heavy darkness will not allow us to see clearly, and we have been admonished not to become like it.

Let us reflect briefly upon the possibility that as life utilizes the mass of this dark sphere to express its living and dynamic qualities, some amount of resistance may be expressed. In other words the very basis of structures and forms borrowed from the darkness, which have been animated by life and sustained by mustardo, have some inherent un-life-like characteristics. At times when these living beings are troubled by low levels of mustardo this inherent underlying resistance becomes more salient, allowing the darkness in. Even with this base possibility, we are left with more questions than answers. Has our voyaging into this darkness placed us in harm's way? Absolutely. Were sleeping demons stirred as we entered their realm? Did we thus create a great disturbance and as a result cause darkness to whirl about? How could life coming into darkness cause such a fuss? Did the space of darkness belong to us? No! Is it painful to any living or existing entity when piercing light meets darkness? Maybe so.

To illustrate this incompatibility, I refer to some impressions drawn from the clinically depressed patients I would attempt to treat during my university days. The clinically depressed may be more subdued by darkness than almost anybody. There is little if any buoyancy in them as they express different levels of despair. At times I would greet them with joy and gladness, which would sometimes seem offensive to them. It was not unusual for them to display their discomfort by responding with angry snarls, spitting, and growling. Clearly my 'up' state or presence elicited very uncomfortable reactions from them. In response to their reactions I learned to enter their personal space in a guarded, even-tempered, almost serious way.

We may have awakened something from a deep sleep. Angry, it may be telling us that our night is its day! The warmth and compassion of life may feel like an infectious pathogen to the rigid cold of the night.

So, though we may have come with life, it may be incompatible with what we have found. The presence within this space of darkness may be mostly inclined toward our consumption in order to preserve the space it occupies. Despite the best of intentions, we may have awakened and threatened a consuming being, the tentacle.

Have I, or has anyone, actually seen this being? Maybe not, but it seems important that we give ourselves the opportunity to conjecture about the nature of what may be happening here in order to better prepare ourselves for what is in our way and to realize the threat of what is upon us, the threat of the tentacle.

I've chosen this name because of the myriad of ways and means by which it draws the mustardo from our lives. Though somewhat interchangeable with the darkness, the term the tentacle may be a more authentic representation of this sinister force, since much of what has been lost and taken away displays some kind of intention in its removal, implying that something with presence from the shadows might be involved.

Whether we call it the tentacle or not, we need to recognize that there is a being or process which is drawing off our mustardo while effectively subtracting life from our world. When we begin to recognize this process for what it is, we can encourage those around us to stop feeding it. Without access to our mustardo it begins to lose its prey. The drinking straw dries up, and the tentacle loses its stealth hold over us.

> There is this something else
> in the equation,
> much in the way of
> the Something More.
> Less is not what
> we were hoping for.

Some may want to call it the dark force or even the devil. Regardless of nomenclature, this something else has taken so much away that it demands our respect, and we need to know how it is manifested so that we can effectively deal with it. My suspicion is that, not unlike the functioning arms of an octopus, the many extensions of the tentacle may be deeply involved in the threat to our existence experience.

We might liken the presence of the tentacle's dark extensions to the physical spaces of darkness between the stars, with all the degrees of cold that exist in those dark places. Where the many octopus-like arms return to a central location may not be unlike the black hole of astrological implications.

Could life slay this beast? I think not. We came with illuminating warmth. Doing this kind of battle is not our purpose, nor has our preparation readied us for such a struggle. Embroiled in confrontation we might find that as we cut off one of its many arms two might return, and engaging this tentacle may lead it to unleash its full rage upon us. We cannot know what ultimate power it may have. Our best effort must be to remove ourselves from it, to understand and accept that it is there, and to avoid it. Its reach seems almost limitless, and nothing good can come from contesting it on its own terms. Is there a way to envision how it has entered our lives and the threat to our existence as well as the Something More?

How It Is and Was

Although I cannot say that I have ever personally seen or directly known the tentacle, I am comfortable with the concept and some of the parameters which characterize it. Directly or through intermediaries, something is drawing precipitously from the promise and purpose of our life's journey. There is a great deal of inferred evidence that points to the tentacle being present. If it is not a being or entity it is clearly a force to be identified and separated from. As a force the tentacle may very well be unintended yet dangerously inseparable from the darkness it is so capable of whirling about. Regardless of what it is, it is capable of connecting with our minds like an electrical charge to a copper wire. When that connection occurs the qualities of darkness like doubt, despair, need, and greed flow readily in, while the vigor of mustardo flows out.

From whence has this troubling being or force come? In so much as it represents the antithesis of life, it may be difficult to know, but we can assume that the edge of darkness is where we have made contact with this tentacle and nighttime will refer to its presence. Although we were sent as a creative breath to bring the light of life to this great space of darkness, we did not know that such a taking force would inhabit it. Thus, I question our ability to successfully deal with this nighttime resident beast. It may have been that we came with a day vision and did not possess the nocturnal faculty of seeing necessary to know that the great realm of darkness was involved with such a contradiction of life and light. As a result the length of time we have been present in this time and space of so much promise, intention and purpose are coming up short and are even threatened.

I share this ancient story.

Other vessels came this way, journeying into the edge of night. The travelers were shackled with unknowing, which caused them to be set adrift upon the great sea. For unknown reasons a web of darkness ensnared them. Losing their mobility they become lost from where they should have been. Some of these vessels seemed scorched by fire, while others appeared iced over, saddening the entire creation that so much was lost.

But the breath of creation has been set forth again, and now here is where we are. Is there something to be salvaged of those great losses? When we look around ourselves, we must agree that much has already been taken away. Many among us seem to be asleep. The question is, can we do it? Can we make a difference in this space of night? If not, then let us be on our way toward the eternal life from which we parted so many ages ago. This is such a critical personal and collective time. It is a time of preparation, a time for us to lift anchor and move out upon the open sea.

The call has gone out
to which we must respond,
listen now to what's being asked
that our life must last.

We must commit ourselves to the preparation for the onward journey. If, during this time, something else can be done, we will know. One is our beginning number. As we prepare within and around ourselves we will complete these preparations together. As we answer the call of parting, we shall leave as one as well.

Life is just too precious
to leave it all behind.

This will not be as simple as lifting our ship's anchor and unfurling our sails. The vessel of earth will need a renewed reverence and kindly stewardship, which must be proclaimed in order to ready her for passage upon the etheric and open sea. Great effort will be needed to reclaim those of life from the encroaching night that threatens to surround us and lock us in its clasp. We must awaken again to who we are and simultaneously separate from who we are not. This is possibly the most critical process at hand. The tentacle is characterized as a taking force and is speculated upon as drawing off life's river. It is not our lives that it wants, but rather our mustardo, the essence of what moves us.

> We will be well again
> and also well on our way.

In the midst of all this preparation how can we know where the many extensions of this tentacle might be involved? By its very nature, we can't really know it. We would have to be of it or kin to it to penetrate the great depth of darkness in which this force or being resides. What we can know is that our critical, sustaining mustardo of life can be and has been taken and not returned. Intellectually, again, we may need to be content with observing:

> Much of the loss,
> conflict, and confusion
> which we see
> is caused by
> something we do not see.

The notion of the tentacle is a point of reference for the subtracting function of this adversary that we cannot see. Some degree of confirmation may result from looking for its tracks.

The Tracks of the Tentacle

Before leaving this discussion of the tentacle's threat to us through its access and subsequent manipulation of our minds we must again assume that much of the pain, unnecessary hurt, and loss that we experience is caused by something we do not see. The tracks of the tentacle are abundantly clear. Consider this metaphor from the farm.

On the farm the fox was a foe with considerable skill and cunning. There was almost no thought or deed this mythical four-legged predator could not accomplish. Stories shared around the winter fireplace would invariably touch upon the slippery wiles of this nighttime robber. Every so often accumulated evidence would reveal that the myth had its roots in reality, as it became clear that something had been in the henhouse.

Chickens would be skillfully stolen, often without evidence until their numbers were noted to be appreciably less than what they should have been. At this point, the fox would no longer be the cunning subject in late night tales, but rather it became a formidable adversary that needed to be addressed.

One of the fox's unique qualities was his skill of deception. Taking his prey to his den left very little obvious evidence of its theft. However, when it became clear that a thief from the night had been about there was little doubt as to who had feathers in his teeth!

Two questions were immediately placed before us. Where was it getting into the henhouse, and where was its den? The detective work began by looking for tracks. Depending on weather conditions and where we were looking, the tracks might be easy or difficult to find. If we could find the tracks we could find the fox. But could it have been a raccoon or a woodchuck? It was always the nature of the taking that gave the offending identity away. The fox was just so sly! The prey and its carcass would always be taken away. No other farm predator was as cunning and as skilled. For all of the other predators such as the wildcat, hawk, mink, and raccoon there were always signs of struggle. Feathers were strewn about and carcasses left behind. But the fox was different. So much damage could be done before anyone knew the chickens were taken, and then when the discovery was made exhaustive efforts began to out-fox the fox. Finding and following the tracks was critical. Nothing facilitated this endeavor as well as freshly fallen snow. Footprints leaving the henhouse almost always led directly to the fox's den, making cornering the elusive quarry easier. But tracks in the meadows or woods, leading ultimately to the henhouse, were a more difficult challenge. One could become exhausted while attempting to follow the many twists and turns of the cunning predator.

With regard to the taking away from creation, we may never completely know the den of the nighttime thief. Clearly, many tracks may lead from a cold and dark sphere, but that place is always dark, and unless we are of the darkness we will never completely know it.

As with the cunning fox, the theft of life's mustardo is so incremental and neat that the earliest evidence may be deduced from the accumulated loss of another's character or saneness.

The fox was so slippery that the remaining chickens seemed not to express an alarm that might indicate the farmers' loss until the crime screamed out by the sheer loss of eggs in the basket.

Where and how the theft from our lives is occurring is something we can begin to understand. The hand and mind of humankind is clearly implicated in these times of subtraction. How is the mind contaminated, and how are the hands being moved against us? Are the hand and mind of humankind among the telling tracks?

We are so accustomed to pointing a finger to explain away a misuse of law and custom. He did it! She did it! They did it! But did the accused, who may very well have guilt written over them, and may even have blood on their hands, really do it? Or are he, she, and they tracks of a cause from something we do not see?

Sometimes it's the really bizarre theft of life that allows us to open our eyes to consider what may be going on. When an otherwise good and caring mother throws her children off of a bridge, she may be charged with taking these children's lives, but did she really do it? Or are these precious, lost lives tracks to something else? Who or what compromised the mind that guided the hands that released these young lives into the water?

If we are willing to study the process of our personal losses then we may come to recognize that tracks are here as well. Something is happening. It may not be clear what it is, but there are correlations that begin to look like causes. Tracks of the tentacle may appear as predator 'foxes' in our personal lives. If a subjective sense of loss correlates often enough with someone's presence, we can be sure there is some relationship.

As is true in general, losses of our personal mustardo will occur most often when we are tired, depressed, or running on empty. At these times it may be most important that we know who is slipping into our kitchen in fox feet. We need to trust our feelings, and we will know who or what needs to be avoided. We must also look for tracks directly connecting us to taking forces in our mind play. Again, it seems evident that we are most vulnerable to the mind's manipulation, from within or without, when we are exhausted. When our vigor is low, our confidence in ourselves is depressed. We become vulnerable when something leaves us fearful, angry, or hating for whatever reasons. In these states of being we are most inclined to reach out into the world to fill a void, which we sense within us. We must be careful of what we reach for, for we may not get what we need. Seldom can something beyond us satisfy an emptiness felt within us. In the words of a visionary student of enlightenment,

> "Don't just do something,
> stand there."

In the face of challenges with unclear consequences we must first nurture the inner sanctuary of our being. We should rest, listen to our favorite music, embark on a refreshing hike, or share good times with a friend before choices are made and lasting decisions are acted upon.

It really challenges us to reflect for a second on the cosmology of this assumption of the tentacle from the night. Some suggest that these truly hurtful acts are a condition of our world; that the stress and uncertainties cause the structures of life to fail and turn against itself. But if wrongness was in the air around us then our creation may never have come so far. We could also expect many more illustrations of other than human life forms deceiving and maiming their own kind. So if we postulate this taking force emanating from the inky sphere into which creation journeyed, it becomes much more comprehensible and helps us to understand how our highly developed central nervous systems can also be utilized to move humankind against itself in incremental, but effective draconian like acts.

I have to believe that the tracks of the tentacle are evident in most of the really severe trespasses by one man upon another or upon the natural world. I do not believe that men and women are singularly responsible for the sinful bloodletting of insane proportions so evident in our recent history. One bad human hand could not do this deed without an outside dark force companion, the tentacle, playing a part. There is nothing within the genesis of life that could account for such cruel and taking actions. Hitlers are not born but rather become.

On a larger scale, war is an equally difficult thing to explain away without speculating about something at play beyond the obvious powers. There may be no clearer illustration of how intrusive thoughts and beliefs can aggress upon people and cultures. Here offenses are said to have occurred, and lines are drawn. Peace is foreclosed, and aggression is parlayed behind guns and bombs. Eventually the combatants tire and the conflict ends or is put on hold. The underlying differences often remain, but no longer seem so unacceptable. Great amounts of spent blood have been poured over goodness, and many who have outlasted the struggle are left wondering why. Why indeed! Who or what fomented the need or cause of this great loss? Beyond the actual loss of life, the spilled blood, and the contaminated water and land, is the long lasting disruption of people's sense of safety and basic trust. Large shadows derived from the conflict combine with the unknowing darkness that initiated the war, and precious ripples of good intent are lost from life's river, evidencing a drop in the flow of mustardo once again.

War, with its taking of life, always seemed accursed to me. Growing up in Gettysburg, the site of gruesome battles in the Civil War, surrounds a person with clear evidence of both the curse and the celebration that conflict can bring upon the life of humankind. My father and uncles told one particular story that left a deep and frightening impression on me. Their father had hopped and walked for three miles upon the battle carnage without his shoes ever touching the ground. His pathway was so thickly paved with the corpses of soldiers and horses following Pickett's Charge that he could stride effortlessly over one after the other. Death and dying had become so intrusive in this life that the moribund cries of suffering soldiers did not interrupt his play on the war's ravages. Despite his wretched footpath, he trudged onward, making his way from his family barn, which was being used as a Civil War hospital, deep into the battlefield where the bodies were being retrieved and thrown onto piles.

Hearing such a story from my kin made me shiver, and I often pondered its implications. Even as a child I suspected that something in my world was terribly wrong! On other occasions, the many stories of the Battle of Gettysburg held out some perplexing hope for my world and me.

Sitting on the large granite boulder known as Little Round Top, I was completely intrigued by the historical accounts of the Spangler's Spring. During the first and second days of this ferocious battle these springs offered refreshing water to the soldiers of both the north and the south. Opposing soldiers, sometimes brothers, would leave their weapons at a distance and gather as fellow human beings at these thirst-quenching springs. There they would drink, have a conversation, and perhaps share a cigarette. It astounded me that five minutes later they could be dying upon one another's bayonets. In the face of war the opposing combatants could agree, for the sake of this water, to allow their humanity to hold sway over the dark killing fields. Today's low flow of mustardo is equally as precious. It is as necessary for our lives as the sustaining waters of Spangler's Spring were for these warring brothers. Differences between men and conflicts, between our vessel and us, might be equally mitigated if they were put on hold. Wouldn't it be something if we could all quench our thirst for the kind of sustenance that might allow life to know the full measure of her inhabitants? One such day might provide the collective opportunity for all of us.

One day of sharing
Against the every day of taking
That we might see
And understand
That which truly matters

So often after bizarre crimes and brutal acts, the perpetrators may be at a loss to explain what happened or why. How can it be that an otherwise caring mother suddenly hurts her own children? Unlikely acts of devastating proportion often leave the apparent perpetrator speechless and lost. Some might suggest that the devil made them do it, which may have an element of truth considering that this is an often-used caricature to explain the otherwise unbelievable. When we are able to elicit a response from these people, something is invariably said to have happened in their minds; a voice was heard, or an unbearable thought overwhelmed their actions. The tracks of the tentacle are evidenced upon them.

Recently in a moderately rural county in Pennsylvania, a teenager shocked the community and the nation when he confessed to the brutal slayings of a childhood friend and his parents in their home as they slept. With no apparent motive, this typical high school sophomore, who worked part time in a fast food restaurant and was well liked by his neighbors and schoolmates, viciously stabbed these unlikely adversaries to death in their beds. This boy was such an improbable suspect that the crime went unsolved until he tearfully confessed to his own father. Shocked and horrified, his father contacted the authorities. His acquaintances described him as happy, smart, funny, and gregarious. The police and the community struggled to comprehend how a slightly built, mild mannered child could single handedly wreak such havoc. Even more incredible, how could this socially normal young man behave in such a beastly manner against his best friend? And all of this contradictory havoc occurred in a short, thirty-minute period of time against a life of good and caring acts.

It is startling to witness the responses and looks of dismay that come from those close to the perpetrator following this type of anti-social behavior. Invariably we hear a friend or parent say, "This is not the person I knew. He would never do such a thing." If it's not the person they knew, then who is it? Perhaps it is their friend or relative, but with the boundaries of the night intruding upon him. The tracks of the tentacle are more than likely traversing in close proximity to their minds during these tragic events.

There are many instances of bizarre and unexpected hurtful acts coming from otherwise good and caring people. Other than keeping our lives filled with goodness and avoiding empty or depressed states of being, it seems that there is little we can do to avoid manipulation of our minds by outside forces. If there is such a prowling, invasive tentacle force, can we know and understand more about it?

How perceptible is this taking presence? A homicide detective from the city of Los Angeles confided, " I have personally investigated over eighty homicides in this past year. I collected information and compiled notes. I was so sure I could identify some basic cause that was underlying these killings."

"And have you?" she was asked.

"No, she replied, "I thought maybe drugs, then perhaps economic conditions, then maybe gang politics. None of these causes could explain the death and brutality that we are experiencing."

"Is there nothing you can point to?" she was asked.

"Yes," she responded, "on each occasion there was one constant, the smell!"

"The smell?"

"Yes, the smell of evil was in the air!"

Time and time again the lady detective noted this perception. Looking over her notes, she was shocked at the constant connection. The cause could not easily be explained, but it could be perceived.

<blockquote>
If you do not belong to it
you cannot know it.
If you do belong to it
you cannot separate from it.
</blockquote>

If we are behaving in such a way as to be withholding life from ourselves, then we are less than complete and we are making ourselves available for the tentacle's taking. In such a case we are losing both coming and going. Sadly we are incrementally becoming lost to life.

Becoming Lost to Life

<blockquote>
It is in the creation
that is born to all.
It is what is made to be
as is what surrounds all life we see.
When the mind is engaged without the rest
then self-centered acts may be the best.
When the next voice is, "Oh we must!"
then the acts of taking end in dust.
</blockquote>

"But these are mine for the taking!
What value? You say I'm forsaking
whose hands which hath so seen nature's fall,
these hands which hold the dying call."

If the tentacle has been involved in our lives, a concerted effort will be necessary to unleash ourselves from it. The most direct avenue to separating from its taking habits is to revalue our lives in the way we live them. If we remember to factor in our feelings and compassion along the way, we will always have an intuitive counterbalance against life-taking coercion when it comes from our minds.

When we feel a persistent urging such as, "Do it, they deserve it," "Don't let feelings get in the way," "We can make a great deal of money here," or "What an advantage we can gain!" we need to step back and wonder. Whose mind is saying this, anyway? To whom does it really belong? Is this how the tempting serpent utilizes us to justify life-taking deeds?

In this light, some of us may come to suspect that we have been tempted. As we have reached out into the world in efforts to find or take things to make us more complete, hurtful acts and thoughts may have become part of us. We may suspect that some of our needs, thoughts, and acts have been manipulated, and perhaps they were. Our minds may have granted so much access to the tentacle that nighttime has become our frequent and familiar guest. It's true that we need this mind faculty to negotiate our way in the world of time and place, but it was never intended for it to grant debilitating access to the center of our being.

We grant it an opening while we are awake
and it sneaks in while we are asleep.
The tentacle's presence
with its extensive reach
has taken so many
to its lair of sleep.

But we do not want to fall into the cold of never-ending night, as so much and many before us have. Now is the time for us to guard our mustardo, to recuperate, reinvigorate, dare to believe again, and dare to awaken from our sleep.

If we answer the call of life to clarify and express the qualities of goodness within us and toward the world around us, we may quickly feel or face unexpected resistance. In place of clarity, confusion may seem to rule. We must remain strong and not be surprised by this. We are, after all, breaking out of a web that was wrapping us up for the night. We may sense a concentrated effort against us. When we attempt to extend a helpful hand it may seem to be bitten. Are these tracks that are beginning to emerge from freshly fallen snow which is, of course, our renewed value of ourselves? The resistance we now experience may be the result of something bigger and more shadowy than the doubt and confusion of those around us.

The struggle to awaken almost always meets reluctance, often indicating the tentacle's tracks. If the conflict is a result of the bigger force from the shadows, the tentacle, then we must be prepared. There will be nothing fair or open about the combat set before us and against us. If there is to be any direct acknowledgment of its presence it will only occur when we are beaten down. By day it may come in the form of a human face we've tried to help but whose countenance bears a sickly smirk as they imply we had it coming. By night, a tentacle keeper in the form of a troubling ghost or phantom may enter our sphere by way of a nasty dream or troubled sleep. How might it look if we should ever encounter its presence or tracks, showing the effect of its hurtful involvement upon a human's face?

> Imagine the face of absolute fright
> and then you might know
> that you are seeing
> the foe from the night.

In general, the presence of the tentacle's work can also be seen in a fellow human when we have been betrayed in trust or friendship. What a disgusting look we may encounter. When the betrayal has been most hurtful and complete, the nighttime server may display a pathetic look of gloat and sick success. If we are able to recover from this open-heart wounding, we will better understand the field of battle and never be quite so vulnerable again. Others who assist us in our recovery might explain that this injustice and abuse is human nature. We will know differently. The pain has been too deep, the timing too critical. Yes, our pain may have been delivered through the mind and hands of a human looking person, but clearly it was someone who was manipulated by a very dark force.

Assessing the timing of betrayal and its resulting pain, we may be left to believe that it was very calculated against us. We can't help but wonder, "Was our one time friend or lover targeted by the night?"

Do we wear down and become
available to the night?
Does the darkness have its servers
just out of sight?

Are some among us chosen, contaminated, and designated to do the tentacle's bidding? Though we can't know the tentacle directly, we can know that the threat to our voyage is most effectual through the use of the human mind. The process is one of taking the life force of mustardo from the planet and her surrounds. The human mind may have unwillingly become a target for its confusion and control. Imagine the long-reaching effects of wrong thought and wrong action by the duped and compromised human mind. Influenced by the darkness it may unknowingly be working toward maiming our vessel of earth and threatening the creation upon, within, and about her.

The Mind

Another look at the mind shows us that as we depend upon cognition more and more, we may tend to move more closely to the nighttime in our taking from and manipulation of the world around us. It's uncanny the way our minds seize control of our reins and less and less validity is given to our feeling and intuitive centers. The threat here is not so much our minds' abilities to understand the everyday but their reluctance to perceive beyond the ordinary as they practice not seeing. They say, "Nothing new, please. Just keep the old and the usual coming!" As our minds take control our presence may quickly become out of balance. Instead of expressing a life of integration our minds, with their many judgments, separate and divide us from one another as well as from the More of our lives. Ultimately, as the situation deteriorates, the reins of our minds tighten upon us yielding robotic, mechanical people that move aggressively through the day holding up their cold fists to anyone or anything that sees or feels things differently. From this authoritarian place of judgment, separation and division typifies the way we see. What we see, of course, is essentially black or white and the many colors of life are locked out. This type of mind-only seeing obscures another's value and diminishes us as well.

> This voyage of creation
> belongs to one and all.
> Nothing can be gained
> by separating and dividing
> these lives which
> to us do call.

Studies have found that neural impulses are often in place in the mind that can precede conscious decision making by as much as half of a second. In other words, even before we decide our brains decide. What a convenient way for an outside force to impose its directives upon us. These preconscious, cognitive signals can allow us to be influenced in unknown fashions and may be so compelling that afterward we are left believing that we have made a conscious decision of our own.

> Things that we think
> we see and do
> may be caused by something
> we do not see.

The message for us is not to rely solely on the incredible faculty of our minds. If we integrate feelings into our decision-making we are much more inclined to act from a position of amalgamated awareness.

When we allow our feelings and intuitional thoughts to be involved in our being we will be guided more effectively through our world and we will be acting with greater understanding of our place in it. The signposts that have often accompanied us along our paths will guide our thoughts.

In the ideas-only minds of some, the otherworldly essence of the tentacle is allowed frequent visitation within their physiology. The mechanisms of the brain may respond to this intruder before conscious directives can be empowered. Therefore, there may be some truth in "I can't believe I did that!" and in "He's not the person I knew," as well as "I heard something strange in my mind," when they are offered up as a means of explanation for incredible or bizarre behavior. Did something outside the person make a decision for them?

Early in our lives our minds do not seem to be so hardened in their perceptions. We seem much more capable of seeing the unusual, and we possess a refreshing flexibility that allows us to connect things, not separate and divide them. Unfortunately, the development of mental constructs often implies a narrowing of our range of openness. We become much more inclined to fit our perception and knowledge to ideas that can be objectively defined and discussed. This loss of openness during our mental development should raise some concern for us. It is almost as if blinders are added to us, which sequentially squeeze out a great deal that truly matters so that we can better master our limited mental domain. Thus, instead of becoming more intelligent with greater range of seeing, our vision becomes narrower and narrower, until we are able to see almost nothing new at all.

Long in time

as the mind has played
it's left us in some pain.
Lostness and loneliness
are what we've truly gained.

Note how the mind justifies its exaggerated place in the scheme of things. "At least I still have my mind. If I lose that, I've lost everything," is something we've all heard at one time or another. Is our exaggerated dependence upon our minds, with their limited knowing, withholding us from Something More? On an incredible extreme, some scholars have suggested that faith and God are inventions of the mind created to fill a void or need in the human hierarchy of values. Incredible! How limited is our seeing, and how dangerously close we are to a long and lasting sleep.

Coming back
to where we need to be,
loosening the latch allowing
what is what we see.
Our minds must look
into the world
where the world looks back at me
saying, "Ah, it is good!"
but not to want
to take from it
as any advantage would.

There, within our minds, reside the thought forms that have led the hand of man to perform so many threatening acts against the well being of our own vessel, without which we go nowhere. The thought forms that align us with the taking are often fueled by our essential sense of emptiness, which leaves us motivated by fear, doubt, confusion, and despair. This emptiness seems to grow in need relevant to the degrees of separation from the More of life we experience.

Insulation from the Darkness

To one degree or another we all are involved in the struggle to free ourselves from the night. It is doubtful that anyone who is of life willingly serves the tentacle. However, as we become aware of the impact of it and our vulnerability to the loss of our mustardo, it becomes obvious that we all have been and will continue to be involved in this struggle.

There are certain strategies that reduce our vulnerability to being easy targets or victims of the nighttime phenomena. What the tentacle wants, and thus what we need to protect, is the resource of mustardo which flows through and around us. We must protect our reservoir or fountain of this fluid essence of life. Our best strategy to avoid the unnecessary loss of mustardo will be to stay as completely as possible in the expression of life (the top line of life; life for life's sake). A constant expression of our joy and compassion for our everyday world will offer a great deal of protection.

It is helpful to spend some time away from other people, relaxing and enjoying the company of pets and the natural world around us while integrating our thoughts with sensual perceptions from the animate world. How wonderful it is to retreat into a balancing and healing exchange with our more-than-human personal world! Keeping a foot in the natural and animate world can also offer us even more protection. Our relative protection here is derived from our connection to nature's abundance of mustardo. Because our natural world offers very little direct connection for the access of the tentacle, the sustenance of our surrounding world is free to continuously pour into us.

Thus loosening the grip of the tentacle's taking teeth is enhanced when we avail ourselves of the bigger animate arena around us. We can be freed from the darkened, descending road to the nighttime's lair when we embrace the expressive spirits of the natural world. Breaking free of our minds and into the living world refreshes our being and simultaneously provides us with valuable insulation from the darkness of Less.

Staying in the top line of life is more easily done when we trust that there is Something More to our lives. We don't have to squeeze something out of this world to fill a void and add value to a life that is much bigger and longer lasting than what is reflected in a mirror.

As we come to trust and touch our different faces in different places, a greater courage and confidence is added to our presence in the wondrous journey of creation. As we awaken to our complete selves we begin to connect again with other realms. The other realities to which we belong can offer us strength and support. Being open to the Something More of our lives may allow many protective vibrations of help to come our way. Remember, we are not alone!

If we become adept at opening doors or lifting curtains to these other realms or realities in our meditations, dreams, or reflections, we must remind ourselves we may need to guard the door. Remember that the fox will always endeavor to find a way into the henhouse. We must learn to keep it out. We can't always be open. Sometimes it pays to be boarded up tight. We should focus on or entertain only those fluid, phantom like presences that come to us with comfortable qualities such as warmth, sweet fragrances, agreeable sounds, or familiar faces. We must never hold our attention on apparitions that feel cold, smell nasty, sound abnormal, or express threatening demeanors. We should lose no time wondering what ugly could mean.

Ugly is ugly.
Turn it away.
Don't bring it in.

We need to trust our guts and allow our feelings to guide us toward comfort and meaning as we discover ourselves and the More to which we are connected. Remember, the tentacle's manipulative darkness needs our minds to allow it in. The truth is that there are many Night Servers that walk among us doing the tentacle's bidding. Early on we must trust our feelings and avoid people and situations that seem to serve the night.

Perhaps, as we have implied, the greatest influence of the tentacle upon this life's voyage has been through the minds and hands of her human sailors. For one reason or another, some have become more impaired by the night than others. Some, in fact, are so afflicted by the night that they no longer respond to the wonder of life. Instead they busy themselves doing the tentacle's bidding. In effect, they have given up or lost their mustardo to the tentacle and now, without thought or deliberation, they effectively feed off the vigor of others and essentially serve that up to the night as well. Not only have they become lost to life, they are also helping others lose their way.

We must remain vigilant, protect ourselves, and remember that our greatest threat from the darkness comes when we are exhausted, overwhelmed by others' expectations, or depressed for whatever reason. Our moment-to-moment vigilance will remind us to protect our comfort zones by avoiding relationships that demand that we completely give up conscious control of our presence. Some of these might include exacting and rigid initiations into religious or cultural ways of life, or total trust in and compliance with practitioners of the psychic arts. Also, we should diminish our involvement in spectator events of overwhelming noise and bravado, which can unknowingly draw off our mustardo while totally dominating our senses.

With regard to other people, there are some characteristics that may give us reason to pause or at least to limit or measure our contacts. We should always be suspicious of relationships that demand our total dependence. We should never completely submit our sense of self to another regardless of how important or powerful they may seem to be. If we give up even a small part of self to satisfy another, the big picture of ourselves will be difficult to perceive.

Some human dispositions should give us reason for concern. People who are blindly attached to a religious or cultural belief system may display compliance to these institutions not unlike a child to its mother. Their moods, which vary between exhilaration and depression, may control or subdue those around them.

Of equal importance, we should try to avoid people who make us uncomfortable. It is not important that we can put our finger on why we feel that way. We just need to trust our gut. We should always be concerned about people who have no real interest in the natural world, except for what they can utilize or take from it. Their mantra is, "It is here for our needs, it is dangerous, and we need to control it and have dominion over it!" Extreme mind-people also need to be measured with caution. For them, everything and every thought has a definition or explanation. They are very uncomfortable with intuition, feelings, or basic emotional expressions. Their minds have seemingly become separated from the rest of their beings with very little integration of their hearts and souls. Every moment of their lives tends to be filled with chatter. Pauses of silence are very difficult for them.

Clearly, we do not want to disassociate with all of these types of people. Some we may know as friends, and others may be as close as family. But we may want to limit our vulnerability to them, especially at times when they appear exhausted or spent. It will be at these times when they will, unknowingly of course, be looking to hitch a ride, to draw off our mustardo to replenish what they have lost.

There are inner tendencies which can indicate taking tracks that can be understood and thereby offer us insulation against the power of Less. We must celebrate our passions, those high frequency tendencies which create such meaningful ripples of goodness in the world around us. But we need to know when passion is being exchanged for anger. Initially these powerful emotions may look and feel similar, but they have very different consequences. Anger, even if kept within, hurts the house in which it lives. Passion excites and lifts within and without, while anger throws open the door that allows the fox an entryway.

Another vulnerability results from our attachment to specific results and outcomes. When we are not attached to the results we are affording ourselves insulation against disappointment. Disappointment tends to weigh us down, leaving us more vulnerable to the tentacle's taking. This does not mean that things and expectancies don't matter and that being casual in all things is preferred. Life asks that we care and we involve ourselves completely, but living reminds us that results can not be determined or always known. What matters most is our strength, vigor, and wellness.

Avoiding competition with others is another means of insulation. Entering into competition can be an insidious process of outcomes with degrees of personal ruin. Competition may begin innocently enough but may soon mix our passion with aggression. Anger from us or against us may result. Someone here wins, thus someone over there loses, and in the process the goodness in us is lost or denied while relationships can be wrecked, and a fox has slipped into our living room.

We must make a good, reflective accounting of our subjective state of weakness and strength as it pertains to others when they come and go in our lives. We must ascertain our feelings of fear, anguish, joy, depression, exhilaration, etc. and understand our vulnerability by correlating these feelings with the comings and goings of others. We need to be willing to distinguish those who build bridges to More from those whose bridges end in the land of Less. Relationships with those who may bridge to the Less are often punctuated with incessant talking, a little pouting and 'woe is me' and 'I really need you' routines.

Briefly stated some of our vulnerability is of our own making while much comes by bridges into our lives. Regardless of the points of origin, insulating ourselves from the taking process of Less equals health and wellness in our lives; the tedious gives way to meaning and the world of good and plenty opens up for our participation.

So together we must beware of those tracks. We cannot always benefit by questioning who, what, or why. More preciousness may be lost which we cannot afford to lose. We may fairly ask, however, "Is that a fox in my garden or knocking at my front door?"

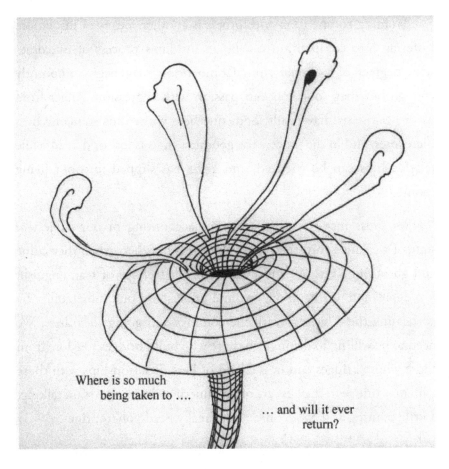

Where is so much being taken to ....

... and will it ever return?

11

The Darkness is Served

We have now come to a point in this book where we must speculate upon how the tentacle and the darkness reaches into our world with so many life-taking consequences. In this time of subtraction, the losses which we do see must have some observable mechanisms, which help explain what we don't see. At the risk of over simplification and even callous observation, we will imply that much of the loss of this world's life-keeping mustardo has much to do with the mind and hand of humankind.

Many of life's losses may be directly related to man's sense of need, entitlement, and control implemented by effective mental manipulation and assisted by our technologies.

The following pages will attempt to identify those who knowingly or otherwise serve this taking tentacle from the night. Unlike those whom we have referred to as Life's Keepers or Sailors of Fortune, whose preponderance of thought and behavior facilitates life, these will be referred to as Night Servers. Night Servers will be generally identified as those whose preponderance of thought and action comes down on the Less side of things and belongs to life-taking forces.

Night-Leaning Hybrids

As was mentioned earlier, it is the nature of these times that we all are hybrids of one degree or another. We all have aspects of both night and day within us as the call of life vacillates with thoughts and behaviors that both enhance and limit life. You might ask, "How do we differentiate a life-leaning versus a night-leaning hybrid?" This is not always easy to determine within the hybridized mix of caring for life as opposed to the disregard and taking from life. As the progression towards More or Less occurs in one's existence it becomes easier to know at the More side of things. Life Keepers are clearly different from Night Servers. So ultimately it is what we value and the behaviors which reflect these values that are defining. What we value, expressed by our embrace of this living creation, defines each individual in how they approach life and whether they support life in all its forms or look to take life away in service of the darkness. These are not just casual questions as to the quality of life on this planet, but they impact the existence that follows when we pass beyond this time and place. Will we have more life? Will we enter another room in the wondrous house of life? Much is at stake in that our deaths will come as extensions of how we have lived. If we have lived in the light of More full of caring, warmth, and giving; our mustardo will fill our sails, and our passage to another realm will be assured. If we have lived our lives in ways of Less using the tools of manipulation, greed, and self gain with an intent to control and take, the passage will become more complicated and maybe even denied. Our time in No Man's Land may find us wishing we had taken the opportunity when presented to grab hold of our eternal birthright by supporting the call of life with every ounce of our being.

At the outset the tentacle may have initiated its control over our world as a response to its discomfort and surprise by the arrival of life, with its warmth and illumination. It may have simply wanted to ease its discomfort at being disturbed. However, over time it has become clever and quite adept at fighting for the dark space it calls its own. It has worked in insidious ways that have unexpectedly permeated our being, bit by bit, leaving many of us with Less and diminishing our ability to feel value or purpose. The all of who we are may be forgotten while doubt replaces basic trust, leaving us to feel alone and wondering what we are doing here in the first place. In response to this, the quality of life has shifted and some of the original elements of More may have been traded for mediocrity or even less as many of us have come to accept our loss of mustardo as something that simply is rather than something we can choose to change. Through an opening granted by our minds and the shortsighted needs of our confused egos, we have been made vulnerable to the subtracting power of Less. The straws of the tentacle have been inserted, and day by day the beast may drink deep of our life force leaving us exhausted, hopeless, and steeped in fear that takes the form of embattled self-esteem, broken hearts, and a less than joyful existence. Life Keepers, while touched by the darkness in different ways, are steadied and empowered by living their lives for life's sake. Still they sense the great losses to the creation around them. Many Night Servers have been misled by the night and conditioned with life-taking ways to attempt to fill the emptiness within from external sources related to power, money, and fame.

The complexity and challenge of these times is that as hybrids, we do in fact hold the key to our own recovery. Some will need to change how their unconscious habits have allowed life to slip away. Others who serve the night must be willing to change and live from life affirming principals that will allow them to break away from the tenacious hold of the tentacle, rebuilding life centered and caring relationships. Our earth is also crying out in many ways to be valued and allowed to carry us beyond these times. If we will work toward cleansing the darkness within us by clarifying what matters, we will be simultaneously giving standing and value to our earth. A sense of renewed value and meaning will assist her in a big way simply by demanding less from her and thus freeing her of the devastating forces that have drained her life energy in deadly increments.

It is critical that Sailors of Fortune understand their role as protectors of life's mustardo in these times, for we will be asked not only to value our own lives as precious, but we will be asked to help our compromised colleagues who have succumbed to the tenacity of the tentacle's taking. It is important that we chance to understand what defines the Night Servers so we can detach the drinking straws and reclaim our lives in full celebration of the giving horizon before us. It is equally important that we recognize who among these fallen colleagues still has a chance of taking a hand that is offered before it is too late to reclaim their place in this wondrous creation.

Night Servers

Night Servers are not all so far removed from life that they can't awaken to the revealing windows of More before them. However, we must recognize that there are those who are so fixed in darkness that they are a cause for concern. While generalizations can be dangerous, it is important to understand that there are various levels of Night

Servers defined by a common group of people with similar ways of manipulating and taking life for personal gain. Calling upon my edge experiences, what ultimately defines a person are the things that motivate him, not the final results that are achieved. I have seen the aftermath of this struggle on the souls of Night Servers in No Man's Land. Some held a ticket of sorts to a place beyond this world, but many did not. For these many we must be concerned because beyond the experiences granted of this world there may be nothing more. While the message in this book is so much about living fully here and now, it is also about living in such a way that we may be alive continuously. Living fully here also prepares us for that necessary passage between worlds and beyond death. This critical attunement with life assures our individual after death experiences, and also extends our reach toward helping the unknowing servers of the night who do the best they can with what they know at the time. For so many of these, what they identify with through their values, beliefs, and ideas of right and wrong can actually be chains to the darkness which now is seeking their service. How can we help them to throw off these limiting chain-like habits? The best we may be able to do is to extend our warmth and illumination. It cannot be known how many drunken sailors, inebriated by the night, can turn in their rum and choose to come back to life. We cannot easily give up on the many chained who may have even fallen. In this last light of day it is our imperative to be available to help each as we can. Some, referred to here as Scavengers and Dead Enders, may already be lost to the night. However, there are others referenced as Bottom Liners amongst these Night Servers whose patterns of abuse and manipulation can be shifted with a willingness to reframe what they value and trade in their misguided thoughts of self and fortune for the real fortunes that come from living within the circle of life.

While generalities can be misleading, there are different levels of

Night Servers defined as Bottom Liners, Last Standers, Scavengers, and Dead Enders. Their differences are indicated by how their thoughts and behaviors manipulate and take from life as they intentionally or not serve the power of Less. Each is different in how it serves the tentacle with an individual degree of taking. Their separation is based on their leanings and behaviors that identify them as being on the less side of life and thus providing service to the tentacle of the night.

Bottom Liners are socially and culturally conditioned for their habits of accumulation that reflect a sense of entitlement. At work they are hard hitting with anything that impacts their bottom line. However it is almost as though a veil of darkness is lifted as they come home to families they may adore and cherish. They are frequently kind people who love their families, are involved in their communities, and address their children from kind hearts. They are often misguided individuals who have bought into a particular lifestyle emphasizing having stuff, the more the better. Their aspect of taking comes from their egocentric, 'take it if I can' view of life.

Individuals who are referred to as Scavengers or Dead Enders are driven by a foul breath of life that has been flushed with the essence of the dark. To the core they are abusive, taking people who will stop at nothing to have their own way. With so little mustardo left within them, they proactively look for ways to steal it from others, squeezing every ounce of life they can from those upon whom they prey with their tentacle like straws. They drink until the well is dry, leaving their victims to suffer intensely. Where previously there may have been an oasis, now there is only desert. Again and again they move on to the next vulnerable being they can trick into giving up the keys to the sacred garden.

Many Night Servers were inherently good people who were

corrupted by the night and now use a value system that celebrates individual profit, fame, and power as their driving force. As we learn to recognize who is still connected enough to life and who has completely let go, we have a better chance of maximizing our efforts to reach those now deeply in trouble.

Bottom Liners

The largest contingents of Night Servers are the Bottom Liners. These people represent a critical percent of the earth's population. Not only are they numerous, but their control over our world is great. It is difficult to recognize Bottom Liners as Night Servers, because so many of them are good and caring people much of the time. It is their individual and collective orientation toward accumulation and self-gain that takes away from our world in a frightening fashion. We must see their place in this struggle for what it is. Their identity is one of manipulation and excessive consumption of resources, and there is no reason to think that they will change any time soon.

I have made efforts to break through their heavy headedness for some time, but to no avail. It is my hope that those on the side of life might develop some inroads with them. We certainly don't want them all to roll over toward the night. What a hurt that would put on our world!

Bottom Liners are identified as those whose value and worth is defined by how well they are doing on the bottom line. To this end they masterfully outwit, manipulate, and take at will. If laws and standards do not permit their taking, they exact changes to allow their gluttonous appetites to proceed. One typical arena for their excessive taking is the natural world. By transforming naturally occurring resources, they skillfully put the value of these resources in their pockets. Vast amounts of precious mustardo are lost from our world, and what is left is often clouded over by pollution resulting from the processes of the taking. "What's the bottom line?" is their common refrain. The top line qualities like the value of life and its joy are of little concern for them.

Most Bottom Liners demonstrate a great, if not excessive, dependence upon cognition and the mental constructs that support their accumulations. They really don't look beyond the now, and they never consider that there could be future consequences to their current manipulative actions. They prefer the touchable, the objective, the rational, and the seeable. The disproportionate dependence on and exaggerated use of the mind and its mental processes are used to their advantage.

The Bottom Liners are so busy practicing the art of manipulation and verifying their value through accumulation that they are difficult to reach. The More of life does not exist for them as they focus on their strategies and gains and place no personal value in faith, the mystical, or the unseen. The subjective introduces discomfort and seems too messy, as they prefer to deal with the objective or the knowable. That is, of course, until something important to them breaks rank with their expectations. Then they can become subjective and messy in a big way. This is not to say that these people will not entertain thoughts with some expressed hope for their immortality, but the subject of what awaits them beyond here and now is often entrusted to the care of a religious institution.

By birth, book, hook, or crook, many Bottom Liners are offered a religious plan or a perspective of God that may sound good and convenient, and with expedience they may follow this prescription of how to live and stay safely on the good side of the almighty.

God or Jesus will come
for you.
Sacrifice and believe.
Tithe now liberally
and you will see,
a seat in Heaven
is where you'll
be.

While the mustardo of the plant and animal kingdom is not directly available to the manipulation and taking of the tentacle, it is indirectly assailed when it is intruded upon and transformed by bottom line motives. In this way huge amounts of vigor and green is quite effectively served up to the night. Thus through the mind and hand of humankind our natural world's life and mustardo are being greatly diminished. For instance a great deal of vigor is lost to the planet when a vast swath of forest is expediently removed so that bottom line motivation can build a meadow of houses and maximize their profits.

Many times I have asked myself how it is possible for the developers, architects, contractors, and purchasers to be blind to the resource of life that is already present in the area that will become their development. A common response from the bottom line driven developers when I try to speak for the trees is, "Don't interfere here, Redding. It's our ground, and we want it to have a certain look and feel." They don't seem to recognize any value or be possessed of any true feelings as I try to reach them with my attempts to salvage a grand statement of life, a tree. The life in these trees does not matter to them. They want to get on with the plan and get these objects, these sticks in the ground, out of the way. Instead of attributing true value to these trees and making every effort to save them, there seems to be a cold and calculating imperative to wipe them out and create something that bears their own image. Whose image is it? I often wonder. Here is where their otherwise capable minds seem to serve another keeper. Will they plan their construction in such a way as to preserve some of the trees? Probably not, but they will agree to a trade-off by planting numerous two-inch hybrid trees to replace the grand, centuries old ones that were bulldozed out of the way. Therein lies another unnecessary loss from the river of life.

From my perspective the forces of darkness are effectively slurping up mustardo through these people's minds and needy egos. Meanwhile, these people feel satisfied because their efforts at tearing away the living and giving mantle of green puts some green in their pockets. Easily and callously they add up and justify all of this havoc as a bottom line gain. I can only dare to imagine the inner emptiness and cold, manipulative minds that kill off and waste unnecessarily, throwing out existing life and resources to satisfy their own appetites.

My experience has continued to show me that these people work hard and are formidable foes in the face of preservation, making great personal efforts and putting in many hours while building their world and stamping their vision on it. They tend to express an almost desperate need to do things their way. Anger quickly rises to the surface when someone steps in, says, "Whoa!" and asks them to re-look and re-think what they are doing. Clearly they are feeling a thirst of sorts, which seems somewhat quenched by their bottom line accumulations. So much life is lost and maimed as they hurry about to complete their projects of construction. Or is it destruction? There must be another force at work here, a force other than that of giving and caring, an insidious force influenced by the great taker of life.

It amazes me when I see how their trained and guided mental processes deny other points of view and justify their own. A shadow seems to have entered their otherwise adept minds, limiting access and withholding the wider view of life from them. Their minds, with their limited seeing and accumulating expectations, continuously slurp up the mustardo, or vigor, from the natural world around them. They are, in effect, taking something that belongs to all of us.

The health of our earth is clearly threatened by the Bottom Liners' traits of over consumption, and the consequences are most telling. In the natural world the tent caterpillar illustrates many of these habits of excessive taking. The voracious appetite of the tent caterpillar chooses the cherry tree as its target, not unlike the way in which the bottom line types go after the fruits of the world whenever possible. Almost unnoticeable, the eggs from which the caterpillars will emerge are bonded in geometric masses encircling the twigs of their prey. Just as Bottom Liners are often protected by layers of insulation from anyone or anything that might want to take from them as they so freely take from the world, these egg masses are covered by a varnish that protects them from the weather and possible predators. With uncanny timing the consuming caterpillars emerge as the tree is unfolding its early spring leaves. En masse they spread into the canopy of the tree, choosing certain crotches in the branches where they spin their protective tents. The size of the tent grows as they grow. Like the Bottom Liners of our times, these insects with their great numbers, hairy-thorny bodies, and sheltering nests are very well protected from naturally occurring controls like birds, weather conditions, and common means of pest control. The Bottom Liners with their aggressive taking, bully their way along by huff and puff. There are not many who even question them because their power is almost absolute as they control our civil, legal, technical, and political systems. Though many of us can see what they are doing as a result of their taking and manipulating, we choose not, or we are unable to stand up to them. They are too overwhelming. As tent caterpillars continue to develop, their gluttonous appetites grow and grow. They consume vast amounts, and almost as much comes out of their back end as goes in the front end. This reminds us of the indirect but equally harmful consequences of bottom line behaviors of consumption. What is not maimed and lost by direct taking is often left compromised or polluted as a result of the expedient processes of taking. There could be many trees left standing following construction of a wooded housing development, but it is more expedient to get them 'out of the way' and thus avoid having to work around them. Sadly, within a few weeks the entire canopy of the cherry tree is consumed, and the arboreal being stands barren under the hot summer sun, exposed to its dangerous ultra-violet rays. The cambium tissue bubbles and burns on its naked limbs and inflicts lasting damage that can't be undone. With all of its leaves gone the tree has no means to feed and cool itself. Its pain is evident and easy to see. It may call out with biochemical signals to other trees nearby. Other members of its family within the circle of its roots will attempt to send it some relief. Carbohydrates and repelling chemicals may be ushered its way.

And what of the caterpillars and their bottom line behavior? Only their nests remain. They have pupated and gone. They can be found in other locations in protective cocoons until the adults emerge. Then they venture forth to lay their eggs to begin the next cycle of taking from the cherry trees, just like the Bottom Liner developer who moves to clearing his next forested acres to satisfy his voracious appetite.

In this illustration the naked tree, with its exposed and weakened structure, provides clear evidence of over consumption in a hurtful way. When individuals, communities, and the natural world are infested and worked over by the bottom line advocates we are similarly hurt and weakened. We are left feeling abused, misused, and taken from, and life loses some of its charm. Our spirit may wonder why, while the night of this world begins to creep over our souls. That which matters is lessened while the process of subtraction is strengthened.

How do we moderate or control the damage? The eggs of the caterpillar, though difficult to see, offer one of the best means of getting some control over the next season of consumption. Rub them off before they hatch. The Bottom Liners are essentially mind heavy people. Controlling their taking will depend upon defending the world from their ideas and thoughts. Once their ideas are hatched and subsequently approved, they are free to practice their taking. A feeding frenzy is initiated, and much is lost. As the mind is honed and honored it becomes a tool to their advantage. It allows them to take from here, even though they lose their way to the More of life, eventually becoming their own worst enemy.

As is true of the tent caterpillars, there are many Bottom Liners, and they are very much alike. They are able to quickly and efficiently dismantle communities, ecosystems, and even cultural identities and redo them in their likeness. As a result color is often diminished, diversity is limited, and true passion towards others is discouraged in their lives. It gets in the way and conflicts with their bottom line consciousness of manipulative taking from the world. Sameness rules. Outward differences are very slight. We can almost identify them by the houses they build and the cars they drive. Life is fast paced with one foot on the accelerator while the other foot steps on more stuff.

As the Bottom Liners' minds dominate our world, their habits of short seeing and repetition rule the day. Integration of their thoughts with feelings that value this creation are often discouraged. Feelings in general and speculation regarding the intrinsic value of our world are dismissed as unpredictable and beyond our knowing. Therefore, they are considered bothersome and not worth our while. As a result of leaving so much of real value out of their lives, these people become flat-sided and sense emptiness. Something essential is missing, and they continually seek meaning outside of themselves. Frequently this meaning is based on what their peers may think of them and how others may see them. Extraneous efforts are made to bolster their fragile personal identities. These might include a vicarious sense of achievement gained through the efforts of others such as a team or a party, whose wins might satisfy their insatiable yearnings for success. Of course along with the wins are always losses, so efforts to gather more stuff are continuous and always the call of the day.

> But the wins stop coming
> and the stuff soon loses its shine.
> Then what we are left with
> is loss and rust in kind.

At some point along the course of their lives a valueless and fragile ego may begin to cause them dismay. If this inner discomfort can be tenderly nurtured, some hope of awakening is warranted. However, in the face of entrenched habits of their consuming lives they may be unable to come free and thus might sink even deeper into self-indulgent behavior. In response to their aroused despair, they may strengthen their allegiance to fairly rigid social, political, and religious associations.

Do not worry
everything is fine.
It's all working out
in accordance with
some plan divine.

There are many examples in which these mind and idea dominated people have been responsible for throwing life away, thus threatening our journey upon the vessel of earth. When they unleash their perception of need upon the resources and many life forms of this planet, these highly capable and highly manipulative people with a singular bottom line agenda can do immeasurable harm with one bureaucratic or governmental decision. Again from the eyes of an arborist take, for example, the idea that we need more and bigger homes. That thought morphs into an order to essentially let loose our technology on a grand scale. Devastation of forests or woodlands may be initiated, and as a result of our failure to see and value what is being thrown away, so much green energy is unsettled in such a short time that much of it is lost to the darkness or slips into the night to feed life's foes. Thus in one fell swoop, another helping of mustardo disappears from our earth. Every loss of this magnitude diminishes the life force that breathes wind into our sails. This is not to say that trees should not be harvested and houses cannot be built. Rather, it implies that sensitivity must be involved as we initiate our projects, and we must proceed with a caring, inclusive plan. When we employ clear-cutting techniques in the name of quick, efficient results we impose a brutality upon our forests that demeans our stewardship.

On and on and on.
The taking becomes
our losses,
soon then
our emptiness.
What we thought we need
we must need more.
The mind and hand of man
open wide the dark door
allowing the night in
forever more.

Since we are using trees and the forests to which they belong as illustrations of the consequences of night-leaning bottom line motivation, we should also touch upon another loss that is occurring when we wipe our forests clean. Not only do we lose the structures and functions of the trees that are sacrificed, we also lose one of life's most available and securing repositories for the essence of one time existing life upon our world. I have so often witnessed the obvious life of a tree when burning its wood or touching or leaning against its trunk. But what isn't so apparent to casual observation is that there is something more to these living beings as well. (see 'Life of a Tree' and 'Secret of the Wood' in *Something More*)

If these bottom line minds served the preservation of life instead of life consuming tendencies, they would proceed with sensitivity toward their goals, which in this case would incorporate a basic appreciation of a tree's wonder. Many trees would be preserved, resulting in a meaningful integration of man with his world. This more orderly and thoughtful way of living with our earth would frighten the essence of life much less, while allowing the transfer of mustardo to other life-expressing beings. The elemental reserve of life resting in the trees slated to be removed might be able to find another repository. It might become part of a new tree or acquire residence in another arboreal being.

Volumes could be written about the consequences of man seeking an advantage by employing thoughts that have pulled at the threads of creation's fabric. Entire species of trees and the forests to which they belonged have been threatened and forever changed as a result of self-serving 'good ideas' initiated to improve someone's bottom line. The assault on the nation's forests by the gypsy moth, a creature introduced to the western hemisphere in hopes of producing cheap, plentiful silk, speaks loudly to the devastating consequences that may result from out-of-control thought losing its way. Millions upon millions of trees have been lost to an invasive insect that produces inferior silk, but consumes massive amounts of foliage. Our native forests became a smorgasbord of edible delights for these voracious offenders. Dutch elm disease, chestnut blight, and even the invasion of the kudzu vine further illustrate the devastation that can result when the threads of life are pulled and carelessly reinserted into its fabric. So many of this world's invasive pathogens and species have gained their advantage when man thought there was some value to be gained by moving them around.

When so much bottom line motivation depends on the manipulation and leverage gained from the mind, not only does cognition build fences against experiencing More, it also places reins against a reverence for our vessel. A person with these night leaning, bottom line type motivations will only venture within a self-imposed, comfort limiting zone of restriction. No greater purpose or vision is inferred or even speculated upon. Limit has been reached, and the Bottom Liners assume a contentedness that their skillful manipulations of the world have gained the desired advantage.

But is this the advantage the pulse of life is looking for? Do we really want to have more, be better, or feel greater than another? When materials, status, or power put us at an advantage, it usually implies a loss or deficit to another. In fact to outwit, outthink, or outsmart another has never been life's intention as we express and discover ourselves in this existence experience.

If gaining an advantage is the Bottom Liners' orientation, they may be outwitting themselves as they forfeit and lose the wondrous way that could lead them to the More of life and the eternal highway. If calculating mental gymnastics is their way in life, then surely they will gain an advantage over others on the planet Earth. However, in the process they may lose themselves from the onward journey, and finiteness and mortality may be their personal resting place, as they discover a one-way pass to No Man's Land.

Here may be the end of their line.
The road to nowhere
is nowhere they want to find.

Once again, the way in which we orient ourselves has so much to do with what we are and what we may become. If we will allow compassion for the vessel of earth to surround our minds, so much goodness and wonder awaits us. On the other hand, if we continue to consume our world with bottom line motives then soon, very soon, the sea of darkness will surround us all.

Feeling and appreciation
returns wonder and goodness unto us.

Scavengers, Last Standers, Dead Enders

What distinguishes the Bottom Liners from the more hardened Night Servers is that the losses to the living world, and thus life's mustardo, occur without a conscious intent. Instead, these losses are coincidental to their bottom line driven motives. In contrast, the remainder of the Night Servers are practiced and proficient at drawing off our mustardo. While the Bottom Liners sometimes live in ways that result in throwing life away through their manipulations and consumption, they do not deliberately concentrate on taking life away from others. In contrast, the Scavengers, Dead Enders, and Last Standers use personal interactions to seduce life giving and caring people into relinquishing their trust, confidence, and enthusiasm for life.

Almost all of us have been betrayed and hurt as a result of a trusting love or friendship that has exposed us, through the space of we-ness, to the selfish motives of another. Intentionally or not, these abusers of trust serve the night as they feign loyalty to their relationships and practice the pretense of we-ness. Going from one phony relationship to another, they fill their tanks with our mustardo. Through their pretense and deception in the space of we-ness, they damage us while strengthening the hand of the night.

As we come to understand how these nighttime types serve up the darkness, we also see how the tentacle uses them. My suspicion is that their taking efforts may be directed from outside of themselves, by way of their minds.

An example from the natural world may serve as a useful illustration.

There is a species of black ant that comes to mind. These ants enslave aphids for their purposes. They find them, carry or nudge them, or place them in a specific tree. Once these aphids are under the ants' control, the ants encircle them and vigorously protect their investment against outside influence or predators. Meanwhile, the aphids do what they do best – and what the black ants can't do directly. The aphids insert their feeding mouthparts (drinking straws) into the tree's vascular tissue that contains the plant's life fluids and effectively draw these fluids off. While separating and utilizing the nitrogen for their own sustaining needs, the aphids digest, secrete, and discharge the sugars from these plant fluids. This is what the ants want. In this scenario, both seem to benefit, which provides for us a way to understand the relationship between the tentacle and its keepers. If the tentacle is nudging and moving Night Servers around, it is done through a preconscious dialogue with their minds.

The Night Servers are transferring the mustardo from the living world to the tentacle's appetite, while the tentacle is empowering them to extend their hold over whatever it is that the servers think they want, whether it is money, material wealth, power, position, or person.

In this scenario the aphids are the Night Servers, and the black ants represent the tentacle. We can look at the relationships in our lives that may pre-suppose us to their taking. Individually, these Night Servers are most taking and devastating when we allow them into our personal space. Why would we ever be inclined to allow them close contact in our personal lives? Why would we want them as friends or lovers? We wouldn't, but they are good at deception and pretense. Coming to us they can appear kind and look regal. After they have stomped upon us and taken what they can, we will see them as the dangerous intruders they truly were.

A Night Server

As we begin to separate the night from our lives, we must begin to identify places and people who take our mustardo from us in the form of trust and love, and thus withhold much of life's essence from us.

Those who manipulate our love and friendship, trash our faith, and draw off our mustardo often use relationships to misapply our trust for their advantage. Beware of their coming. Know them for the Night Servers that they are. Glen Wheating was one who was in bed with the night. His chilling life and character disastrously affected our neighbors' family, particularly one of their daughters.

Glen came their way as a suitor of one of their girls during her early years in secretarial school. The first impression of Glen with his roses, broad swift smile, and 'so good to meet you' salutation was very positive. Their daughter seemed really happy with him, and it was easy to understand why. He came with fresh flowers, good manners, a box of chocolates, and many admirable and appreciative comments made toward her and her family.

With all of these positive aspects, we were surprised by her father's reaction to Glen. At best he was lukewarm. Her father could sense something that triggered his dislike and mistrust of this man. Glen, noticing her dad's reluctance to sidle up to him, brought along a bottle of wine and a big voice proclaiming his respect for her father during his next visit. To her father's credit he was a straight shooter and called things as he saw them. Instead of being swayed by Glen's gift and big voice, he was even more sure of this man's threat to his daughter and her family. The following morning the dad approached his daughter and declared that this man was not going to be 'worth a damn.' He said that he would appreciate it if she ended their relationship.

The daughter was much like her dad, strong willed and controlling to a fault, and she continued on in the relationship, sensing that love was there to be had. On one occasion Glen mistimed his visit to the family farm in the midst of the haymaking season. Her dad was there and saw an opportunity. Handing Glen a pair of work gloves and a hay hook, he told him to join his sons on the wagon.

Her father was just this way. He managed his farm fiefdom with a level hand. If someone was visiting the farm and didn't want to be involved in the labor, their visit was best timed on a Sunday following the obligatory Catholic church service. It mattered not who it was; salesman, church deacon, teacher, politician, or neighbor; if the family was working when someone came to visit, then they were likewise working during their visit. Otherwise they would be 'in the way' and told very directly, with the point of his finger, to hightail it out the driveway. In retrospect, I often think that successful farming wasn't so different from the workings of a beehive. There is a certain constant hum of effort necessary to accomplish all of what needs to get done. Should someone show up that interfered with the work getting done in the hive and was not involved in helping gather the pollen, they just might risk getting stung. Time and time again on our own farm I would get a laugh watching salesmen, whom Dad seldom enjoyed, react to being put to work while they attempted to impress Mom or Dad with some new product for the farm. In particular I recall a recently graduated technician shoveling chicken poop in his white shirt and tie while trying to convince Mom of the benefits of a just-on-the-scene miracle drug called teramycin. I can't say if he made any headway with Mom, but I do know he never again lost his way up the half-mile lane to the brightly painted and polished buildings of the Redding family farm.

My Dad had a way with his soft voice and clear instructions that left no doubt of who was in charge. It was his principality, and being there meant joining in with whatever was being done. Of course a visitor could also be treated to some delicious homemade soup and bread along with roasted chicken and a garden fresh salad, depending on their timing. If Dad didn't just point back down the long lane, then for the duration of the visit a guest would do and be like family. Some of our best entertainment and introductions to worldly life as it was beyond the farm were given by the visitors who would take their places on the benches alongside our long table. Fifteen places were set along those benches, but another place setting or two could always be squeezed in. Mom and Dad sat at the table ends. If there was an abundance of sweet corn, peaches, fresh eggs, or freshly made sausage, a package was prepared and given to the visitor at the time of his departure, along with a handshake. This is how things were done on our large, family farm, and this scene was mirrored in varying forms at the other working farms in our vicinity.

The work Glen and the neighbor boys would be doing was on a wagon pulled behind a hay-baler. They were to stack the bales of hay as they exited one by one from the baler. Keeping up with the emerging bales of hay and stacking them securely on a wagon was always difficult as the wagon bounced over rough spots in the hayfield. Aspects of this torturous farm experience were varied and painful. This work took place on an unstable, bouncing ten foot by fifteen-foot wagon in the full sun and relentless heat. One hand was extended, not unlike that of a rodeo rider, to maintain balance. The other hand held a sharp, eighteen inch long hook, which was used to snag the heavy hay bales as they exited the chute of the baling machine and drag them across the vibrating wood or steel bed of the wagon. Each bale of hay was placed in an interlocking pattern that would hopefully secure a hundred or so of these four-by-two foot by eighteen-inch bales for the duration of several trips back and forth across the field until the wagon was loaded. There was a hurried aspect to all of this, as there was a need to keep up with the emerging bales of hay while simultaneously stacking them securely. If a worker was late returning to the baling machine, a hay bale might fall to the ground through the space between the baler and the wagon. If it fell beneath the wagon's wheel and got run over, the carefully stacked load of bales became dislodged. Haymaking was one of the most difficult assignments of the 1950's and 60's farm life.

On the bailing wagon in very short order, the laborer's body broke out in a drenching sweat that caused severe itching, as hay pollen and husks stuck to the perspiration. This led to one of the worst scratching reflexes imaginable, as every movement felt like sandpaper was working under the arms, in the crotch, and every other place two or more body parts rubbed together. It wasn't unusual to see a wagon tender standing spread legged with arms at right angles after this nasty chore until someone showed up with soap and water or a rinsing hose.

As if all of this was not enough to make the haymaking, wagon-tending duty distasteful, there was one last peril worth mentioning. The green head flies were biting, bloodletting villains. Flies were always an issue with farm life, but the green heads delivered an enormous wallop. While occupied with the hook and the hay, they attached themselves to the body delivering their ferocious bite. One might feel them but could not deter them. Their presence was so distracting and their bites so painful that hay workers would sometimes reach over their backs with a swinging hay hook, occasionally impaling themselves and suffering wounds from the misapplication of this implement. Hay making was one of my worst nightmares, and it seemed I so often was appointed to this duty!

To have Glen along to assist the neighbor boys seemed like a good idea, but what happened to the avid, always talking, always laughing Glen Wheating? Grim faced, he accepted the gloves and tagged along, but his disposition was troubled. The next couple of hours in a hot and miserable hayfield were especially trying for the neighbor boys. Glen quickly gave one of the boys his hook as the wagon rolled over the uneven field. He did everything to avoid helping, but he could not escape the heat, the itchy shaft, and the flies, and he cussed continuously. Glen fell apart by degrees and showed himself to be just what the father had feared he was. Not only was he not helpful, his constant complaining and cursing made the whole task more difficult. Not helping would have been okay, him being a city boy, but the negativity coming from his mouth was hard for the boys to take. As the wagon slowly filled, Glen continued to dissertate. What? Did they not hear him swear under his breath at how their sister set him up? He said, "I only came up to this damn farm to take your sister out for some fun!" Soon they were thinking even less of him than did their almost always critical father. Their dad was right about this man. They wanted him off the wagon. The next time they would see him would be too soon, and they worried for their sister. How he was tricking and misleading her!

What it was that their sister thought Glen could do for her was not completely clear. Perhaps it was an inner need of we-ness, love, or companionship. In this case, had Glen Wheating been a giving and sharing person, everything may have been okay. Behind his bravado, he was a timid and somewhat submissive personality. This would do for this woman at the time because she was of a dominating, tough girl disposition.

To this day I can still share in that father's pain. What a grimace he wore upon his face when he walked his daughter down the church aisle to give her hand to Glen Wheating! Father and daughter had always been very close, and for her he would follow the protocol of this special day. His daughter was to be married, and he would be there for her.

Not much interrupted the task oriented family farm, but there would be a few occasions, such as Christmas and Easter, when work and machinery came to a halt. Weddings and funerals were also such days, and they were given the collective family attention. Our neighbor's daughter's wedding was one of these special occasions, and I had the opportunity to witness this father's reluctant preparation. His sense of despair over his daughter's marital selection foretold a looming disaster. For a dignified and reserved man, the patriarch was very worked up. It was clear for everyone to see that this celebration was going to be less than enjoyable for the bride's father. Growling under his breath, he told his sons to wax the car and shine his shoes. You could actually smell this dad's sweat in that last hour before giving up his daughter's hand. He was on fire. On the outside, however, he continued to look the part of a proud father, not wanting to dampen his daughter's giddy joy. But that final walk down the aisle of the church was most revealing. With his daughter at his side, he began the procession with a soft grin that was replaced by an ever-tightening facial grimace with each step. This may have been one this father's most difficult days ever.

I felt that the father's pain and fear over Glen Wheating was in part apprehension about his lovely daughter's future, but it was also fear for the collective family unit and the conflict and decay that might be introduced into it. He was also deeply pained that for the first time ever, his daughter was not open to his point of view. She was not even open to listening about how he saw it. What he 'saw' was what he felt. This man just didn't feel right, not by a long shot.

It wasn't long until the confirmation of her father's fears became apparent. Children were born and preyed upon by their father. This Night Server emotionally and physically beat upon his wife. Glen Wheating soon quit his job, drank beer, and enjoyed a couch potato dependency. As her father feared, Glen Wheating introduced a cancer of sorts into that lovely farm family, which took dearly from them and so devastated their daughter that she has never recovered. Glen Wheating lasted long enough to drain an excess of mustardo from a lovely, hard working farm family and left a vibrant young woman in such a state of deterioration that it is still painful see. Once this Night Server got in, it was very difficult to get him out.

How is it that an intelligent, strong willed lady just could not see or even listen to what was so obvious to her father and the rest of her family? How could she squander the treasure of health, family, and belonging to this thief from the night? Clearly she had somehow felt an emptiness that she thought this man could surely fill. It's not so different than the case of Marie who felt such a need to 'know' that she totally submitted to a night serving 'psychic' to clarify a need for her to understand. Although the consequences were much more devastating in my neighbor's experience, the process of intrusion and taking was much the same. In both cases a need was felt which allowed the opening for someone outside to bring the darkness in.

The space between us can be so giving.
Or it can exact a loss that is most unkind.

We-ness

Although the circumstances surrounding my neighbor's failed and injurious relationship were very different from Marie's preposterous and leaching 'reading,' they both illustrate a similar vulnerability. In both cases a space of trust was deceived and manipulated, which led to a great loss in mustardo. In both cases, I believe that a deep sense of emptiness led to the painful consequences. The space of we-ness, which can be so giving when love is authentic and trust is returned in kind, was the space where these two ladies let their guard down. The spiritual and mystical type need of Marie allowed her a disproportionate confidence in someone motivated by business to fabricate his skills and abilities. Marie went into this reading with far too great an expectation that a 'psychic' could reveal to her some deep truths, for which she was willing to trust implicitly, leaving her vulnerable to the drinking straw.

Never go out beyond your self
to fill your bowl
with another's overcooked stew.

One might admit to seeing how my neighbor could be hung out to dry from a perspective of failed love and abused children. The feigned intimacy and manipulative sense of love in this marriage happened over years of time, which allowed the tentacle, by way of her perpetrating husband, numerous opportunities to hurt and abuse her. As I see it, this effectively drained so much vigor and trust from her that she was left empty from the very thing she was hoping would fill her.

One might wonder how a one-hour session with a clumsy 'psychic' could be comparable. The time was short but the dagger of the drinking straw went deep. Her blind faith in a 'psychic,' along with an empty feeling of needing to know, caused her to sacrifice the otherwise natural protection of herself. This deep sense of 'needing to know' established a false sense of we-ness and trust, which was easily manipulated when this 'psychic' pried open her inner being, allowing her reserve of mustardo to be drained.

I can almost hear a similar internal dialogue in the heads of my neighbor and Marie. Marie's might have gone like this:

"I really need to know. I trust you explicitly as a psychic. Yes, I understand that you need me to relax and respond only to your suggestions. Have at it, I have thrown wide the door to my soul. I hear you and, yes, I understand that you are watching me on a historic battlefield where I've been mortally wounded."

Perhaps the wound is what happened just then, and the battlefield is the edge of night.

As for my neighbor, perhaps it is a more conscious dialogue, but it comes with equally unseen vulnerability:

"Hello, Glen Wheating."

"I have strong feelings for you."

"Yes, it is love. Isn't it?"

"And you are sure you love me too?"

"Take me, please, to be yours."

"I certainly will, and I will care for you on a daily basis."

"So let us have a family and walk together, hand in hand until our last day."

"We will prove to your father that he is wrong about me."

"Yes, we will. It's just that he is not ready to allow another man to come between him and his daughter."

"Glen, I truly do love you, so come into the carpeted sanctuary of my being."

In this case, love was blind. The sacred space of we-ness was contaminated by deception from day one. Her need to fill something inside allowed the Night Server access, and when her mustardo was finally extracted from her life, she had paid a very great price. What she thought was love was left bruised and bloodied.

My neighbor never recovered from the pain and abuse of this relationship. She went on beyond it, but she did not fare well. She could not give up her anger over what had slipped into her life. The years following this relationship evidenced her dismay and high levels of stress, and her countenance always bore a visage of sadness.

The grasp of the tentacle became very personal as it hit that family full force with its cold taking of life. A close and potentially loving relationship was compromised and manipulated. This should have been a special space of we-ness, where love defined two or more individuals in a fluid give and take as their separate selves were mixed and blended into something greater than the parts could have been alone. Instead it became a torturous hell.

The magical and giving qualities of friendship and love that exist between two separate people occur in the giving space of we-ness, the space between self and others. Much can be learned by reflecting upon what we-ness can give us as well as what this space can take from us. If both people are true and honest with one another, then the space between them is sacred and becomes most giving, rewarding, and protective. If the commitment or trust of this space is feigned or manipulated, then this space of we-ness can be hurtful and maiming. Through the manipulation of trust, access may be gained to one's mustardo, and health and happiness can easily be compromised. When that space of we-ness truly exists between one person and another, then one's emotions, thoughts, and behavior are available in part to the other as well. Thus we-ness can be a most giving or most taking space of life. It can be filled with life's trust, love, and purpose or it can be accessed, through betrayal, by darkness and pain.

Once this intimate space of we-ness is compromised, the user's darkness seems to gain entrance into other intimate relationships in the victimized person's life. A cancer seems to set in. Where understanding and caring was intended, misuse and manipulation rear their ugly heads.

The most common spaces of we-ness occur naturally in family units. When a night stalker gains access to any member of the family, they can access the mustardo, to one degree or another, of the entire family. Such was the case with the Gettysburg farm family. As my neighbor's manipulative husband served the night and took from his wife and children, he also took from the entire family.

When the tentacle effectively taps his drinking straw into us by one means or another, we may be left so drained that we unconsciously borrow or take the mustardo from another just to keep going. Family, friend, and love relationships can be borrowed from quite freely because our spirits, passions, and lives are often mixed in a similar bowl of we-ness. The bond between Marie and her mother was quite obvious and clear to see. Again while we-ness can be most giving, it can also be a space of vulnerability in our relationships and in our lives. In close relationships the we-ness is experienced as an arena of trust. The danger here is that if one person in the relationship loses their mustardo for any reason, it can be unconsciously borrowed or taken from the other simply because the connection exists. As others suffer a loss of mustardo, it leaves them less than vigorous but typically unsuspecting of what has transpired. Love and friendship can quickly become suspect if this trust is compromised, because along with disappointments, vigor is drained, sometimes precipitously, from the offended's life.

If and when we-ness is trespassed upon, there can seldom be a cure. "Let's fix it!" rings hollow. If trust is lost, the space of we-ness is diminished as well. For our own protection, we must change the picture. We must seek to regain the personal space of our lives, putting us back in control of our mustardo before we lose our balance and our way.

How regal they may come!
Time passes, damage is done.
How pathetic is their departure
when their hurt has come,
and they are on the run.

Does the tentacle directly manipulate these servers? We can't know this for sure, but by intention or happenstance they steal our lives away, which feeds the night.

For the fortunate ones, one incidence of abuse by these Night Servers is enough to develop a gut reaction and avoid them when they come about. This is a necessary response because the very quality of our lives and personal mustardo depends upon our ability to identify these stalkers and effectively slough them off before they play out their moves on us. There are clues that might alert us to their act, which will often be hidden behind a pretty face or kindly smile.

It is ironic that they suddenly appear in moments of joy and satisfaction when we are fully engaged in living our lives. Not unlike a fly circling about, once they decide we can offer up some sugar they will immediately initiate their practiced moves upon us. If their first act doesn't capture us then another one is quickly forthcoming. These early acts of pretense come quickly and often involve a good deal of commotion. "Oh my this! Oh my that! Awesome! I love this about you! I've been waiting so long …" This early stage of inducement is often connected to some kind of gift that is more splash than substance. It is almost always party time for these Night Servers as they initiate their "Oh my!" interest on us. They seldom arrive when serious work needs to be done, and if they do they skillfully avoid getting their gift-giving hands involved in it.

We might expect to hear from them, "I wish I could be of help to you, but my back is acting up. I'm going to the chiropractor tomorrow," or "My shoulder has been killing me lately. I wish I could do more," or "Well, I just stopped in for a moment. I have some serious business to attend to. I'll call you tonight."

Another clue is that these users become too comfortable too quickly with our surroundings and us. As soon as they gain our confidence, they may begin to cling to us for one thing, reason, or another. This may be our first experience of discomfort coming from this other who seems to care and love so much. This clinging is not unlike a scale insect on a magnolia leaf, which inserts its proboscis to draw off the trees' life giving juices, leaving a healthy green leaf yellow and wilted. For us, this clinging comes at an equal cost of vitality and joy as our mustardo is being siphoned off. The needs of this server begin to seem like a sucking sound to our psyches and we should be alarmed.

As we understand them for what they are and initiate attempts to cast them off or separate from them, we will be met with emotional pleas of love and caring. Quite a fuss will be forthcoming. "I really love you. Give me another chance, and let me show you how much I care," they proclaim as tears roll down their cheeks. Worldly gifts, as peace offerings, are offered to us as they renew their pretense with us.

Know these nocturnal snakes
who with pretense and practice

wrap themselves about you.
Your love and your heart
are what they come for
and what they want to take.

Last, they may refer to the stress they have been under and say, "Please, tell me that you will reconsider." After a moment to wipe some tears or catch their breath the message is, "Please don't tell me that everything we have been through will be lost." If all their cards, played quickly one after another, fail to achieve realignment, then out comes the guilt trip. If you are not caught up in their feigned emotional drama, you will note how pathetic looking they are at this point. "This is killing me, you are really hurting me. I can't tell you how much I have loved you. I gave and gave for you." On and on it goes until we push them out and close the door on them.

There is no one fool-proof way to avoid these servers, but once we've been worked over by one of them, they will not easily access our love and trust again. If we know one to be a Server, there really is no threat to us. They may be annoying, but we can co-exist without losing something sacred to them. And if, like flies, they circle and bite at us, we'll quickly bring out the swatter.

Let us briefly attempt to distinguish between some of these life-invasive and life-taking Night Servers.

Scavengers

Scavengers skillfully utilize the space of we-ness to put themselves into a taking position. Acting with polished pretense they stalk, they take, and then they take even more. Scavengers swoop in with uncanny timing. When we are troubled and experiencing anger, fear, or depression, our condition will somehow beckon to them, and the eventual consequence will amount to more pain being added by them. There is often confusion within us as to where the added doubt and hurt has come from. We can't imagine that this one who has just arrived, with gift in hand and promises of how things aren't as bad as we think, may be hooking us up. Our minds and perceptions may not be able to sort it out, but we need to remember to ask ourselves, "How does it feel?" We need to notice that something just doesn't fit. Something doesn't smell right. How did this one know to come now? I should be appreciative of course, but …

The pain we are struggling with may equal an opening for the darkness, which almost instantaneously can be connected with the shadows that are always about. If a Scavenger is let in from out of these shadows or from behind the face of a neighbor or even a friend, more darkness will surround us as available light will be taken away. In the long run, our experience may be hellacious. Initially, we sense added sadness, loneliness, fear, and depression. Whatever has brought us low will be magnified by the Scavenger's presence. While they know not what they do, they do it well. The longer we tolerate these people in our company, the more we will be victimized by their presence.

Beyond their skill of pretense they seem not to have mastered other vocations or professions. Part of their deceptiveness is an apparent lack of motivation to do anything in particular as they just hang around. They will often make themselves available when you need small things done like fix a tire, carry some groceries, or change a light bulb.

As we become comfortable with their hanging around, they bide their time until an opportunity arises for them to seek an advantage as they begin to feed upon our mustardo. They most often target the naïve and vulnerable. As they skillfully begin to draw off our mustardo, they may also pick our hearts clean. So much vigor may be taken that our ordinary hopes and aspirations may no longer seem to matter. While they are there ostensibly to help us, just the opposite happens as our feelings send up a red flag signaling that we are weakened and alone.

In some ways the Scavenger's operation on others is like the preying mantis upon its prey. A proboscis, its drinking straw, is inserted into the body of a chosen insect. Frequently the prey is not even aware of this intrusion. Feeding begins, and after some period of time only the skeleton is left. The difference here is that the Scavenger of the night wants to create a weak and needing condition so that its prey can be utilized time and again. Mustardo from life's river may be completely withdrawn, leaving only the exoskeleton along with the slightest amount of physical vigor. We might ask, are they aware of their allegiance to the tentacle of the night?

Are they aware of their acts of taking? Maybe. They are conceited and self serving in all things. Do they have inner reflection? Is there ever an inner for them?

There are probably moments when they do acknowledge that they are manipulative, vengeful, and hurtful; that they are poison to the free and loving life around themselves, and that's the way they like it. After all, they are responding from a cold and calculating place, getting even with those who seem to have an inner warmth and value. Theirs has been lost or thrown away. Why should anyone else express a warmth and giving life that now, for them, is just a troubling adjunct to how it might have been.

Last Standers

The Tentacle
The deep-deep night cold as ice
is where it's from.
Warmth and passion it knows not.
Our minds have given it
the hold it's got.

Last Standers represent people who are of even stronger mindsets than Bottom Liners. While Bottom Liners may forget themselves and put a foot in the emotional realms of caring from time to time, Last Standers almost never will. For them, perhaps even more than the night serving Scavengers, the slide into darkness appears to be more complete and irreversible. Their absolute reliance on their cold and authoritarian mind set is frightening.

It may be very difficult for Sailors of Fortune to melt away these mental blocks with light and compassion. It would be like throwing oil into water. Last Standers, in their righteous indignation and thirst for always being right, are almost inseparable from the chilling essence of the tentacle. The notions and beliefs that justify their need but keep them inaccessible to our ministrations may be the likes of, 'We are the children of God,' and 'Man has dominion.' This is another example of justifying attitudes and authoritarian mental constraints that serve to separate and divide them from the circle of life. Collectively, Last Standers exhibit strong mindedness with an egocentric disposition. It never occurs to them to reconsider because they are always right. They have a cold, plotting, and essentially emotionless nature about them. To reach them is most difficult. Many of them live in homogenous communities and operate in bureaucratic centers of control around the world.

The average person would rarely come into contact with them, and that's the way they want it. They are important people who have no time for the average. If these people were to be compared with something from the natural world we might liken them to an invasive species that slowly and steadily snuffs out other life forms. Eventually, these invasive species collapse in on themselves, and then all is truly lost. How can we alleviate their mental locks and loosen them from their mind fields? With just about all of their other senses closed and off limits to us, we almost need to begin by appealing to their rational minds. However, that is not easy. For instance, if they are approached about preserving the resources of the planet with its very important quantities of mustardo, they will declare that the resources are already well managed and that human beings have God given dominion.

The dialogue might unfold like this:

"But isn't global warming a concern to you?" says the concerned Sailor of Fortune.

"No, not at all, I think it is overblown. The earth has always had its cycles, this is just another one of them," the self-righteous Last Stander might reply.

"Well, shouldn't we begin to control these greenhouse gases to be proactive in our approach?"

"Without a definite study that is conclusive enough to sound a global alarm, I say no because of the economic downturn that will affect our profit margins."

Social or health issues will demonstrate even less of their willingness to listen or show human caring and empathy.

"Should we attempt to alleviate some of the suffering of the sub-Saharan Africans? Thousands of children are dying day-by-day from the AIDS virus," asks a compassionate life keeper.

"We have already offered these pharmaceuticals to them at ten cents on the dollar, what else should we do?" replies the hardened life taker.

"Well, sir, they just don't have the means to pay even one cent on the dollar. So, a discounted price does no good for them. Why can't we make the formulas available to them? They do have the ingredients to produce these drugs."

"That is out of the question! These are patented formulas, which will not be divulged to all. I have what I have and if you think I am going to share what is my God given right with those who are less, you have another thing coming."

What a bargain these Night Servers have struck with the tentacle to treasure and protect such shallow gain in this world at the cost of what they lose in the next. They truly might be the lost souls of this life.

These mind games can be exhausting and we need to guard against spending too much of our time and mustardo trying to bring back these Night Servers. With their inner beings running on empty and compassion lacking in them, they are living on the surface of things in a big way. Their egos and sense of self-importance impose their social and economic will on others. Their interest in controlling and managing the part of this world they are interested in finds them imposing their will upon others. Here is where the danger lies for the rest of us. Their way is so contrived and demanding that they demean the value of our lives by selectively rewarding us with the materials which they control while hoodwinking us to believe that what they have and what they ration out to us is what it's all about.

It may not be possible for them to feel love and express joy. On occasion, we might witness them mouthing the words, but when an opportunity arises for them to show the meaning of these emotions they tend to come up empty. This may be the single biggest characteristic of all these Night Servers. They simply fail time and time again to express a true connection to other people and this living world. Being connected to others is so indicative of those who do, in fact, possess and benefit from the expressions of love, joy, and friendship.

Locked up Tight

Their wrong seems so right._
There is no feeling or caring behind a door so tight.
But if only we could
loosen their hold on us
like WD40. Loosen the rust
before their needs end in dust.

Another step deeper into the darkness brings us to the Dead Enders. Regardless of how they may appear to us now as fellow humans, soon they will be irreversible shadows of the night. Unlike the Scavengers, I feel that on some levels they are aware of who they are and that their allegiance lies directly with the dark tentacle of the night.

These are hurtful people who feast upon and celebrate the pain in others. A great natural disaster excites and satisfies them. War and large-scale bloodletting entertain their consuming minds. These are things they can stick their imaginary knives and forks into as they feast on the many losses.

They know they are vengeful and hurtful people, and behind a few beers they might easily admit it. While they may have business associates or partners, typically they are loners. Few want to connect with them. Even families choose to lose them. There is an undefined darkness about them. They tend not to measure themselves in particular societal roles, but some will strive for and attain professional clout. They excel in accomplishments that do not demand teamwork. The night is where they are at home.

They are alone in this world. Who would want to be their friend or lover? Mustardo is all but completely gone from them, and by some means or other they are nurtured by the night, siphoning off others' vigor as it moves through the metaphorical drinking straw to the night. As the mustardo is passing through them, they are allowed to draw off some of the vigor, which supports their needs. Of course, the majority of life's nectar passes directly to their keeper, the tentacle.

Some might liken Dead Enders to fallen angels who have been completely transmuted from fellow sailors into servers of the darkness. They may seem to be so far removed from our cares and concerns that they appear to have an entirely different genesis from ours, as though they have ridden a separate ship into this place and time. But no, they have journeyed with us. More recently they have identified with the never-ending night. Why would they do this, and how could they become so completely lost to us that they must be considered a force against us? I am certain they have forgotten how they got here and why they do what they do, but it has become their comfort zone as they serve the night.

Though they walk and talk among us, they are true outcasts of life. As we come to know who they are, the most we can do is avoid them. They are already gone, lost to the night where they will forever belong.

When we sense who they are, they seem to know that we know. At this point, they seem willing to allow us to maintain a certain distance from them. If circumstances allow, and they perceive they haven't been recognized, they might attempt to move close to us, almost to the point of causing us discomfort and even fright. If their hands touch ours, they feel cold and clammy, lacking in any life affirming mustardo. Their decaying and repulsive breath hits us as waves of empty and lifeless words emerge from their mouths. For those who have had constant and close contact with these people, something doesn't feel right in a big way. On a casual level as business associates, neighbors, club or church members, their deep and dark character may not be so obvious. Frequently there is a creepy, uncomfortable edge to their presence.

On the surface these people are often very capable at the jobs they do, and many are very accomplished in some of society's most public roles. So many of them are driven individuals who are concerned only about making a name for themselves. On first look, they may appear to be gifted and capable people who could contribute greatly to our world of existence. They have the keys to influence many as public personas in positions of leadership. However, they serve another master, and if opportunity allows these people a trusted place in the scheme of things, they can become quite dangerous and destructive in their positions of power. They can appear as people who gain our national trust and then abuse the limits of power. Hitler would be an agreeable comrade for their association. Perhaps they will show themselves in the form of an entertainer who celebrates the base and ugly or as a trusted man of the cloth who feeds on the fear and developmental vulnerability of our youth. While they walk and talk among us, they drain our mustardo by serving false hope in place of real substance.

Once their earth-bodies are spent they willingly snuggle up to the night, feeding the tentacle in its unquenchable thirst. When they pass from this life they inhabit the edge of darkness that surrounds our world. Joined as one with the night, they appear as some of the most troubling ghosts and phantoms, which we need to avoid.

> Due to their darkness
> light that comes to us
> must through them pass,
> and upon our world more
> shadows are cast.

Beyond these times these Dead Enders will manifest as frightening nighttime dreams, poltergeists, boogeymen, and ghosts. If they gain access to us, in our conscious minds or in our sleep, they will leave with varying amounts of our mustardo, which they will add to the night.

> We are most easily stolen from
> when distracted, exhausted, or depressed.
> Find time for life and love,
> do not withhold it from yourself.
> If you are not empty you
> will not be tempted
> to allow these shadows
> to set up in yourself.

The truth is that in this world, at this time, there is no garden or sanctuary where we can completely avoid these Night Servers. As keepers of life's fortunes, we might attract even more than the usual amount of their attention. Relationships with others may prove to be difficult because, if less than authentic, the we-ness allows an opening by which another can leave us quite vulnerable. So, for many of us, singular may need to be our disposition. Our greatest challenge is to answer a call to awaken those around us, and relationships may prove to complicate our work. There are also relationships that nurture and support our work and play. The way for one will not necessarily be the way for others.

Our work is to be done among the many of this world. Among the Servers and Night Stalkers, many will be found asleep in the night but not corrupted by it. For these, a foggy sleep has affected them, but they will prove to be good and reachable people. In time, many will make their way back from the edge of darkness as we illuminate their way.

As the newly awakened begin to reclaim their place upon life's deck, they may assist us as effective and needed comrades speaking for what is right and good within this world. Individual thoughts and acts of compassion will go out into the world as a ripple of comfort and a drumbeat to awaken, adding to the safety of our journey.

Those that look kindly upon us
are those who most need us.
Help them on the bus.
Those most inclined to trouble us
are those who are taking from us,
even while they make a fuss.

We have journeyed long
upon the trying sea.
We have come too far now
to let it slip away.
That glint before us offers
the protected harbor
of our destination.

12

What Time Is It?

Time remains with us, but is it getting late? It is difficult to ask this question without admitting to a sense of urgency, an urgency that is completely cognizant of the widely differing implications contained in *More or Less*. At this juncture it would be helpful to again touch briefly upon the shadows lying before and behind the human eyes that have put in our hands the responsibility and thus the opportunity to make all the difference. As we have speculated upon and gained some understanding into the genesis of these shadows, we may be helped to fathom what can be done about them and how we can work with them. Let us reiterate some of the most telling attitudes and behaviors which are so decisive in the struggle between More and Less.

At a time when the threat to our personal and collective lives as well as to our earth seems so obvious, it is amazing how many people seem to be free of concern. Do they just not get it in their unconscious state? If we raise the issues of subtraction to them, a subdued concern may be their only response. Not responding or not seeing is equal to a limited willingness to react to what some of us feel is necessary.

Expressed naivety seems to characterize their limited concern. Their typical response may be something like, "Darkness! What do you mean? There is as much light in every day today as there has ever been." The light from the sun that shines upon us belongs to this existence experience, but this is not the light of our immediate concern.

The light upon this world is but a candle against the vast spaces of darkness which separate the nighttime stars. If the existence experience is to continue, then this vast sphere of darkness will need to be clarified as our journey of life crosses through it. The darkness that needs to be diminished in order to allow this voyage to continue is the misunderstanding and confusion that allow so many hurtful acts to get between the good ones. When the hand of care and compassion is devalued, and the cold hand of taking and manipulation is extended in its place, darkness may be said to be deeply involved.

Pass the Night Through

The light that is diminished
is the love and care of man.
With our compassion lessened
we have freely taken from the world around us.
Much we have thrown away.
The rest we have put in a can.
What is wrong? What great storm?
And why should we be concerned ...

420

When justifying the way of our lives, certain humanistic concepts of God that allow us a special status have been used to give validity to all sorts of naivety. "Look at how we have evolved from the limits of Stone Age man to today's highly evolved, technologically advanced human beings. It is clear that God has marked and chosen us, giving us dominion over all the earth and all the creatures thereof. Our spontaneous creation, development of technology, and control over the earth confirms our place in God's plan!" It does? Was the plan at our inception to dominate the earthly scene? "Yes, of course, it was given us to do with as we see fit." There must be some confusion here for we as God's children have acquired an un-God-like human appetite, which is consuming our very home. I think it is time (and please ask God if he doesn't agree) to place reins on our appetites. Many of us are busy extracting all available resources and utilizing the planet's other life forms to ease our way and elevate our assumed special status. If we continue this way, then soon there will be nothing More as the very essence of life will have been squeezed out by the consumptive greed.

Could this God have really sent a life with a beginning and an end? If we accept this scenario then we can expect more of the same as we mere mortals attempt to get it while we can because this may be all there is. Pacifying ourselves with these futile efforts of validating, we will continue to elevate ourselves upon a pyramid above the rest. And when we've taken all the best and left behind all the rest, we will surely know that it is cold and it is lonely up there. We will then watch the shadow grow as it sets upon and darkens the world around us. We'll then surely know, as we curse our situation, that we are stuck, and a once promising journey has been forever lost as we enter the last of the evening light.

Come back now off this lonely height.
Join again in the circle of life.
This pyramid climbing is dangerous stuff.
Much has been taken and much has been lost.
But what we have is still just enough.

The truth is that for every advantage gained by a country, a people, or an individual, there is an equal or a greater number of people who feel some deficit. In these times the majority of this world's people are left to struggle mightily. The general health of our vessel is suspect. The earth is clearly being diminished of its resources by the ravenous appetites of those who have attained a high standard of living. Climbing high comes at a cost to those who cannot or will not share the altitude. Regardless of all of our evolutionary and developmental advances, peace can never come to a world where so much has been taken away from so many. Instead we have more war and bloodletting on our planet today than ever before.

Others naively might hold out the 'hope of heaven' scenario. "It is all in God's plan. He's (never a she) looking over us, and if he's pleased with my obedience (whatever that means) when I die I will be carried into Heaven (wherever that may be)." Frightfully we must suggest that if this is enough for them, then maybe there will be nothing More. After our best intentions and extensive dialogue, they may conclude by saying, "Even so, this talk of other realities is just so much hocus-pocus. This is it. This world is all that I am concerned about. When I die it's over and done. Why should I worry about the Something More, which is imaginary at best?"

But for many nothing More will just not satisfy. Accepting the above beliefs for those who still sleep will not preclude us from having more, much more. Thus the message of awakening, remembering, and discovering may be for the many who have always suspected that there was more to life's grand design, and that we are entitled to know it and be a part of it. For us the Something More will be compelling and will feel right. It may not be exactly this or exactly that, but there is more and we want to be open to it.

For those among us with a conscious acceptance of the More before us who are touched by the grandeur of life wherever it meets us, we must continue in this everyday world with an abiding enthusiasm. As we have noted, here and now is where it needs to get done. As we quietly play out this commitment we have implied a willingness to perform as a Sailor of Fortune for the world around us. Dedicated to our calling we will continuously extend our care and trust, even in the face of others' doubt and pain. As Sailors of Fortune we will also perform valuable lamp lighting functions for others, illuminating their way while we navigate our way out of the darkness. Mindful of the great promises before us, we must continue to function at a high level as we go about our everyday expectancies at our jobs, in our families, and within our communities, while sensitively articulating what can and needs to be done.

Whoa – all our fellow mates
Awaken now if you are asleep
Follow this lamp from the darkness held
Unto the deck we keep
Turn your face into the breeze
Open your hands to our vessel's needs
Opened hearts with much hope we hold
Before darkness upon this time is told

So much darkness has been so effectively introduced to our world by suspect ideas of entitlement, perhaps best illustrated by our assumption of manifest destiny. A self-serving consciousness has supported and approved the taking, while our minds have developed the technologies and guided the excessive extraction of resources from our living planet. The consequences have been painful at best and devastating at worse. We may not have needed any of it! This purist position holds that life was complete in its inception and remains complete today. Life is not about gaining an advantage but rather experiencing understanding and interaction. Kahlil Gibran reminds us that:

"Life needs naught but itself
and takes not but from itself."

Life may not have needed institutional type religions or large bureaucratic governmental systems either. Nor do the expressions of trust and celebrations of life need manipulative mathematical formulas or artificial processes of any kind. In this regard I am reminded of a telling experience afforded to me upon my return from the edge following The Sting (see *Something More*).

Return now to where life is from ...

... or suffer the loss (less) in the shadows
through which we have come.

The River Divide

As I was making my way through a nexus of realities adjacent to our world I found myself looking in, and this is how it was.

I was moving through a forest and soon came to the wood's edge. With my back to the woods I looked through tall grasses to a large stream that wound its way before me. On the other side the land rose quickly to a knoll upon which was located a settlement. People moved about the settlement and seemed busy in general upon the distant hill. Was I going to attempt to cross the river that divided the forest and tall grasses from the neatly kept meadowland on the other side? Looking about me as though to receive guidance from who or what I am not sure, as happened so often during my interworldly travels, I saw that I was by myself but did not feel alone. On this occasion, I felt a strong suggestion to remain where I was standing. I would go no farther. Continuing to study my surroundings I noticed a large reptilian form stirring in the creek side grasses. Built low to the ground with powerful movements, it looked much like a gator.

A momentary impulse of concern suggested that I should protect myself, maybe by sliding behind a tree. Soon I noticed a sprinkling of people coming out of the woods and attempting to cross the stream. The reptilian beast moved quickly along the stream edge, consuming most of them. Fear and panic was obvious in the way these people from the woods dropped belongings, leaped, ran, and otherwise attempted to avoid this hungry reptile. Some could be seen emerging from the far side of the stream even as the consuming beast was entering the water to snatch those that had gotten by it. I was amazed as this drama played out in front of me, but puzzled that I did not hear the screams or see the panic that I would have expected. I was also surprised that the villagers upon the knoll just a couple hundred yards away seemed totally oblivious to what was occurring on the far side of the stream. Those who safely reached the other side were making their way to the village. They did not look back! The stream seemed to be a clear divide. The consuming reptile belonged to one side, the villagers with their work and play were protected on the other. The people fleeing from the woods belonged to another world. Obviously they were fleeing from something they were no longer happy with. Why else would they risk an encounter with the beast in an effort to cross this divide?

Here again, I was just looking in. The edge experience had broken down my earthly restraints and I was allowed this opportunity to step into and see from another reality. As I felt carried away from this scene, I was left with many questions. Now time has passed and allowed me to reflect, and I sense that I have some answers.

The people coming out of the woods may have been those who were in one way or another separated from the knoll. The villagers upon the hill were focused now and focused always upon the circle of life, and they were content to belong to creation's meadow of existence.

The people running from the woods in a desperate attempt to cross the river and return to the peaceful village on the knoll indicated that something was going terribly wrong for them. The consuming beast may have been kin to the taking forces from which so many were trying to escape. They seemed utterly surprised to meet this devastating beast so close to where they would be protected.

The river represented the line of division between those who lived and celebrated life from those who had wandered off to find and practice something else. Perhaps they had left the Garden of Eden's meadow of good enough in an attempt to find something else in the slippery shadows of the woods.

The unknowns of the poorly illuminated woods eventually led to an even deeper darkness, and now in this day of the river divide many were trying to return to where they once belonged. Most were not successful in this instance. They may have remained in the darkness just a little too long. These people, unbeknownst to themselves, had traded off the More of life and were now getting much Less.

The consuming beast belonged to the limiting Less, which these many beings were hurrying to leave behind. While something from the woods must have initially enticed them, it was now clear that it no longer satisfied. In response these woodland seekers were wanting to return to where they were once from. Their losses were huge and painful to see.

> Now that you have come
> you cannot leave.

It was interesting how the villagers in the protected meadow were totally unaware of the great struggle at the river's edge. They had never yearned for anything but what life had given them. They were not tempted by the obscuring darkness of the woods on the far side of the river divide. In this way they were protected from the havoc now playing out at the river and wood's edge. It was interesting that those who got past the riverside beast and crossed the divide never looked back. They knew they had become lost, and they knew they were being found.

> Why look back at what was wrong?
> Why look back where darkness was found?

Will it need to come to this for many of us? Or will we awaken in time before being held in the tentacle's lair? If we choose to awake to what we are and were, we shall forever put the wrong behind. We must be clear in our intentions and true to our cares.

> We must be here,
> not over there.
> We must cross that line
> of the river divide.

Leave everything from there behind.
No one will carry us from
the night-like lair.
If you have lingered there may be time to run.
Follow the light of the setting sun.

The gift of creation has asked us, during the time and place of this existence experience, to express this life by carrying a warming compassion as an illuminating light into the vast sea of darkness. Thus we need to be guided by the directive, which in these times is now an imperative; to love the life within us while caring for the life around us.

Creation's love was sent
as a light
that would warm
and illuminate the night.

By what means could this simple and protecting admonishment have been forgotten? How did the obscuring darkness so effectively creep in? Our minds were given to us to navigate the great sea upon which we journey and to create order between the many forms of this life while validating the place of one and all in the great circle of creation. But, oh, how we have become distracted! Over time our manipulative minds have assumed a false ascendance over the entire vessel. This has allowed separation and division among us. An arrogance has been displayed by those who have sought an advantage by identifying and withdrawing riches that belong to us all, then calling them theirs.

Those in the shadows of the manipulative mind have utilized and taken resources for what seemed like their needs. They have separated and insulated themselves from those who had little. Religions were created that could justify their deeds. From a manifest destiny and dominion point of view, a rationalized aggression was galvanized against anyone or anything perceived as a threat to this elevated status. This aloofness by way of emphasis upon mental gymnastics implies a real separation from much of creation itself. Not only have we forfeited a critical balance so necessary to navigation, but we have also removed ourselves to a great distance from that which really matters. The critical balance that has been lost regards the integrated path of knowing, which implies the intuitive and feeling centers of being.

Getting Lost

It's getting dark out there
and I may be getting lost.
The way in which I came
is coming to such a cost.
My mind can't seem to help me
find my way
out of here.
Trusting my gut might be a start.
I'll also start by opening my heart.

For those of us who feel and sense that much is being lost and that Something More of great value lies before us, an accounting of our situation is important. We must actively begin to clarify and enunciate our position, and we must distinguish ourselves from the many others who are content to play out a repetitive tune, "Everything is all right, everything is fine; just take a nickel or maybe a dime." For us everything is not all right, and it's far from being fine. We do not want the nickel or the dime!

Accepting that we are concerned, that things are less than okay, and that much of what matters to us is being lost or taken away may allow us to agree that much of what is wrong that we do see may have hidden causes in something that we do not see. A recurring theme throughout much of this book, this assumption may go a long way toward understanding our present situation as well as helping us to appreciate the work that needs to be done.

What we don't see
may be causing
what we do see.

That we as a collective are out of control is almost a given. Where upon our way did a weakened resolve expose us to wrong thoughts and wrong acts? A bigger and more difficult question remains. Was this wrongness inserted into us from without, or was it developed from congealing ingredients present from our inception? This would mean that it was in the batter and is thus now in the bread.

It is my belief that it met us along the way, lingering in the darkness through which we journeyed. We may have allowed it in. Over time we lost our reins, and now in part we reside under the reign of a taking force. We must loosen the control of this cold and shadowy hand upon us. Then we might be able to move away from the edge of night and raise our sails into the spirit winds of the open sea, venturing into the splendor of our destination.

Has the dominance of a mind-heavy means of existence forfeited our control to a dark and using force? It is certainly an important possibility to consider in our want of understanding. Has a tentacle moved out from the darkness and extended its cold and taking force over much of this existence experience? Has the extended use and reliance upon our cognition opened a door for our own demise? As we have gone out beyond the true intention of the mind we may have left a way open for something on the outside to reach in and manipulate, if not control, this powerful axis within us. If this potent structure, our mind, has indeed been compromised, we really can't know who or what is ringing us up or who or what is running the show.

> From who or what
> is the way I am living?
> From who or what
> are the thoughts I am giving?

The bold assumption that has been presented suggests that not only are the elements of the nighttime such as misunderstanding, lack of caring, pain, injustice, and greed beyond need obscuring our vision, they are also home to a devastating force, the tentacle.

Who or What?

> Is it an entity, guided and directed?
> Or an amorphous force
> with a sucking action and vacuous need?
> Darker than dark and colder than cold
> occupying our place between life and more life
> it is clearly more than just a space.

Where to those who are lost to it?
And what does it do with our mustardo,
which it skillfully takes away?

How this control over creation was initiated has been speculated upon. It seems clear that a means of control from this forceful, outside entity is through the manipulative mind and taking hand of humankind. Our mind, the primary focus of control, may be implicated as being out of control, thus allowing devastating manipulation of the entirety of our vessel of earth and the many wondrous forms of life upon her.

So much of the cruelty and pain that is loose upon the land seems connected to the darkness of misunderstanding and unknowing. Remembering that more life implies other sister vessels and realities (with differing designs and forms) is important. The concerns of so many of us in the world today are not so different from the combined sentiments of other realities and worlds into which my edge experiences have allowed me to glimpse.

Nothing More

A cry of deep concern has been heard throughout the near and far reaches of the great sea of space upon which we have journeyed and upon which we must continue on this most incredible voyage.

This unsettled concern speaks to a strengthening tide of confusion and despair upon the vessel of earth. Those who speak out from the etheric realms and guardian spaces that surround the planet have deep concern about a storm of unknown origin bearing down upon the vessel of life herself.

Some of our sister ships that also set out to bring expressions of life to the space of night wait in calm and starlit waters just beyond the edge of darkness. Others, however, have not been heard from, and it is feared that they are lost. Clearly the ship of earth and the existence experience to which she belongs is threatened by a loss of mustardo, as is the well-being of the planet herself. So much of the life upon her is distracted or imperiled and is not capable of adding its spirit wind into her sails. Word from the hold of the vessel suggests there is a destructive taking force which is somehow part of the darkness. Is this entity inseparable from the darkness, or is it indeed the darkness? Regardless, it has not responded willingly to life's light or the sailors who carry it. Yet it does seem adept at consuming it.

If we can not ultimately free ourselves and our world of these subtracting forces, what might life's distant eyes see? Our space, time, and place will become guarded and clarified with nothing in and nothing out. In this late hour in twilight's last glow a bridge will be offered to those who stood for life as they could. Despair, confusion, and uncertainty will surround us on all sides. Then, a grand but blinding light will greet our troubled selves. Prepared or not, we will acquiesce to it for it shall be a light more intense than any light yet witnessed or even imagined. This shall be the hour of resolution in the day of clarification. Darkness and its shadows will be separated from any life to which it is bound. Mustardo will be loosened from where it may be tied up or congealed and returned to life's river.

As this scenario unfolds, a fiery transmutation will quickly follow. As with fire unto wood, this inferno will melt everything away, drawing to a close the existence experience. The wrong will be left in ashes, and everything else that matters will be returned to the batter along with life's river back to where life once began.

That which we had become
would be given back to where from.

The journey was lost.
The wrong came at such a cost.

The shame in this and maybe sin
all that we were
and might have been
couldn't find itself again.

In protecting ourselves against this coming storm, awakening and seeing becomes critical. While we are still gifted with time we, individually and collectively, must return to where we belong, immersed again in life's river and not attempting to fish from it. How might this happen? With the challenges and opportunities noted throughout this discourse we can envision what we wish but cannot know what will be. Of course we would like this awakening to involve one and all, but as we orient ourselves toward the More, that to which we aspire may not be easily transferred to others. Yes the darkening skies are gathering about, and so many have not yet evidenced concern. For those who have been looking, awakening has been unfolding; perhaps for a lifetime or more. The others who still sleep may yet be awakened, albeit by extreme shock. Awakening can be a process or possibly a shock which brings us back to life's embrace and may be confirmed through a single, significant event. While the preparation for this awakening may have occurred over an extensive time in the person's life, there is a moment in time when we know that something has changed, something is different. This awakening to the More of our lives may seem like something new has been born in us and for us. The birthing of this discovery may come in different ways and with different degrees of difficulty. Some will experience this birth of newness as an initiation. For others awakening will be experienced as a shock event of pain and discomfort that nonetheless introduces us to the More.

Along a continuum of least to most, a process of initiation will imply much less overall disruption than will awareness by way of shock. Initiation may be analogous to a hatching egg or a developing cocoon. For quite some time the egg is just an egg. Within it life is steadily forming. Then comes that amazing developmental moment. Within a few minutes, the egg bursts open and a new individual life is manifested upon the earth encountering an entirely new world in which to experience existence. Once an egg is joined with mustardo through fertilization, the preparation for life is fairly predictable. Cell division and differentiation occur over a set period of time with predictable sequence. If life is to come forth from this fertilized egg we can almost predict its arrival. The conditions needed to allow the awakening moment of hatching are essentially continuous warmth and protection.

At another extreme awakening may come as a comfort shock, and the quantum leap to awareness will occur in the midst of a great deal of discomfort. This would not be our first choice, but to avoid the lasting condition of not seeing, we will take it. This author's edge experiences were all initiated this way, albeit through the pain and discomfort a great deal was given to me. The violence surrounding the emergence of the sequoia seed may be seen as analogous to awakening by shock.

In the case of many grand trees, the seed (of opportunity) can remain dormant for almost endless periods of time. When some kind of outside condition such as fire, severe cold, or moisture awakens the genetic material from its sleep, cell division is initiated and a fairly predictable sprouting and growth is underway.

In the case of the tree, many years of leaf litter may have covered and hidden a sequoia seed from the light of day. Only a severe environmental act such as a fire can reach the hidden seed and free it from its sleep. From all outside observations, and possibly even for the sequoia seed, the means of this transition from static promise to living manifestation might seem harsh, disruptive, and painful. Much of the existing life of the forest will be maimed and lost. Many plant and animal forms will likely perish in the fire.

I question if awakening needs to come at such a disruptive cost for all of us. I envision humans as kind, alert, sensitive, and able to know what is needed before our earth shakes, rattles, and rolls in her necessary sorting out to achieve balance and realignment. Can we awaken to what is important, or will we need to suffer the full force of nature's shock and rage?

If we choose the process of awakening through initiation, then clearly what is needed is a caring and wholesome integration with our earth. In this scenario we implement a kindly stewardship with our natural world. Human-earth interactions must reflect living with the world from a circle of life perspective. We must come down from our 'above all else' pyramid attitude and understand that the notion of dominion is a curse of our own making. The consequences of this cold and superior relationship to our world have been referred to and can't be overstated. There are so many signs and signals that the well being of our vessel is threatened. Many of her cherished life forms have been diminished, and some have been lost forever.

Could the earth communicate her fragility to us? Would she call out with a plea for her human residents to discontinue their appetite of excessive consumption, which is creating so much loss and pain for the entire family of life and their vessel? For those of us with eyes ready to see and ears willing to hear, her plea has been heard.

A sense of urgency has been born in me during my time upon the earth as well as from the deep concerns from other realities experienced during my edge travels and experiences. More recently I have heard and witnessed the desperate and alarmed signals from Mother Earth on two separate occasions. The first one happened in the early evening four or five years ago.

It was an early spring evening. A chill was in the air as I turned my head skyward in appreciation of the pinks and purples splayed above me. The sky was lickable, asking to be savored. A loud crack shook the woods all around me. It sounded like the crack of thick-layered ice on a frozen lake that was under so much pressure it had to find a release. But the echo from this crack was from above. A long and continuous fracture suddenly appeared in the sky above me. Evening light was still available as I looked to one side of the separated sky. There, in full sparkle and glimmer, were more stars than I had ever seen before. Not only could I see them, but it also seemed like I could reach up and touch them.

A line of separation as straight as an arrow divided this fractured sky. There was nighttime black on one side, starlight on the other. The multiple colors present just moments before were completely gone. The line of separation appeared to run north to south. An entire galaxy of stars seemed to fit into the eastern sky with only deep darkness in the western sky. Leaning against a tree I steadied myself, for surely something momentous was at hand. As I looked back toward the fracture in the heavens my earth eyes seemed to see forever into the vertical height of the fracture. Light was streaming over from the starlit side of the sky and filling the gap with illumination. The vertical edge of darkness seemed to be walled off against this light.

This clearly seemed to be a separation with great implications and magnitude. As the starlit side of the sky passed its light into the fracture, it illuminated the edge of the dark side. Pitch black and deep indigo, it left a fright in me. "Is this the day?" I thought, "Am I standing at the cusp of yesterday's end and tomorrow's beginning?" For an hour or more the fractured sky held its place above me. All the while my gaze remained upward, as sensations of meaning poured into me. Eventually the stars thinned out, the fracture eroded, and a typical sky took its place above me. To this day the thought of that momentous sound, the fractured sky, and the clear division of the heavens lives within me. Was it perhaps a message from the universe to earth? Even now I await the revelation of the full meaning of this skyward phenomenon. The one lasting impression is that a great change is soon to be in the offing. How soon is not presently clear. It has been a few years now, but in astrological time a few years is a blink of the eye. If it was a signal from this world and to this world, I'm thankful for the time allotted. I want to be on the side of the stars when and if that fracture completely separates and divides this realm.

The early years of the twenty first century evidence much talk and international concern over global warming. Some suggest that extreme conditions with historic records of heat, levels of low pressure, wind speeds, and incidents of hurricanes and cyclones are normal cycles of the weather. Their response to the many that feel we are being forewarned is, "Let's do another study or two."

At the time of this writing there have been no globally successful efforts to relook at our relationship with our world. Giant waves, devastating earthquakes, and great storms, along with a rapidly warming globe, might give attuned people some reason to pause. However, in the years 2008 to 2009, prominent governments are still resisting the simplest first steps of assessing our need to reconsider our living habits and the devastating pollution resulting from them. This global first step of the Kyoto agreement still remains unsatisfied because some of the powers-that-be are not ready to make changes that might put a small dent in the bottom-line materialism of their populace.

Time may be running out for governmental institutions to respond to the big picture and begin to initiate meaningful changes. Individuals and small groups may have to double their efforts toward our world's needs, standing in as a pervasive advocate for her in these times.

Some of us will hear the call of the planet, feel her needs, and understand the signals. But if enough of us don't respond soon, many of us are going to experience some messy events in our near future. It is not clear how much nurturing and caring will be required to heal this planet's wounds and return her to a natural balance of health and life. A new and compassionate attitude towards our world seems necessary at this time. With this, so much of the wrongful taking and destructive behavior could be quickly modified. For such a sensitive attitude to emerge among us we must consider how we perceive our earth. In observing the contemporary relationship between industrialized and technological man and our world, we might infer that the earth is just a huge rock covered with some water and a mantle of green. But for those of us who heed her call, the assumption is that she is very much alive. For us the indigenous properties of Mother Earth seem so animate. The Gaia principle of a living and spirited world resonates with us as central to our perception.

To lessen our needs would reduce the pain.
Our world and her life would together gain.

If this attitude of consideration is not forthcoming, what messy events might we expect? That they would be unsettling and overwhelming is guaranteed. As uncomfortable as it seems, comfort shock may be our last, best hope. Our earth's efforts at regaining her balance and vigor will be akin to the experience of troubling fleas on the back of

442

an elephant. If bitten often enough by a large enough infestation of these blood-taking irritants, the elephant is going to act up. She might throw herself against a large tree, smashing many of her pests, or she may splash into the mud or water, where many of her inhabitants will perish. When the elephant does respond to the unacceptable level of irritation, the results can be unpredictable and indiscriminate. Many of the kindly life forms living on her immense surface will suffer along with the offending fleas. As this elephant may be likened to our world, many may feel as though some have brought these conditions upon the rest, and anger may rise like fire upon the land.

The hope of her resident population will be that the elephant will soon recover from her state of agitation and return, temporarily at least, to resting or grazing. Many people believe that the extensive storms, great waves, earthquakes and fires of the late 1990's and early 2000's are just that: a troubled, agitated world trying to relieve the excessive pressure that her inhabiting parasites, humankind, have placed upon her. Is our world striking out at us with intention? I think not. I feel that the forces of nature are more kindly than aggressively resentful. My closest day-to-day connection to the earth is in my life as an arborist, caring for the trees. It is from an arborist's point of view that I draw many of my clues regarding the health of our world and what the vessel of earth might want us to know. In my many years of working with storm thrown trees I have often had occasion to muse, "I can't believe it didn't hit the house. I can't believe it missed the car or the child." More often than not, falling trees come down in a safe and kindly way, testifying perhaps to their intimate and protective relationship to our earth and her life forms.

It is not that the earth is getting even, nor is it that we, as humans, have a price to pay to a vengeful Mother Nature. The simple fact is that she hurts, like we all hurt when we are continuously wounded. At this point we might reflect back upon the response toward wounding of one of her favorite life forms. Trees' ability to ward off infectious pathogens reminds us that the ancient wisdom of this world does possess the option to wall us off. How sad that day would be if our world felt that unleashing and surrounding her human population with deadly microbes was her only recourse. That she would remove us as a last, desperate act to preserve the diminishing life upon her demonstrates how desperate our situation is. As a living and spirited being she may allow us a reprieve if the first meaningful steps of reconsidering our relationship are evidenced.

The time for truly caring for our vessel has arrived, and the initiation of our interconnectedness must be underway. She will know that we are awakening of our own accord from a deep sleep, and no end of effort will be made by this world to keep us well and to steady any tempest blowing about us. Mother Earth's understanding and forgiveness will not be lost on us, but instead will comfort and protect us in every way possible as we come back to life in these late hours.

The second sign and signal that others and I witnessed in southeastern Pennsylvania was a startling atmospheric phenomenon that left a strong impression. It was a late on a January evening. All light had departed from the sky when I first noticed what seemed to be a light bulb flash, followed by a sound akin to thunder, but resonating more like the grunting of a beast. "Shetlinn," I said to my son. "What was that?"

My son replied, "I can't say but it seems to be grunting."

After a short period of time, as I walked under some leafless trees, I noticed another soft flash coming not from above the earth, but from my surroundings. It was not exactly a lightning strike or bolt but rather like a very large flashbulb. Again the evening-into-nighttime sky was filled with a loud growing rumble. My mind wanted to call it thunder, but it was clearly something different. The rumbling was loud and quite long lasting. It seemed to stay in one place above and around us. The rumbling, tumbling, unnerving sound persisted for five full minutes. Over and over again there was a short pulse, another flash (sometimes barely perceptible), and more unnerving vibrations of uncertain origin and meaning. Our minds wanted to suggest a fighter jet circling overhead or maybe a huge freight train rumbling down its tracks. But there are no train tracks and there was no aircraft. What there was I believe, was another sign and signal to be vigilant. "Awake and know that an alarm has been sent!" I couldn't clearly decipher the message, but I'm absolutely certain there was one. Maybe it was, "Call out your name! Signal your intentions!"

Yes, we heard the thunder,
and it would not stop.
Time was set,
I checked my clock.
The signal I did receive,
indeed it is time to believe.
Get up! Sit up!
Before this time
before us
leaves.

The call of life has gone out. We are highly motivated by this late hour opportunity to avoid unnecessary loss and pain. We understand that the time is limited during which we can awaken to the Something

More of life. Being open to receive will in large part define these moments of initiation and signal the newness before us.

While clear understanding of these two skyward phenomena is incomplete at this time, I will not forget the signal and will await further revelation or explanation. I realize my limited understanding, but I also know that I got it. I was there, I received the signs, and I will be ready when the additional call is sent!

Additional time will be necessary to parlay the meaning of these two incredible events. I sense an awakening to their meaning is unfolding within me and I remain quietly anxious to know more of the message.

Let us not be as the sequoia seed lying dormant under years of leaf litter, where only a devastatingly hot fire will initiate our awakening. Imagine the potential loss and cost of freeing this seed from its sleep.

From a static
and sleeping seed
a tree will never be.
Now if this freeing heat
will set the seed to growing
then the wonder of life
will rise from a sleep,
from which there was no knowing,
to become all that it might be.

Recently, in a most enlightening experience under a starlit sky, some deep impressions were imparted to me. They lend themselves to a hopeful reflection and understanding of the above-mentioned phenomena.

I was awakened in the pre-dawn hours by the screams of a bobcat. I wanted to be up anyway, so I rose and made my way out onto my bedroom balcony. The excitement I always feel during the infrequent visitations of the bobcat to our Pennsylvania woodlands was accentuated by my anticipation of observing the astral event of planetary alignment, the conjunction that had been foretold for the early morning hours of that day. I gazed skyward, and accompanied by the persistent cry of the wild cat, I observed the unusual alignment of three of our planetary bodies. Standing there in my nakedness in the cold and splendor of night, I was struck by the symbolism of this conjunction. Warm tears trickled down my cheeks as the enormity of it all touched me deeply.

Three heavenly bodies, each with its own particular and separate orbit, had come together in a single alignment. How appropriate. How splendid. How peaceful. How inspiring. Why can't we as people, cultures, and countries find a way to line up with one another over a common cause? Why can't we find something bigger than our individual belief systems, cultures, economies, and world-views to which we can all belong? What could we identify that would be so compelling that we can't help but respond and align ourselves to it? The creation, our earth, of course! There may be nothing with greater magnetism for bringing this human conjunction into focus. This could be our collective opportunity, and it may also be our collective imperative.

Whatever our personal beliefs or individual orbits, caring for this creation to which we all belong is the 'pearl of great price.' If we do not care for our world and its place in space there may one day be nothing left upon which we can continue to celebrate and express our personal beliefs, cultural aspirations, and religious traditions.

Did I not feel a sense of urgency in the guttural cries from the bobcat that awakened me? The cries of our world are equally clear and compelling. Standing there alone in the cold of night I was both humbled and gladdened. The planets, like oranges hanging in the dark sky, seemed overwhelmed by the vast darkness. Yet this night, in this astral moment together, they were not alone. Our world today, much like the night sky, is often more dark than it is light, and its darkness is more cold than it is warm. The call to us all is clear. Let's get together on this and raise the voice of caring everywhere. Right here, right now is a good place to begin. We can do it from where we are by opening a door for another, diminishing our need for belongings, and practicing small kindnesses whenever we have the opportunity. We've journeyed too long and given too much to leave it all behind. The common imperative is to utilize the waning light and limited time to hold onto what we've been given. We are called to enter a new and lasting day together. Otherwise, we may be experiencing the evening light of the late, great earth and the creation that has sent it forth.

Let us respond to the call of life, hear its signal, and come forth from our sleep. The message from my own inter-reality experiences, as well as that from others with edge or near death experiences, seems to carry the same message: what lies before us is potentially wondrous. We have all been sent back to be here now for this world. She is not a lame duck. Earth very much matters to this creation, and we must go on together into that day with a beginning but not an end.

We Are the Ones We Are Looking For

The heavens were opened
in sweet, telling chimes.
An angelic song
called to our duty
and sang to our beauty.

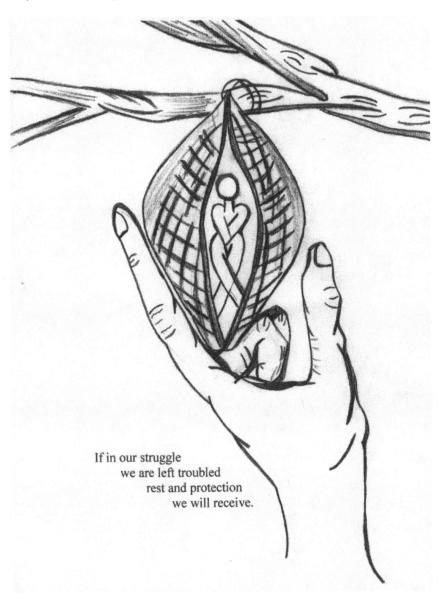

If in our struggle
we are left troubled
rest and protection
we will receive.

13

What's Next for Us?

The flower cannot last
but
the bloom will not die.

Letting Go

Many of us are inclined to live today as we lived yesterday. We allow ourselves to be guided in the present by values and beliefs that have worked for us in our recent past. If we are extending right thought and right behavior into our living experience as it regards the More of life, then our everyday world is valued, and this is as it should be. If we are caught up in habits of living that are devaluing our relationships and ourselves, it is my hope that we take the initiative to make value and meaning our morning call into our days. Living day to day by going along to get along without insisting that we feel valued can have huge consequences. The end results of the way we live our lives are never as obvious as when we are closing out our time in existence.

Dying becomes a defining moment as there is so much before us if we have embraced life, while maybe nothing more if we have wasted it. The way we live will have clear and profound implications in how we die and the options open to us at that moment.

There are many good reasons to reflect upon our eventual deaths. It permits us to practice and be prepared. With this preparation we will be better able to walk upon the bridge between worlds, as well as open the door into our continuous tomorrows. Our presence, essence, and soul will move along together in a successful migration into other worlds where more of us and ours will be received.

Individual deaths can occur at any time. We must remain aware of the troubling implications of this time of subtraction, which could affect huge transfers at any moment. The value of being prepared cannot be overstated. Being prepared can allow more clarity when meeting more of ourselves beyond the door. An added advantage may be the sloughing off of limiting doubt and fear, which may have withheld so much of the wonder of our continuing lives from our participation.

We now get it!

The meadows of life are endless

and

our place in them is timeless!

It is said that dying is an event we cannot practice for, but this author disagrees. Allowing ourselves to slip-slide away into the last moments of evening light without some preparation would be foolhardy. "It's something I really don't want to think or even wonder about," is an often-heard refrain. If there was nothing more beyond the time of this world, that might be okay. But if dying is but the first step in traversing a bridge to our next incarnation, then surely we must practice, practice, practice.

In the long and the short of it, practicing for our passing is the prescription for a complete and valued life. Much of the preparation for the next room in our house of life will also nurture our time here upon the earth. Much of this is about unlearning; letting go of limiting ideas and habits that have kept us in a small meadow.

What specifically can we unlearn? The many bits and pieces of information derived from our analytical minds, which have closed out or limited our interconnectedness to creation, have objectified our existence. We want to let go of the 'rules' of intelligence which have led to the tendencies of looking and learning about aspects of life at the expense of removing ourselves from the whole of life. These 'rules' allow us to see only bits and pieces of a much larger picture. We can only lose something valid when we attempt to fit pieces of an indivisible whole into our intellectual 'rules' of engagement. In this we are often losing our intimate and necessary embrace within the context of our living creation. In place of belonging to it we are left looking at it, playing out a cognitive riddle of who, what, and why. Unlearning in this instance lends us the sense of being woven within life's fabric, not standing outside looking at pieces of confusing yarn. We want to return to life's river where we clearly belong, benefiting by its encompassing wisdom with a deep sense of belonging to it. Moreover, what we are unlearning and letting go of is an existential condition that finds us sitting along this river wondering and worrying about what's coming next with our best clue being something some authority may have said about it!

The sooner we get started in this process of unlearning the more comforting our preparatory work will be. Extracting ourselves from the sticky, obscuring webs of limiting thought and behavior will allow us more joy and meaning in the here and now while also benefiting our eventual transition. In this way we can work free of one web at a time while sensing that we are sloughing off burdensome skins which did not really belong to us at all. As these skins are cast off, the celebration of who and what we are will comfort and assure our passage onward. What might some of these weighty skins that are bound to us by these sticky, obscuring webs look like?

The first skin to let go of may be the most trying because it is often something we have hidden from ourselves. This would be the skin of doubt and shame. These are often deep underlying conditions of our psyche that have constantly accompanied us in negative thought and behavior. I have witnessed people in their last days refer to these as skeletons in their closets. Practicing reflection and meditation can be a very effective means to observe these closet skeletons.

We can begin this personal exercise of observation with a willingness to expose these bones and dust them off. Essentially we will be transmuting this negative into something positive as we acknowledge the time and place of their genesis. This process of courageous looking allows us to become free of the weight of any guilt or shame that may have been associated with them. We must allow our emotions to wash us clean as this process of transmuting the negative builds us anew. Acknowledging these negatives is a very important first positive act toward removing the shadowy weights of guilt, doubt, and shame. Life's embrace will lift us into a more meaningful present while removing chains against our free and clear passage. In place of spoiled and bitter fruit this process of honest looking puts a nurtured seed in our hands and hearts. How can this fruit of goodness grow from where spoiled fruit lingered? Life places her sweet kiss upon those who ask her.

Now that we are learning to forgive ourselves, we may benefit even more by knowing that much of the wrong and negative actions in our existence here upon this world are in large part a condition of our journey. These old skeletons we have pulled out, looked upon, and dusted off will be left behind forever in that same box in which the other skeleton, the exhausted structure of our body, will now belong.

As the negative thoughts and memories are pulled out of us and transmuted in the openness and illumination of our willingness to be More, healing and caring tendencies become operative in our lives: our thoughts and words become incapable of wounding us or the world around us. There is no longer a need or want to deprecate ourselves or others. At the same time we are cleansing the pain behind us, we will be preparing the road before us. Our feet will be tendered by the pulse of our heart. As we give up our negatives of guilt and shame there will never again be a need to step on ourselves or our world in harmful ways. As we give up these negative tendencies a warming and giving wind will begin to fill our sails, carrying us within and beyond this world.

Another of these really difficult skins to slough off, and particularly in our western cultures of bottom line conscience, is the ensnarling web of possession. Shedding the first skin frees us of inner darkness. Shedding the next skin will allow us to see the unnecessary hindrances of possession. To effectively get out from under the enslavement of material goods or stuff, we must simultaneously free ourselves of the idea (another dangerous idea) that it is ours. There may be nothing inherently wrong with possessions, but when they become characterized as 'mine' then a great deal of distraction becomes involved, allowing Less to further its hold over us. Yes we can have material possessions, but at what point do they have us? Ah! Here is the rub. Can we possess the thing without the thing possessing us? We begin to see and understand how we have failed continuously to separate this hook from our lives. We suffer to get these things, then we suffer to keep them. How distracting! There is no room in life for the excessive celebration of stuff.

We suffer to get this stuff,
then we suffer to keep it.

Another correlating burden from these possessions is the distracting emotion of fear that somebody or something will take this stuff from us.

What is the right and purposeful thing to do? Give them up. By process or single act, only we can decide this. Clearly all these possessions are perishables, trinkets of this world. In preparation for what's next for us the sooner we begin to relinquish them the sooner our distractions and fears will be replaced by a lasting radiance, the light of our passage.

Honor the life within you
and
care for the life around you.

If we see life's grandeur within ourselves and begin living this way, possessions can never own you. We will want instead to protect and nurture our enduring qualities of presence and essence while gladdening our soul eternal; mine-only gets in the way implying that it is not ours, and life would never want it this way.

As we give up this skin a thin veil of austerity will become our way. Implicit in this will be a renewed free and expressive self that has more consideration for the world.

Without loosening our closed hand upon this world's trinkets we can not open our hand into the life around us nor can we reach for the eternal life beyond it!

With these considerations and preparations we have gained immeasurably in our time in this world, our walk between worlds, and how we will be received beyond the here and now. We can now better glimpse how our passage might be. Through these reflections we may be greatly soothed in an otherwise difficult time by the image of our walk upon the bridge. From a position of comfort we could include our significant others in our choices of how it might be for us. Our last days here will also be our first days there.

The passage between worlds and the doors and bridges we utilize is always an individual experience, and preparation for leaving is supported by our singular focus. Participation in our death is not necessarily enhanced by a congested space of friends and family. This may work for us if we believe there is value and comfort in the support they provide, but it is our time for our work, play, and preparation. One or two comfortable caregivers on the scene may be quite okay, but they must move gently and quietly about us with little or no fuss.

Many of the personal emotional scars from the passing of my grandfather and father resulted from the circus scene surrounding these events. People came and laughed, drank, and cried, proclaiming their close relationship or fondness for the deceased. I found the commotion offensive and wondered where these grieving people were when those close to me were living their lives in well and healthy ways. It felt as if I was being elbowed out of meaningful moments of letting go as all this unnecessary commotion encircled me. My personal reaction to this craziness was to swear off funerals and make it a practice to be with my friends and family as they live their lives.

As part of our practicing for letting go we might benefit from envisioning a how-it-might-be scenario for ourselves as we approach our bridge beyond. For me, I wish not to entertain my passing with many others. I would hope that those who might want to impress me with their presence would do it before that parting time. I want to be about my parting in a familiar and comfortable surrounding with soft background music, birdsongs, or the sound of the blowing wind. The illumination of the space in which I'm packing my bags should be soft and natural, and the mechanical sounds of this world should be as nil as possible. Little should distract or interrupt this passage. I want to go unencumbered and enthusiastically.

We may ponder how we can practice something we can't control. It is true that many endings are abrupt, and this is part of the value of practicing. Our subjective sense of time needs to be considered when talking about passing between worlds. Time can become very elastic, and a split second can become a very long time when it is our end time. Regardless of how fast the scythe of the reaper falls, we will benefit from preparation. The farewells, the bridge, and the doors will not blindside us. Against the considerable love I have for this world, my family, and my friends, I am not afraid. I am ready and even excited for what may be next for me.

How do we reconcile and prepare for the pain and suffering often involved in the process of dying? We need to remember the nature of the journey and our value in participating in it. This may be our finest hour of service toward the onward journey of the existence experience. In many ways our pain belongs to the struggle between the splendor and hope of life and the obscuring and taking force of darkness. The conflict and unresolved struggle between these disparate forces is the willing service of life. Even our seeming deaths belong to this struggle.

Our great hope is that eventually we will arrive comforted and gladdened in a place of protected harbors where dying is no longer necessary, belonging only to the distant past. It always needs to be remembered that this is why we journey. Life is not a given and greater force in the edge of night. Rather, it is very fragile and survives and expresses itself in a very narrow range. Life is a phenomenon of the miraculous in this world and whether it be human, or coral, or forest, it lives in a very thin place. But that life within and around us is our celebration. That the forces of less will pummel and beat upon us evidences the difficult but highly valued cause of our passage in and through the encircling dark and unknown property of this distant place.

So die if we must,
but live beyond this time.
Life will be given back
to me and you in kind.

We should practice when we are well and healthy and practice when we are falling asleep at night. We must allow ourselves to fade into the sleep of our night, then sit up in the embrace of the next morning's light. We should prepare ourselves from a position of strength, envisioning letting our useless stuff go and then giving it all away. We should experience our fear of the unknown when we are fully conscious and taste the debilitating conditions the walk from this world might entail. We should wonder about it, and then wonder about it some more.

Death is the Dark Side

Many people view death as the dark side of the struggle between More and Less. It's true that the process is never pretty. Being prepared, however, will extend some advantages to us. Participating in our own deaths invariably confronts us with a subjective appreciation of the power of Less.

Less is not just an abstraction. It is not something that is there because we didn't do more. At the very least, Less is a subtracting force generated by the anti-basis of life, perhaps the force of the darkness during our preparation for parting. We may suddenly become acutely aware of those who served up the Less side of things to us. Simultaneously, we can appreciate the value of letting it go, knowing they had no particular intention to do so. We will not want to carry additional weight from old burdens. It will be moving on time, and we will need to be light on our feet.

The breaking down of our personal bodies, loss of basic functions, and all of the unknowns of aging and debilitation are essentially ugly things. We can be comforted however, in knowing that beyond this structural deterioration we may celebrate in life once again.

once given

never taken

We know that a basic aspect of dying greets us with the breakdown of our forms, but how are our essential qualities of spirit, essence, and presence managed at life's door? Briefly stated, spirit implies the unseen but lasting allotment of mustardo from life's river. Our essence implies the ripples that extend out from us that influence, in right or wrong ways, the space around us. Presence is the state of our being from moment to moment.

Spirit, Essence, Presence

Our spirit is not completely housed within us but rather surrounds us and is entwined through us. It is most necessary and also most tenuous. It is the lasting allotment of mustardo given to us in the beginning, and as long as we stay in life it will keep us through all time and beyond time. The most remarkable attribute of our spirit is its relatively constant nature, when compared to essence and presence in this existence experience characterized by so much development and change.

Our faces will change
but
our spirits remain the same.

Having said this, our spirit belongs first to life's river and will return there if the beings it supports throw life away. Our spirit is a very elastic property of life and can be found closer or further away as we live in the More or accept Less as good enough.

`Frequently people, or their behavior, are characterized as being evil or dark spirited. In the context of this perspective, spirit can never be adulterated. If the beings referred to are living this way, spirit is already gone from them. Presence can imply corruption and negation, and essence can likewise be dark and compromised. The quality of spirit, however, is born out of the impulse of creation. The life it supports is also the life it keeps.

Our presence is how the everyday world sees, senses, and feels us. It is indicative of who we are minute-to-minute and day-to-day. Our presence includes our entire functioning being with the integration of our mind, psyche, and body. It will be very much the same beyond the door as it was just before the door. For better or worse, who we were embodied is now much the same disembodied.

Essence, on the other hand, is the value of our vibrations. At times essence may move far from where we are physically. The ripples of our being go out from us and can affect the world in real ways. Upon our death our essence will signal what is next and who or what will come for us. Our presence, with or without spirit, will remain fairly static while what's next for us is sorted out. When we die, only our presence participates in the deterioration of our form. Our spirit is slip sliding around us. With one last kiss upon its structural house, it accompanies our essence to brace our passage through the reception beyond the door. Together they will adhere to our phantom presence and await movement into the next room of our home.

The hidden beauty of dying is living on. The eventuality of More is earned and deserved by what we are doing now, right here, today. The prescription for our recovery beyond this time is the exercise of joy and celebration in our everyday lives.

By caring for the life around us,
very soon
we will be living the life
within us.

If we have lived this life, our last hours will find us accepting our vulnerability, knowing that the hurt will not be long lasting. We come to understand and find a beauty in this dying. The flower cannot last but the bloom will not die! Before this death and beyond it a basic trust secures us. We know that there is More beyond the door. It does not end here. With this confidence, our letting go can be one of the most dignified times of our lives. It may be a time of brute courage as well

– akin to looking down the barrel of a forty-four with a grin pinned ear to ear.

This trust and confidence can comfort others and us as well. It can be most giving to those who love us. We fear not and suffer little, thus none among the party of separation can find anything to feel guilty about. It is difficult to feel angry when one is going into another room but staying in the house.

We are now exercising the highest power of resolve as we respond completely by answering the challenge from the chicken farmer from Gettysburg. We are not attached to the results. It is not easy, but a giving smile forms upon our lips. Voices are calling, opportunity is waiting, and we are passing through the veil. Another room in the house of our lives awaits our reception.

Briefly stated, dying here can mean living on with much, much more, but it can also foreshadow nothing more. As was briefly noted, it is important that we take charge of our lives and participate fully in our deaths.

To die upon our feet
is to live beyond the end.

Practice can comfort us against much of the end pain. In this way, the bridge will open up to us and not confound our crossing over. With practice we shall be prepared, and confidence, not confusion, will greet us on the far side. Regardless of the nature of our transition; whether it is a continuous flow, taking the ticket, or even being stuck; preparation will be helpful. Being prepared will add wind to our sails, which is so helpful when moving beyond.

What's Next?

At this juncture it may be helpful to look at some of the options and how we may choose between them when our walk through this world brings us to the door of the next. What is meant by continuous flow, having a ticket, or being stuck? How are these options at the end of our earth time different from one another?

In the best-case scenario we achieve a continuous flow transition. The celebration of our lives carries us into More of our lives.

The house of one's

life

has many rooms.

Being received and conscious in our next room or world will occur without notice. We will immediately be dressed and defined by the designs and relationships of this new place to which we already belong.

In this continuous flow situation we will be present almost instantaneously. Only reflections or dreams of the earthly place we inhabited less than a moment earlier may allow it to be conjured up, and at these times we might be inclined to say, "Imagine that ... it was only a dream."

The continuous flow is available to those life keepers we have noted as the Sailors of Fortune who almost completely live on the More side of life, continuously caring for the life around them. These people typically leave this time and place of earth with a profusion of mustardo, and thus they have an abundance of wind in their sails. They have a serene acceptance in their last days and hours, though they are never in a hurry to go. They will often take their parting wide-eyed and with smiles upon their faces. They have loved this world without condition, and they express a basic trust, which serves them well as they span that space between worlds.

If it is indeed their time, without regret they flow into another room of their extensive house. They are always well received. Their glow in life upon our world precedes them, and beings of similar essence celebrate their coming. There is much to share with those who receive them, not the least of which will be questions regarding some of the mysteries of the universe. In this remarkable reception of kin they are simultaneously given to smiling upon those whom they have recently departed. A particular glow or vibration touches and soothes those who so miss their presence upon the earth.

The ripples of our essence will continue to nurture that world from which we have come, comforting those who were left behind and gracing the living world we lived upon. From our present room much help can be directed earthward. Our earth being is now among the wedge. A new face emerges to carry on upon life's deck.

Here and There

We are here and also there.
Life is connecting, congealing.
Familiar voices surround us.
The sweet jellies support us.
The face of our presence is elsewhere.
The force of our being remains here.
Preparation to break from the hold of night is underway!

This particular transfer closely parallels the personal accounts of near death experiences in which the people who are dead or dying refer to a bright light and a comfortable, if not exhilarating, reception before being sent back. They are not sent back because it isn't yet their time, or because they still have something to learn. In fact, they now have so much more to give that they are now capable of being of great assistance as they have seen beyond the veil and can affirm the More of life.

Not Yet, Sweet One

Accept our healing and be
warmed by our welcome.
Accept our choice to turn you around.
You are still needed on earthen grounds,
but do not forget; and none ever will.
This is your coming home.

There is another continuous flow transfer that is much the same as noted above, with a few variations. For those of us with near death experiences wherein we felt warmly received by kin and were surrounded by familiar voices, this may pertain to us.

Familiar voices and angelic music, soft and pervasive, will carry us beyond the door of yesterday and into our tomorrows as we witness the subjective experience of passing over a deep gorge or void. We have passed above and beyond No Man's Land. Our spirit, presence, and essence move along nicely together. What propels us are those who await us. We have simply given life its complete do. We did not manipulate for our own gain. We respected all life forms, and they respected us in return. Simply stated, life really worked for us, and we lived our place in it.

A comfortable sanctuary of merriment, understanding, and rest awaits us, much like the Benginers of the blizzard experience. A great deal of mustardo is with us. We are very much aware. If we did not know this beforehand, it will be explained to us there. Much will seem almost the same, and we will be looking back with twenty-twenty vision and saying, "Wow!" for so many reasons.

We belonged in life, and our destiny was assured. We will certainly meet the chicken farmer there, as well as Gertrude and a few others noted in this discourse. We will be enjoyed and embraced, and all that we might have worried about will no longer matter; even as our presence in every moment precluded our distraction from the life in which we so willingly participated.

Dying may have snuck up on us without a long infirmity. In fact, we will have barely noticed and we may be surprised that we are passing on. Preparation for our passing was in the way of our lives. We needed to part from very little, because we scarcely accumulated anything. Attachment to what we had was almost nonexistent.

Our interest in life was to always be there planting the seeds that would offer their color to the world, awaiting each flower's bloom. Some earthly joys were missed because we were off planting more seeds and clearing the land of heartache and depression.

So come now, come in. Come back to where we are from. Our choices now are many. We may allow ourselves to stay here in our peaceable space with kin of goodness. With protected celebration, together we may co-create more of this open, fluid, and giving space. Or we may be off to another world of form where we may dance, work, and play in place once again; living life in time with form and structure, or maybe even to return to the world of earth where we lived so wonderfully the life we were given. Or perhaps we may migrate in open space between and through many realities. We may choose to go alone or go with others with whom we are now gathered.

Passing Into More

We have given
and we have received.
Living life in the middle,
not on one side or the other,
has given us
these many choices.

Having a Ticket

Different from the continuous flow transfer is taking the ticket or the doorway scenario. Among other reasons for ending up this way, these people just do not have enough wind in their sails, or mustardo, to break cleanly free of the circumstances of their lives. For them, passing on is interrupted in one way or another. Their experience will definitely be noted by choices at the door, so to speak. Dying here may come to equal living on, with a great deal being resolved in the last days, hours, and seconds. For those among us, it's so important that our dying occurs consciously, as free of debilitating alcohol, drugs, and medical stupors as possible. What's next for us will, in large part, depend on right choices. We must distinguish Benginers from the phantom realm. We must oppose being encircled and held by those from the Less or dark side of things. We must be able to grasp for an extended hand through a mass of confusion and move toward friendly and familiar voices.

Having a ticket implies that, although death has occurred, life will go on. All tickets are redeemed at the door in the space of No Man's Land. "What?" you ask. "No Man's Land?" No Man's Land refers to an adjacent space to our reality on earth which serves as a transfer station. The concept of this phantom realm will be more completely defined as this chapter unfolds. Ticket holders represent a state-of-being transfer to which most of us belong. Rest and recuperation is always implied in this designation after which we will enthusiastically and consciously involve ourselves in life once again.

Ticket holders exercised their life habits and choices in hybrid ways. While most of their lives were lent to the More side of things, there were many occasions when they were guests of Less. These occasions handicapped and diminished their mustardo. It was not that they weren't worthy of what they had, but that they weren't able to hold onto enough mustardo to move them beyond the door and through or past No Man's Land without stopping in.

Ticket holders must remain conscious of the fact that they do not have anything in common with the now disembodied Night Servers, even though they will have to share a common space with them. However, in passing through, they will have imprinted upon them a lasting impression of the despair of the truly lost phantoms that circle about them, who have forfeited their right to life. These phantoms have used up their allotment of mustardo, which was given up and lost in the service to Less. While they aligned their lives with Less, the night was allowed to aggress upon and maim the life of this world, and as a result of this, the spirit they once had fled back to life's river. Reinforced by their experience in No Man's Land, these ticket holders will gain lasting appreciation and understanding in keeping More in their lives in a continuous way for evermore. In telepathic clarity, they will be powerful guides to those of us still on the vessel, helping us to understand the true importance of valuing all life in all its forms.

As life continues on for these ticket holders, there will be a preconscious aversion to anything in thought or act that will support the shadows of the night. Anything which will not vibrate with life will be avoided, almost as instinctively as a young child would avoid crawling over a piece of Plexiglas bridging an open space beneath her. The stay in No Man's Land will be a difficult but necessary correction as they make their way toward the eternal highway.

There are different tickets with different choices and different destinations. The ticket to reincarnate could bring a person back to this world or send him on to another. Briefly stated, more living may be expected, with less disconnected thought. Some will hold tickets to other worlds without the option to return to this one. This ticket will carry them away from this world, where much of their lives appeared filled with boredom as they took so much for granted. That which was offered to them in this world didn't seem to excite or satisfy. There is also a ticket out of form and into the fluid and timeless. These people didn't really thrive in form and time. The mantel of this life appeared much too heavy, and their life's fashions may be much more effective in fluid ways. There is also a metamorphic ticket for those who unnecessarily stumbled and struggled, often living unlike themselves.

While reflecting upon and practicing our parting, eventual ticket holders will benefit greatly by remembering. We have been a very long time upon this journey and have had many faces. Now in this present place and time we may have deviated from who we were and thus should be. Time spent in a long and protected cocoon-like state where life's deviations can be cleaned up and corrected, allows us to emerge with a new and clearer understanding of who we were and who we need to be.

All ticket holders experience much of the same in the time of transfer. The destination outcomes are where most of the differences lie. The choices have been made before the arrival. Each has chosen by the way he or she has lived. As the properties of warmth and care are administered, there will be additional real choices to be made.

Beings from the contingent of Benginers will assist and guide each presence to a protected, warm, and sustaining anti-room type space adjacent to this world in another reality of this time and place. Unresolved experiences of the past life may allow some confusion at the door. Passed friends and loved ones not yet received or found may gather about expressing their discomfort or anguish. Others who may be stuck might express their dismay. The one who is newly passed should not be distracted or preoccupied by the ones they find in No Man's Land. There is nothing they can do to change others' situations. They must collect themselves, settle in, be expectant, and look for an open hand extended out of the confusing and obscuring surroundings. If they take the hand they will be gently lifted and moved beyond the confusion at the door. The ticket they carry will open certain doors and not others. The way they have lived their lives and where they have placed their values will make all the difference. Consistent with all of this, familiar voices with unmistaken comfort and gladness will embrace their arrival. This is now their special and protected space. Opportunities to resolve old issues with understanding will be given to them. Old wounds will be allowed to heal.

Briefly exploring two of these tickets of destination may give us some insight into their differences.

Reincarnation is a definite option and possible outcome for those who have come to the end of their present lives with a substantial amount of mustardo. For these, life has been valued and essentially lived to its fullest. Necessary rest and recuperation for these people will occur in the kindly etheric or phantom realms of the unseen spaces surrounding our world. All the while their old faces join the unseen wedge of life that they stood in for while on the earth's deck.

As part of their learning and healing, opportunities and experiences will be afforded to them. Their spirits, which have been joyful during their lives upon the earth, become even more buoyed as they are allowed to go out from where they rest and experience many other dynamic life forms. They may be invited to experience the properties of flowers and trees, to know the sweetness of the honeybees, to join with the spirits of the wind and waters, or to fly in the wings of birds.

In time, each will be asked to choose which life form they will pick to continue to extend the ripples of life upon this world. Yes, the human form remains open, but so do all the others. Many, if not most, will choose another structure; something that flows, sings, grows, and shines without the burden and confusion of the heavy-headedness of their previous human minds.

Do It Again

You will be tickled or nudged awake
as you are born into another form.

Go out again into the world.
Love this life which has lifted you.

Sing your song,
adding your shine to the world.

Make your way again in time
without a heavy, taking mind.

At this juncture there is at least one more ticket we should consider. This transfer will take others to a metamorphic rest and recovery. Their quantity of mustardo may have fallen dangerously low as they came to the door between worlds. But they have done much for others' lives, even while they withheld much of life from themselves. They understood what it meant to be good to the world around them even while they shortchanged themselves on their own portion of goodness. Basic trust was often an issue.

Here they are at the door and they need this trust more than ever before. Their situations and circumstances will be difficult to clearly perceive. They will look back toward the door not wanting to believe they have passed through it. It truly is a one-way door. Kindness and value, which they gave freely to their world, must now be given to them. They may wish to run from the forlorn stares and the unsettling despair of so many lost souls on their side of the door, but they just don't have enough wind in their sails to break free of the darkness gathering about.

Helpful Benginers will know that they are there, but they will wait until their guests are composed enough to reach through the encircling confusion so they might grasp their hands. In this way, each is calling out his own name, and he will not be forsaken.

For those of metamorphic implications, it is so important that dying occurs as consciously as possible. As these ticket holders begin their passage, so much of their earthly fears and concerns may be resolved in that last day, hour, and minute. It is precisely the lifelong tendencies of fear and doubt which have signaled unpleasantness at the door. Mournful souls and phantoms will come with their cold hands and dark eyes, but these incoming ticket holders never were, nor are they now, one of them. These beings of the dark will be fearsome, but they cannot do any harm. In time they will relent, a hand will be extended, and a good and keeping clasp of warmth will lift their essence up. Thank goodness!

These selfless ticket holders who have done so much for others will now have a chance to receive healing and care. They will be completely and unconsciously placed in the care of the life-serving phantoms and for some duration will be protected, warmed, and wrapped up like a cocoon. While their transfer from this world is being interrupted for this necessary pupa state, dying here will yet become living on. The period of cleansing that must be undergone may withhold an awareness of one's presence from one's self. During this inactive state of suspension their souls will be washed clean. Their former fearing presence will be broken down and reborn into a trusting life in another form. The lasting and giving door may not now work for them, but it will not be withheld forever.

Their presence, or essence, may be carried in fluid ways into the natural world for recovery. Awareness will return to them as their protected, fluid essence becomes a presence in form. The chrysalis, which has been so protective, is opened, and the replenished one is free.

Kindness Carries You

Wings have been given to you.
Open them wide.
Fly for your spirit.
Fly for your life.
Live again in this new form.
Never fold them to ask why.

Their spirit was deeply wounded. It matters not how, what, or why. But their beauty has run deep. They have been guarded and protected because they insisted upon giving others wings, even though they denied them for themselves.

Your spirit, though wounded
could not be denied.
You so completely gave it to others.
Now life gives it back to you.

The transitions and transformations involved with the transfer of ticket holders can be most incredible. Their presence may enter in and out of many realities as they make their way along. The more lasting and giving doors may not now work for them, but may not be forever withheld. They may be carried in fluid ways into the natural world for their recovery, becoming properties of the trees or spirits of the wind or water. Still, they will continue and, in time, be called beyond. They may also choose at the door to remain with this world and reincarnate, in same or different form, and be largely guided in this by where they are best manifested for this time.

As we have already noted, the business of death can have the unintended consequence of discomfort optimized in the degradation of our spirit. Generally speaking, we would do best to avoid some of the business of death. We do not want our physical lives to be stretched out beyond reason and dignity. A tubular termination heavily dosed with narcotics will do us no good. These conditions often impart a debilitating fog when clarity is most important. In our last moments and during that brief time between worlds, there may be options, and we may want to choose.

The leaving time
is your time.

Louise

One night a few months ago I received a call from a long absent friend. Jim and I had befriended one another for many meaningful years and, although he had moved to Georgia with his wife and children years before, the sound of his voice made me feel as if no time had passed at all. He told me he was coming north for a visit with his family.

"We will have a dinner in your honor. The family will be there," he said, and then came the difficult news. "Mom has just come back from the hospital, and this may be our last time together."

"Yes, Jim, I'll be glad to come," was my reply.

Upon arriving at his home, the sounds of family along with the smell of dinner welcomed me and, for the moment, also cloaked the seriousness of the occasion. Louise was in her wheelchair, sentenced to remain there by what was left of her bandaged and raised left foot. Handshakes, hugs, and hellos opened up to mother Louise. I looked down at her, and I received a warm but anguished look in return. Bending low over her I received clarity on some critical issues from this very giving mother. This large family was made up of a devout group of practicing Catholics, and I was a little concerned about how my view of things might be received.

It was soon apparent that Louise would not discount the value of dying on her feet. She even embraced it. She held tightly to the message of Something More, finding comfort and trust in its implications. "Dying here may also be living on! There are other meadows to which we belong."

Louise had been treated in the hospital for a vascular condition in her feet and legs. I told Louise I would help her family understand that she chose not to go back for further flesh reductions and not to again be intoxicated by narcotics and dressed and bound by the many tubes that kept her breathing, medicated, eliminating, and hydrated.

Sitting at the dinner table, her family fanned out around her, I shared with them what their mother, Louise, was asking.

"When it is her time, she chooses to be with you. She chooses not to return to the hospital."

At this, her son Dan came out of his chair and burst out, "What are you saying? Are you crazy? We want to give Mom every day we possibly can!"

Cocking his thumb and forefinger in the form of a six-shooter and aiming up, Dan, with a determined look upon his face, declared that he'd been telling Mom to just keep looking up and further stated that this world is a painful place and suffering is just something we have to get through. The glint through the tears in Mom's eyes suggested that she just wasn't buying it.

It was a difficult night for everyone at the dinner table. Dan returned to his seat and stared at this guest who was no longer welcome. Looking around the table and catching all of their eyes, I felt strengthened by Louise's resolve and stated that their mom was choosing to leave this world surrounded by the warmth and comfort of those she loved.

"She wants all of you whom she bore, all of you whom she cared for, all of you whom she comforted when your father passed to be there when it is her time. She is asking for understanding and I hope you will support her wishes. For all those long days of caring, clothing, feeding, and embracing she wants you to understand that when she leaves this world she wants to be as clear as possible."

At this, in the company of her family, with a clarifying glint replacing subduing tears, she asked, "Mr. Redding, do you think I could die turned toward the setting sun while watching birds at the feeder?"

"Yes, Louise, I think that is very possible," I softly replied.

Dan protested once again, "But Mom's going to heaven!"

"Dan," I responded, "if there is such a place for Mom it will meet her at the door. She has lived a right life, and these last days need not be spent looking for it. Your mom loves this world, and she loves her children, her home, her garden, and her birds. She wants to look straight ahead to feel all of this as she continues beyond this world. It is here where her life was lived. It is here where her life was loved, and it is here where she wants to be until her life moves on for her!"

Louise's request will serve her well in the evening light of her earth life. She will go on beyond this world and live again in a very continuous way.

It is so important that children, friends, and loved ones allow the dying to fully participate in their passing. We must not withhold our support from them or tie them up with our personal requests that they stay a little longer. Instead, we must be ready and grant them our blessings for their unencumbered flight.

The value of the More of life is ever so apparent when we look at the alternatives. There seem to be many among us who choose not to take responsibility for the way they live, or don't live. They look at their time upon the earth as though they are an interesting collection of matter between nothing and nothing. Frightful and limiting conditions may meet them at the door. The transition from the living experience to the realities of the disembodied may not be a kindly one. Instead, what may meet them is a space of the lost and lonely where they are suspended beyond time in a state of non-entity. They have entered No Man's Land. Against these conditions, nothing might be an enviable choice, but it may not be an option.

No Man's Land is a space and time just beyond the veil, which can be cluttered with the lost and mournful. All who enter here would like to pass right through. Some will and some will not. The light burns very low in this space, and the lost are thick and gathered about. Some are stuck and very distracted. Why, you might ask, has this come about? It is because they were not prepared. Some were distracted by those individuals back home that were not ready to let them go. Others never thought there would be anything more, and others fell off the bridge they didn't believe they'd see. But most of these, with whom we don't need nor want to mingle, came to the end of their road without a ticket. They are waiting for a bus, but without a ticket it's not a bus they are able to take. Instead, they will be gathered up and moved into deeper darkness, of which the rest of us can know very little. Thank goodness for that!

Why should we allow ourselves to be stuck in this place of No Man's Land? If we have a ticket, have lived and loved life, we need not experience this lost space of the mournful and disembodied for an indeterminable time. "Yes!" I say, "Practice living, practice dying, and be present when you go!"

Where did the term No Man's Land originate? Early in my youth, when I asked Dad about the myth of the North Woods witch ('Witchie Willie' from *Something More*), he responded with a stern warning to stay away from her domain.

"Dad," I asked, "why can't we go there?"

"Son," he replied, "that ground between our farm and that witch is No Man's Land."

"No Man's Land? What do you mean?" I asked.

"Nobody can go there. If they do, they are on their own. There is no protection," came his stern reply.

As different edge experiences unfolded in my life, I had several opportunities to enter this space, which could be found between worlds. I always felt that Dad's brief teaching was very appropriate for these difficult experiences.

For most of us, one encounter with No Man's Land would be enough. For me, having had several stops before passing through this unsettling place gave me the confidence to share how it might go for us.

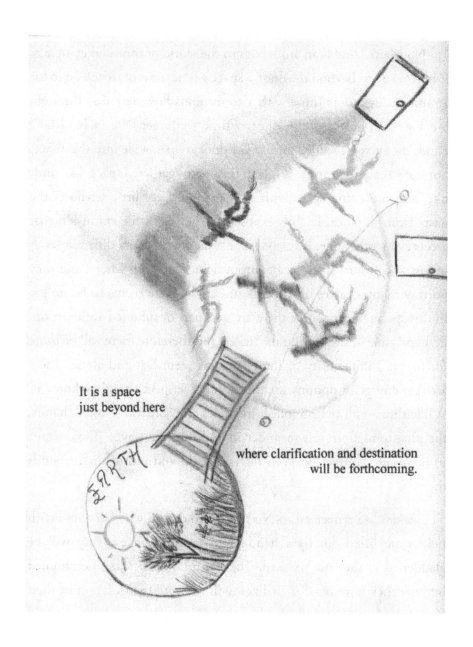

It is a space
just beyond here

where clarification and destination
will be forthcoming.

No-Man's Land

No Man's Land is an anti-room to the world of time and existence. It is a space just beyond the door, a space where most of us will go to for a moment or more. Those with a continuous flow may pass through, but they will not stop. The shorter time we linger here in No-Man's Land, the better it will be for us. The door is open wide into this space, but not so easy to get out. While in this many-gathered space, like finds like, and most find space with similar kind. Very little separates the nasty from the nice. Each is exposed to the very same confusion that greets every other one. It is a populous space with many different levels of loss and future promise. Phantom beings are everywhere, and they portray many degrees of warmth and cold. There seems to be no joy in this space, but for some there are whispers of subdued anticipation. Perhaps some know they hold a ticket, and therefore there will be more for them. The majority of the phantoms seem lost and alone. There aren't many good options for them, and I suspect that they know it. While those with tickets collect in circles and sometimes touch hands, the phantoms from less meander in and out like waves. There seems to be no eye contact between them. A cold and biting air surrounds them.

Tickets are redeemed in No Man's Land, and whether those with tickets are lifted out by a hand or a warming breeze, they will be gladdened as they are released. The nature of the ticket, determined by how they have lived their lives, will indicate the duration of their stay and where they will be referred. Warming breezes may surround some with a hybrid past, and in time kindly hands might appear and lift them out. Others may seem to be lifted and moved out directly by this same warming and comfort-giving breeze.

Others from hybrid lives will resolve and redress issues withholding them from More. Soft voices and warm breezes will soothe their troubled presence. They must hunker down and be patient, although they won't believe that they can, and wait until resolution is completed and life comes in to call their names.

For those who are alone, lost and captured by the night, No Man's Land opens into a deep, deep darkness echoing of emptiness. It seems like the collective misery of so many without tickets to life's doors may have stirred the cold night. A sucking sound preempts a cold wind and causes those in circles to bend down. Night has seemingly come to retrieve some of those who had nowhere else to go. Perhaps there was no intention to take them, but like metal filings to a magnet, the darkness is attracted by their despair. It seems clear to me that the same cold darkness present upon the earth has its extended force in No Man's Land. Something from out of the night effectively interferes with life's play, cuts up joy, and takes trust away; and it is present in No Man's Land in the same debilitating ways.

The Likes of Witchie Willie

Can some of these once night-serving people who are now lost and angry phantoms be moved back into the earth to continue their cantankerous ways? Yes, I believe they can. I cannot speculate upon how this return transfer would occur, but I am sure I have met some of them. The powerful but joyless Witchie Willie might illustrate this phenomenon. Most of the lost phantoms we referred to in the chapter Becoming Lost to Life may have their ghostly essence placed among us in this way. These may include many of those who come to the end of their human time deeply involved in the Less side of things. In one way or another, they cling onto a substantial amount of mustardo.

With their accomplished habits of the night, darkness allows them to continue to do its work in the light of day. This speculation helps me to get a handle on the poltergeist, and even an understanding of a character like Witchie Willie, who in their own ways are very strong and capable. Their cunning craft and unsettling skill are clear to see.

So what happens to them at the end? If they haven't truly lived, can they die? Can they move on to more?

I often peer back into my youth to reflect upon Witchie Willie, that old and lonely lady who was nestled in the long cast shadows of the North Woods. How compelling were the mystery and intrigue that surrounded her. It is difficult to perceive such loneliness without stopping to wonder, "Where is the joy in living? How can someone be so miserable?"

Her cunning and power seemed to deviate from what could be expected from a normal human being. When she finally captured me by the nape of my neck, I was shocked to find her behind me even while I was watching her. Did I look away for a moment? I don't think so. And if I did, how could she move so fast?

Now, many years later, I think I know. She remains here as a guest of a using force. Yes, she once truly lived, but somehow she took her hand out of life and never got it back. Yes, she seemed to be living, but not in the way we think living should be. This juxtaposition of her existence challenged the sense of life in others. Others feared this lady from No Man's Land, and they said so by calling her a witch.

That which found her in their day moved her into its night. Those kin to the darkness residing in this world called her theirs. Her deep and staying sadness held her in their lair. Some get turned around and sent back to the world where they once lived. Others slide into the ghostly realms, while still others are taken away. They journey deep into the cold and dark, out from No-Man's Land and into the place where the mournful and moaning are hanging all about. For them it will always stay this way.

I remember being in Witchie Willie's cabin and the frightful experience of being collared in the light of day. The forceful grasp in that old bony hand was hard to believe, and it was impossible to escape from. When confronted with such a controlling force, most sensible people try their best to cooperate. So did that young farm boy. Sitting uncomfortably, of course, upon her cat-haired couch she stared into my eyes, "Tell me, Boy, what happened? How did you survive? How did you live?"

It seemed like such an urgent request from her. It sounded so very important! Was it the darkness coming through? Was it something else that needed her to know? Did the protection I received defy the control and design of the force from the night? Was this answer it wanted so dearly to gain some advantage that could continue to wrap us up tight?

Very little value can be gained by further speculation, except furthering our protection by caring for the life we've got.

Hello.
Here without a ticket?
What did you give
with your time?
Now you want
some place to live.
Life may not have this
for you to give.

There will be much to sort out for these souls who have entered No Man's Land reluctantly and fearfully, or who have come to this space angry with life denied. The landscape will be murky and clouded over. Many beings of uncertain future will express their forlorn presence. Uncertainty will be everywhere while sorting out gets underway. If we can effectively steady ourselves against the fear and despair of those desperate to escape their certain fate in the cold and deep night, we may be able to notice contingents of those who are stuck. These ghostly beings will be almost frozen in place. Many have been here for a very long time. There never was nor is there now anything terribly wrong about these, but there is little which is right about them either. They never really took initiative in life. They suffered in their dying hours and now express little hope of moving on. The stuck beings have never really expressed caring and love for this life, and thus they withheld it or pushed it away from themselves. A deep sense of compression was apparent in their dying hours. A fear of letting go may have tormented their last days.

For those who might be wearing these shoes, if there is yet time, there is still hope and opportunity. Regardless of who we have been or how closed we may be, if we so choose in any of these parting moments, we may be open to More. Wouldn't that be something if our dark and cold reception was put on hold? It may be most important in this last moment to fight to stay clear. We must resist the end fog as though we are preventing our slide into lasting darkness. Unless we open up to life, as we die the ghostly spaces will be closing in around us. Even though it may be our last breath, life may find us. We should close our eyes, cry if we must, and declare that we are not one of them. After a period of time, a soft and soothing hand, feeling like a light breeze, will lift our remaining essence up and sprinkle it over the world. We will reside in a deep static rest in the form of minerals, carbons, metals, and oils. In this very compressed state of being, the template of our being upon the world will remain intact. Our presence as a continuous living experience is null and void, but something of essence does remain and by a very circuitous route may be assimilated and integrated into life's living beings. We will not suffer. In total unawareness we may be moved around within earth structures as carbons in trees, minerals in water, or calcium in bones. Our return to conscious legitimacy is a future possibility if this voyage of life is successfully completed. If this vessel reaches those protected harbors and is thus secured in lasting life, we will be awakened from a suspended state, our template aroused, and life will extend its opportunity once again. Coming to our personal end this way is very risky business. At best, we will have no control over how it does or does not work out, and at worst we will slip into the lasting terrors of the night. Most suicides end this way, as a result of anger turned against the self. Life has been thrown away, and a lasting state of static existence is the most that they can hope for. Templates will be separated from form, and presence will determine our next room or our elemental return to the world from which we recently left.

The Less Side

Life has withdrawn her spirit.
Its home has been voided.
The windows are boarded over.

Those who have effectively and continuously served life up to the night are represented in No Man's Land by the anguished and frightening phantoms that are moving about. Their individual essence and presence appears as dark and cold shadows. Their transfer out of this phantom space is indicated by a suction sound in the vicinity of darkened doors, as those lost to life are being drawn out.

When the Night Servers from the Less side of things are passing into their last days, an unsettling fear and anguish is often expressed. Their spirit has probably already vacated their premises and returned to life's river. When a persona indicates little warmth and compassion, there is very little space in this life for the spirit. Therefore, from the perspective of spirit, these people are essentially heartless, or dead men walking as they serve out their time in existence. They do feel, but what they feel is hard to know by those on the More side of things. Perhaps the most we can know is what we can observe in the twilight hours of their time upon the earth. What we often will see is an agitated presence with distorted facial expressions. An anguished passing is obvious in many respects, but tears we will not see. In those trying moments we will understand that tears can not flow on a face of stone.

These people are landing with a thud in No Man's Land, and once they are removed from that space they will never be seen again on this side of life. If the tentacle can effectively move them back upon the face of the earth (as illustrated by Witchie Willie), they will occupy the marginal side of things where they will continue to take from life's giving forms. They will continue their work in the time of subtraction, loosening mustardo from life giving beings and essentially feeding the night aspects of life, which they will attempt to draw off. They might return, for instance, as ensnarling poison ivy vines constricting the life out of trees. They may also show up as vectors of deadly diseases, such as blood sucking ticks, or mosquitoes that draw off warm blood and irritate the restful while adding illness to their prey. We should not be hesitant to smack these pests. Some may argue that they are alive, and to a degree they are. Their lives, however, are given to taking, and very few redeeming qualities accompany them. If they occur in human form, they mirror the agitating and taking life forms of the natural world noted above.

How long has it been going on that a one-time promising life returns to our present world to operate from the less side of things? In effect, the ghosts of Night Servers may be here among us as gnats, fire ants, mosquitoes, lice, ticks, yellow jackets, and even people who continue to harass life from behind the dark face of a using and taking force. Even as we are coming to the end of our story, we are left to wonder, "How?" and "Why?" We can suspect that over the long journey there has been a great deal of vulnerability in the passage, the confusion, and the dying. But we really can't know it for sure. It just isn't in us to understand the obscuring twists and turns of the night.

In less challenging times the space of No-Man's Land would be less cluttered and cumbersome. There would be many less residents gathered there awaiting the arrival of one bus or another. Destinations would be clearer, and the obscuring influence of the night would not be the order of this anti-room. With less distraction there would be less delay. Resolution toward our tomorrows would be swifter in coming. But, in these times of subtraction, this is just the way it is.

I make a simple suggestion at this point. Should we fail to find legitimacy in our lives and should we be afraid to practice letting go of this life, we may be assured that we are going to No-Man's Land, and it may be a long time before we are moving on or getting out. With our willingness, however, these consequences can be avoided. In the staying of one's life is the protection of another life. Once again the single imperative central to this worldview and responsible for allowing the eternal More into our lives is to:

Honor the life within you

and

care for the life around you.

With this principled and practiced existence we will remove from death its hold over us.

No darkness now.
No darkness ever.

It is a bridge we wish to take
into the world of the double suns.
It is a place where life lives always
and death can never come.

Conclusion

As we near the end of this discourse we end where we began, with two simple but very different words, More or Less. The More of life seeks to return completely to us as we express our connection to one another and the world of our residence. This celebration of life can be a staying experience if we return to life's river while trusting the destination of its flow. We will then be guided by the ancient wisdom of its source and comforted by the considerable life of its waters.

It is a late hour in our challenged journey for life. We must work together to diminish the Less and allow the More in. As the Less is allowed to fall away from us, the More will become us.

If We Only Will ...

resolve our conflicts with this world

and

give back to life the much it has given us

deepen our commitment to honor the life within us

while

caring for the life around us

appreciate our value, accepting the much that we are

and

know we are far too precious to leave it all behind

know that we have been here for a very long time

and

know that time has been long in us as well

This is all that it would take to allow us to awaken into the wondrous More of life. Accepting that we are all involved in the conflict between More or Less, we will come to know who we are and who we are not. It is this author's hope that the words and thoughts of this discourse strengthen us against the distraction of purposeless thought and excessive service to material stuff. Together we must understand the need to free ourselves from these distractions to avoid the taking teeth of subtraction. We must not allow the Less to occupy our lives, which might permit the enduring illumination of life in existence to go out for us. We have come to a time when we must leave the house of not enough and open a door to the lasting and wondrous. Caring is the key that opens this door. With this key love, kindness, and friendship are released upon our world. From beyond this door the consciousness required to understand the length and breadth of life's journey and our personal place within it enters in.

A Tale of Two Sons

A father had fallen to the weight of time allocated in this world. He lay on his bed, slowly closing his eyes upon his earthen life and understanding that these would be his last hours. With a barely audible voice he summoned his sons. They stood quietly by his bedside until their father awakened from his last minute preparations and opened his eyes to look at them. "Excuse me, sons, but I am very busy preparing myself for the journey onward. My preparations are all but complete, and I will remain with you for only a short time. This will be our last opportunity to exchange words and for you to ask for any final favors or share any parting thoughts with me."

The oldest son stepped even closer to the bed, nudging his younger brother into the background. The habit of being first was always a trait of his, and it seemed even more important to him on the day of his father's passing.

With an anxious voice he extended his arms above his dying father and asked, "What is to become of our estate? I have always worked tirelessly alongside of you and now I hope you have declared that it will be mine. My brother, of course, will always have a comfortable place here, but I think it will be much better managed if you see fit to leave it under my care."

To this his father spoke feebly that it would be done. The older son broke into a smile from ear to ear and raised his hands above his head crying, "Hallelujah!" Seeing the pain of death upon his father's face he leaned forward and placed a kiss on his father's hand saying, "I'll have my brother wait in an adjoining room for a little while to allow you some time to recuperate."

"No, please, allow your younger brother to approach and stand by my bed."

The youngest son cried deeply and could not quiet the quaking within his heart. Tenderly the father pulled his troubled son's head to his chest. "Come Son, share with me this last and longing need. What would you have me do for you?"

"Father," the still quivering son responded, "it is clear that you are leaving without fulfilling your promise to me. You have spoken of a very special place of the soul, but you have not shown me how I might touch it. It remains real only in words for me, so, please, I need to know how to reach it."

"Son, I am sorry for not having given more time to help you touch your soul. But the first and most important thing is to look for it. This you are already doing. The depth of your tears shows that you dearly miss it. When the need to know your soul burns so intently in your heart, you will find it. It is something that is discovered, and once you find it, it is forever with you! You will go everywhere with it and nowhere without it."

"But Father, how will I begin to look for it and how will I know when I find it?"

"The things you will do in this world will be the paths of discovery. The faces of those around you will be a mirror for you to know how you are doing. If the songs from the meadow are sweet, and if the faces that look back at you are smiling with sparkling eyes, then you are on the right path. The world around you will always be your affirmation. I must warn you, the path of discovery can be difficult and sometimes lonely. With intention and persistence your search will take you to a time when you will not easily recognize where you begin or end.

Then you will have fallen into your soul, and you will never feel lonely again."

The young son's ears were now pressed next to his father's mouth to grasp completely these last, parting whispers. "And Father, how will it feel?"

"It will feel as if you have come in from the cold with the infinite wrapped around you. You will be warmed by the significant. Your search will now be over and living will feel complete. There will be an easy smile upon your face that will reveal gladness in you that can't help but lift the doubts and soothe the pain of others. What you have searched for and discovered will compel others to look for their souls as well, and in time the gladness from them will seek out the gladness of many others. Soon there shall be such a joy upon this land that it will never go away."

"Father, Father …"

The time of passing had come. The words would no longer flow, but there was a smile, a grand smile, upon his passing face.

Less or More

Who and how many will respond
to life's last call?

The Great Escape

One cold, mid-December day I was loading short pieces of firewood atop hot coals in the belly of my woodstove. Sitting in a comfortable chair in front of the open door stove, I was enjoying watching the small licks of flames begin their consumption of the newly placed wood.

It soon came to my attention that some little living beings were having a very difficult time of it. From inside a piece of cherry wood, over-wintering ants had been awakened from their slumber by the heat, and they were making their way onto the surface of the wood farthest above the coals. The ants sensed their dilemma and expressed their panic as flames emerged between the pieces of wood. They raced around on the surface of the wood, searching for an exit from their predicament. In the highly organized system of ant life, nothing could have prepared them for the fire that was quickly consuming their winter habitat. What could be done to help these frightened beings? I attempted to utilize a sliver of wood to lift them off their scorching abode, but as quickly as I scooped some up they jumped from the wood splinter back onto their burning residence. This method clearly wasn't working, and the time remaining for rescue was becoming very limited. Singeing the hair on the back of my hand, I reached in wanting to pull them from their diminishing island of safety. But instead of trusting the giant hand, they chose to return to the home that they once knew. I could hear their defenseless bodies crackling, as they were consumed by the heat of the fire. Though my painfully burned hand and the obnoxious smell of my singed hair were testament to my efforts, I sat back in my chair frustrated that I had not been successful in rescuing these innocent creatures.

Suddenly I noticed that there was still one ant running frantically about on a small square of safety on the top of the piece of wood, even though all of the remaining wood was completely involved in the fire. In one last attempt at rescue, I laid the splinter of wood from the frame of the woodstove, across the flames, to the spot occupied by the ant.

"Save yourself," I whispered. Waiting to hear the last body pop before I closed the stove door, I was amazed to see the little ant use the sliver of wood as a bridge and make his great escape. As quickly as I placed it, the ant jumped on it and raced through the flames and out of the stove. At that point he got it. The giant was an unknown, but it was better than his now incinerated home of wood. I put my hand at the end of the sliver of wood, and the ant jumped in it. In a way uncharacteristic of ants, he waited calmly there while I closed the stove door and escorted him outside to a soft place in the mulch in my garden.

What an amazing drama had just unfolded! Touched by the symbolism of what had just transpired I returned to the comfort of my chair by the woodstove and began to wonder. If I had not tried to force the recovery of these ants, would I perhaps have saved more of them? Had I laid the sliver of wood down earlier, offering them all a bridge out of their dilemma, would they have used it as the lone remaining ant did? Why did the ants attempt to return to the cavity within the cherry wood, frying and dying as they did? Why didn't their instincts of preservation keep them on that remaining island of hope above the flames? Why was just one of many allowed to escape the inferno?

While I couldn't answer these questions, they did allow me to reflect upon correlations to present day conditions in our world. The ants were abruptly awakened from their winter sleep by the heat of a fire (an unexpected condition), which was telling them that they had to leave their home. The home for the ants might be likened to the way of life for us human 'ants.'

The heat from the fire that awakened the ants may not be so different from the alarming conditions of our world: global warming, dying forests, super bugs, and disappearing species. Action and movement is urgently called for! For us humans changing behaviors of taking, polluting, manipulation, and blind faith may amount to answering the alarm and escaping the fire. Will we do it, or will we blindly go on with our habits of bottom line materialism and domination of the world? Will we insist on staying where we have known our home to be (our way of life), even as the fire and darkness of a dying world surround us? Will we feel and experience the loss of what was once promising as our lives are extinguished before us? Will we choose the Less or the More? And if this More is what we choose, what will be our bridge out of the consuming fire and obscuring darkness which even now are upon us?

Our bridge will be a basic trust in the promise of Something More before us. The hand that receives us will be the same hand of life that released us. We will have called out our name as our presence in the circle of life evidences our renewed care and reverence.

Darkness seemed set and solid,
and all around
sent upon an arrow
from life's mighty bow
deep into this inky space
night was now set aglow.
Into this place we
journeyed so
flowers might from the heavens
onto the ground to grow.

As I tender my farewell, there are a few assumptions and affirmations to consider. Few will have begun to read this book without having heretofore sensed the possibility of a bigger world. None will have finished this book without discovering that they have already begun living in a better world. So much of our individual and collective success in our search for a more meaningful existence experience is dependent upon awakening and remembering the all of who we are. It is not about becoming more important but rather knowing how important we are. Every moment or act that celebrates life adds value to our presence.

The worldview introduced in this book advocates placing great value in our past and current presence in life's incredible journey. With a renewed sense of our present opportunities and obligations, many of us may want to respond to the challenges and issues before us with giving and purposeful efforts. All the while we must remain mindful that when we strive toward discovering the More of life, no effort is too small or unworthy. It is not so much about assuming a heavy burden or making hurried efforts, but rather living in such a way in which we consciously practice caring for the life in and around us. It is this author's hope that *More or Less* has helped us to discern what we value and oriented us toward the direction that best brings it within our reach. As we move forward, if this is true, there is no need for overwhelming single efforts, nor is there any particular hurry. Let us enjoy our purposeful walk through this world, and know that we have returned to the giving waters of life's river. These waters shall forever quench our thirst and sustain our presence.

The Journey Continues ...

Glossary

anti-room

a space adjacent to this world; another reality of this time and place

Benginers

human like beings who have a consistent and knowing connection to life's journey; they exist in phantom form but are capable of stepping out of their realm into ours to lend assistance or protection; they can come and go quickly, quietly, and effortlessly

curly-whirlys

sketchy outlines; wavy, fluid-like indications of some essence or presence; typically occur at or above our line of sight; always moving, they occur most often in the morning and evening light

Cyclops

a large being showing a single red eye that often appeared detached from its form; very vocal, called with a sound somewhat like a great horned owl; could often be signaled to respond to vocalizations which approximated his own language; a very dramatic and powerful figure, he visited the earth over a three year period slipping in and out of our reality

503

deadenders

    using people whose skills of manipulation take excessively from others; they effectively serve Less into the life of others; when they die to this world they reside in a cold and dark space

edge experience

    where the experience of near death or actually dying has taken one beyond theexistence reality of this world to other worlds and realities

existence experience

    the unique expression of life upon the world of earth; that individual forms such as people, trees, dogs, etc. live in a period of time as separate entities even while nurtured by a similar vein of life; while unique in form, all are animated by the same river of life

having a ticket

    the collective vibrations, or presence, of your life signals to life's keepers; your condition and what's next for you as you make that walk between worlds; ticket holders have more life before them and the nature of their tickets will signal their different possibilities

intuition

    a means of knowing something is real or true for us even though we may not know how we know; this knowing is often accompanied by a strong feeling

life-leaning hybrid

these beings resort to acts of taking and manipulation as a result of subjective states of doubt and apprehension; the majority of their time is spent expressing life giving and caring behavior; these are essentially life serving, not self serving people

mustardo

the fluid essence of life; given to us in our beginning, the dynamic something which helps build life's forms while providing the vigor and spirit which allows our function; this precious underlying something is carried to us in life's river where we may draw from itnight-leaning hybrid while these beings have mixed qualities of both More and Less, the preponderance of their thoughts and behaviors effectively take life away; intention is not the issue but rather the effect of self serving thoughts and the subsequent manipulation of the world

No Man's Land

a space immediately adjacent to this world; a reality of the disembodied where many one-time living beings from the existence experience will enter on their way to what's next for them; it doesn't belong to anyone in particular but is open to all as clarification and sorting out is completed

river of life

a metaphoric illustration for the underlying currents which carry life into the sphere of darkness in which our existence experience plays out; the flow of this 'river' is critical to sustaining the mustardo which animates and sustains life's many expressions

Sailors of Fortune

those who prize life for life's sake; these people's first cause is to treasure the life within them and to equally care for the life around them

subtraction, time of

when we refer to the time of subtraction, we are implying a precipitously low flow in life's river; the decline side of things overwhelms the up side of life as it pertains to a sustaining and living world; the health and vigor of our lives and world are diminishing; the more grand, differentiated, and accomplished life forms are being replaced by more marginal life expressions and decline side organisms

tap screws

indications of a presence from another world or reality; appears to our eyes as a radiating point of light that is usually blue or green; tend to appear on the ground or close to the surface; glowing intermittently, they often appear in small groupings; represent the essence of beings from other realities

tentacle

an amorphous presence that, with octopus-like tentacles, reaches into existence from out of the night and preys on life and life's keepers

ticket

implies our next living expression following our departure from this world